CHIAROSCURO

Achim Gnann, with David Ekserdjian
and Michael Foster

CHIAROSCURO

RENAISSANCE WOODCUTS FROM THE COLLECTIONS OF GEORG BASELITZ AND THE ALBERTINA, VIENNA

Royal Academy of Arts

First published on the occasion of the exhibition

'Renaissance Impressions: Chiaroscuro Woodcuts from the Collection of Georg Baselitz and the Albertina, Vienna'

Royal Academy of Arts, London
15 March – 8 June 2014

2009–2016 Season supported by

JTI

Supported by

EDWARDS WILDMAN
BUSINESS-MINDED LEGAL COUNSEL

The Royal Academy of Arts is grateful to Her Majesty's Government for agreeing to indemnify this exhibition under the National Heritage Act 1980, and to Resource, The Council for Museums, Archives and Libraries, for its help in arranging the indemnity.

Exhibition Curators
Achim Gnann (Albertina, Vienna)
Arturo Galansino
with Katia Pisvin

Royal Academy Exhibitions
Director: Kathleen Soriano
Idoya Beitia
Kitty Corbet Milward
Andrea Tarsia
Elana Woodgate

Royal Academy Publications
Beatrice Gullström
Alison Hissey
Elizabeth Horne
Carola Krueger
Peter Sawbridge
Nick Tite

Translation from the German (Achim Gnann): Michael Foster
Project editor: Michael Foster
Design: Adam Brown_01.02
Colour origination: Die Keure
Printed in Belgium by Die Keure

British Library Cataloguing-in-Publication Data
A catalogue record for this book is available from the British Library

ISBN 978-1-907533-63-1 (hardback)
ISBN 978-1-907533-64-8 (softback)

Distributed outside the United States and Canada by Thames & Hudson Ltd, London

Distributed in the United States and Canada by Harry N. Abrams, Inc., New York

ILLUSTRATIONS

Contents

President's Foreword

The Royal Academy is proud to present the first exhibition devoted to Renaissance chiaroscuro woodcuts to be staged in Britain. An extraordinary group of over 130 prints of the highest quality has been selected to provide visitors with a complete account of the genesis and development throughout the sixteenth century of this revolutionary technique, which introduced colour associated with effects of light and dark into printmaking. Initially prized by the most sophisticated art lovers and connoisseurs, including Duke Albert of Saxe-Teschen (1738–1822), who formed the Albertina collection, chiaroscuro woodcuts have once again become prestigious collectors' items, championed in no small part by such a forerunner of taste as the contemporary artist and printmaker Georg Baselitz HON RA. As one of the few Presidents to have made chiaroscuro woodcut prints, I very much recommend to you the special qualities to be found only in this atmospheric and compelling medium.

We are greatly indebted to our colleagues at the Albertina in Vienna, Dr Klaus Albrecht Schröder, Director, and Dr Achim Gnann, Curator, for their important loans and for creating this exhibition. Our gratitude goes especially to Georg Baselitz, whose exceptional generosity and willingness to part with the many precious prints in his collection have enabled us to display this extraordinary group of chiaroscuro woodcuts, and to his son Daniel Blau, who has supported the project at every stage. They have worked closely with Kathleen Soriano, the Royal Academy's Director of Exhibitions, and Dr Arturo Galansino, Curator, to realise the exhibition's presentation here in London. Idoya Beitia, Exhibition Manager, Katia Pisvin, Curatorial Assistant, Elana Woodgate, Exhibitions Assistant, and Kitty Corbet Milward, Rights and Reproductions Manager, have provided invaluable assistance. The expertise and dedication of the Royal Academy's publications department have resulted in this handsome catalogue.

The exhibition at the Royal Academy has been made possible by JTI, our generous benefactor and long-term partner of exhibitions in the Sackler Wing of Galleries. We are also extremely grateful to Edwards Wildman for their support.

Christopher Le Brun PRA
President, Royal Academy of Arts

Supporter's Preface

We are delighted to support this exhibition, which provides a rare opportunity to enjoy the creativity and technical brilliance of the artists and printmakers involved in the development of the revolutionary chiaroscuro woodcut printing technique.

Daniel Torras
Managing Director UK, JTI

Acknowledgements

All those concerned with the making of this exhibition and its catalogue would like to thank the following individuals for their invaluable assistance: Giulia Bartrum, Karine Bovagnet, Stephen Chambers RA, Hugo Chapman, David Ekserdjian, Ulrike Ertl, Jonas Grimas, Margarete Heck, Maria Metzler, Eric Pearson, Klaus Albrecht Schröder, Monica Sidhu, Mike Taylor, Elisabeth Thobois, the late Frank Whitford

Achim Gnann

The Chiaroscuro Woodcut: An Introduction

This exhibition and its catalogue provide a unique opportunity to study the genesis of the chiaroscuro woodcut and to trace its dissemination and development in various countries in the sixteenth century. A chiaroscuro woodcut is a colour woodcut in which gradations of tone are used to suggest volume and depth. It is produced by printing two or more woodblocks on top of each other. As in a straightforward line woodcut, the 'line block', generally coloured black, prints the drawing for the image as a whole, with the wood cut away to leave thin ridges.[1] The 'tone block', or 'colour block', has the wood cut away in those areas that are to form highlights in the final image: when the block is printed, these areas stay blank, revealing the white of the paper. Often one or more tone blocks are printed over the first in order to create darker areas.

Designs to be printed usually took the form of drawings traced onto the woodblocks. Occasionally, the composition might be drawn directly onto the block. The image appeared reversed when printed. This necessitated transferring the design to the block in reverse if it was to reproduce the composition the original way round. The first block to be prepared was the line block. The cutter drew the lines and the main areas of hatching on the block, then used a cutting tool to remove the areas around them, which would not print. Giorgio Vasari, the first to describe the technique in detail, recommended taking a freshly printed impression of this line block and pressing it onto the second block in order to reproduce the lines.[2] Then, says Vasari, white paint should be applied with a brush to the areas of the second block that are to form the highlights. These sections are then cut away, so that they remain white in the final image. Vasari advocates the same procedure for further tone blocks: each time a fresh impression of the line block should be taken to transfer the outlines of the image to the block, the shaded areas painted on it and the remaining parts cut away. The blocks are printed in the opposite order to their cutting. The lightest tone block, with only those sections reproducing highlights cut away, is printed first, then the block(s) with the shading and, finally, the line block, with the outlines and interior drawing. Each block must be aligned exactly with the previous one(s), so as to avoid blurring and other forms of distortion in the final image.

Some artists, such as Ugo da Carpi and Beccafumi, cut their own blocks; others, presumably including Hans Wechtlin, had the blocks cut by specialist woodcutters. The term 'chiaroscuro woodcut' came to be used for these colour woodcuts by analogy with 'chiaroscuro drawing', employed by Vasari, Raffaello Borghini and Giovanni Battista Armenini to describe pen and ink drawings executed with the addition of wash and white heightening on coloured paper that functioned as a neutral, middle tone.[3] Tonal gradations and strong contrasts of light and dark in these drawings generated an effect resembling that of painted images. Chiaroscuro woodcuts partly imitated the appearance of such drawings.[4]

Printing in more than one colour began in the fifteenth century. Red and blue initials in the Mainz Psalter, published by Johann Fust and Peter Schöffer in 1457, were removed from the text block, coloured, reinserted and printed together with the black text.[5]

1518
H · BVRGKMAIR

VENI
VIDI
VICI
SPQR
CLEMENTISSI
PRINCIPI O M
TRIONFATOR

The printer Erhard Ratdolt of Augsburg played a key role in subsequent developments in colour printing. From 1476 to 1486 he was active in Venice, where in 1482 he produced an edition of Euclid with the preface printed in gold. In his 1485 edition of Johannes de Sacrobosco's *Sphaericum opusculum* Ratdolt used as many as three colours for the astronomical diagrams.[6] That year, in a breviary for Augsburg, he printed the first colour woodcut with what might be termed an 'artistic' motif: the coat of arms of Bishop Johann II of Werdenberg, in black, yellow and red.[7] The first colour woodcut including a human figure, printed in four colours and showing Bishop Friedrich of Hohenzollern surrounded by his coat of arms and those of two other bishops, appeared in Ratdolt's *Obsequiale Augustanum*, published in Augsburg in 1487.[8] Blue features for the first time in a print in 1492, in a Crucifixion canon picture in a missal Ratdolt printed for Freising, near Munich.[9]

Ratdolt's colour printing offered an alternative to hand-colouring, which nevertheless persisted unabated (even parts of Ratdolt's colour-printed images continuing to be executed by hand). In Augsburg he helped to prepare the way for the chiaroscuro print by reason of his collaboration with the local artist Hans Burgkmair the Elder. In the 1490s Burgkmair produced a few designs for colour title-page woodcuts in liturgical works published by Ratdolt.[10] Experimenting with the colour printing technique, he came to rank alongside Lucas Cranach the Elder as one of the inventors of the chiaroscuro woodcut. Ratdolt's prints cannot be termed thus[11] because they feature self-contained, additively juxtaposed blocks of colour. These operate purely in terms of local colour; they fill shapes, but do not model them and do not combine to enhance or complement each other's effect. Furthermore, the paper forms a neutral background: it does not function as light, generating atmosphere or a sense of depth. The introduction of the tone block changed this: the white of the paper now acquired a voice of its own as highlighting. Only when tone and line blocks are used to create gradations of colour from dark to light, and only when colour and light are employed as artistic tools for giving volumes three-dimensionality and generating pictorial depth and atmosphere, is it permissible to talk of a chiaroscuro woodcut as opposed to a colour woodcut.

The development of the chiaroscuro woodcut over a period of some hundred years after its early sixteenth-century beginnings in Wittenberg and Augsburg is traced here in nine sections featuring some of the most important, finest and valuable works produced in the technique. Following its beginnings in the work of Cranach and Burgkmair in 1507–08, it was soon adopted by Hans Baldung Grien and Hans Wechtlin in Strasbourg and by Albrecht Altdorfer in Regensburg. Albrecht Dürer ignored the technique (but see cats 17, 18), though artists of his circle, Hans Sebald Beham among them, employed it. In 1516, barely ten years after its invention, the chiaroscuro woodcut was introduced into Italy by Ugo da Carpi. Antonio da Trento and Niccolò Vicentino, both of whom probably trained with Ugo, continued to practise it there, as did later Niccolò Boldrini and Andrea Andreani. Italian artists developed the technique in the direction of a freer, more painterly approach. This was adopted in turn in the second half of the sixteenth century in the German-speaking regions and in the Netherlands, where Hendrick Goltzius was the finest exponent of the technique.

Chiaroscuro woodcuts were produced for vastly differing audiences. Some were aimed at a sophisticated class of connoisseurs and collectors. Others, featuring more popular subject-matter, were widely distributed in the form of broadsheets. Still others seem to have served artists as models. The effect produced by their colours rendered them particularly attractive as wall decoration, and some monumental prints by Andreani probably even acted as substitutes for paintings.

Motifs were similarly varied in origin. Whereas some designs were produced specifically for chiaroscuro woodcuts, others reproduce studies for paintings. Still others reproduce drawings after finished paintings and sculptures.

Two images featuring emperors are included here. They could scarcely be more different in style and execution. Burgkmair renders Emperor Maximilian in terms of taut, regular, densely spaced lines (cat. 2; fig. 1). They lend the composition a severity also apparent in the stiff pose of the mounted emperor. Subordinated to the line block, the tone block contributes only a single note of colour. Strictly linear highlighting and firm 'drawing' bind the elements together and grant the imperial portrait a dignified and hieratic aura. By contrast, Caesar and his triumphal procession in Andrea Andreani's prints are wrapped in an atmospheric space, complete with clouds passing in the sky and light shown entering the images (cat. 138.9; fig. 2). Contours are loosely rendered, like freehand drawing, and combine loosely with colours that resemble wash applied with the brush rather than areas printed from a block. The figures' movements appear fluent and spontaneous, as though captured in a fleeting moment, an aspect reflected in their facial expressions. Freely orchestrated compositions in which space is animated by figures' movements have replaced the kind of closed, self-contained image represented by Burgkmair's portrait of Maximilian.

These two examples demonstrate the enormous distance travelled by the chiaroscuro woodcut in the space of less than a hundred years. Chiaroscuro woodcuts continued to be produced in various countries in later times. In fact, after a period of neglect, it enjoyed something of a revival in Italy in the eighteenth century in the work of Anton Maria Zanetti. The same century saw it used in France as a reproductive print medium by the Comte de Caylus and Nicolas Le Sueur and introduced into Britain for the first time by John Baptist Jackson and John Skippe.[12] Yet the golden age of the chiaroscuro woodcut was undoubtedly the sixteenth century.

Fig. 1 (Page 15) Detail of cat. 2
Hans Burgkmair the Elder, *Emperor Maximilian on Horseback*, 1508 and 1518
Albertina, Vienna, DG 1934/65

Fig. 2 (Opposite) Detail of cat. 138.9
Andrea Andreani, after Mantegna, *Julius Caesar on his chariot*, 1599
Collection of Georg Baselitz

Collections formed by artists occupy a very particular position within the vast realm of the history of collecting. While there is no documentary evidence of artists in antiquity having been collectors, there is every reason to suppose that they must have owned works of art, whether by their predecessors or by their contemporaries. Moving forward in time, it is possible to chronicle a continuous tradition of artist-collectors stretching from the birth of the Renaissance to the present day. In the sixteenth, seventeenth and eighteenth centuries, when all but the most prized works of art were comparatively inexpensive, even relatively unprosperous artists were routinely able to own important items. This state of affairs gradually began to change in the nineteenth century, and we have now reached a point at which the most admired twentieth-century and contemporary art commands significantly higher prices than all but the most exceptional productions of the Old Masters, and even of the Impressionists and Post-Impressionists – a situation that would have been inconceivable even a generation ago. As a result, extremely successful artists are now not only able to command unprecedentedly high prices for their work, but are equally in a position to collect at what might initially seem unexpectedly high levels.

While it is therefore true that Georg Baselitz is one of a long and illustrious line of artist-collectors, it does also seem important to add that, as will emerge in due course, his is a very particular kind of collecting. Indeed, it would be a fundamental error to imagine that artist-collectors were ever – or are now – all of a piece. This applies not simply to the kinds of art they collect or, above all, to their relationships with the art of the past and present, but also – and arguably altogether more tellingly – to the extent to which they have or have not employed their collections as sources of inspiration for their own creations.

The earliest recorded artist-collector was Lorenzo Ghiberti, who by the time of his death, in 1455, owned a collection of antiquities valued at an impressive 1,500 florins.[1] Giorgio Vasari, in both the original, 1550 edition of his *Lives* and in the substantially enlarged and revised 1568 edition, which together represent the first systematic attempt at a history of art since antiquity, discusses Ghiberti's collection, the cream of which had been purchased by a cleric of the Camera Apostolica in Rome called Giovanni Gaddi, in almost identical terms.[2] Himself a painter and architect, he singles out what was evidently the most notable of Ghiberti's treasures, the so-called *Bed of Polycleitus*, a relief whose appearance is known to us only in the form of sculptural and drawn copies, but which was to influence an extraordinary number and range of artists, not least Jacques-Louis David in his celebrated *Death of Marat*.[3] Intriguingly, what is now the best-known copy of the work, a small marble relief, was owned by the eminent Australian painter Sir Sidney Nolan OM (1917–1992).[4] There can be no doubt that the main reason why Ghiberti set up his collection was to have the opportunity to absorb the art of antiquity, which he clearly studied extensively for his own work, intimately and – so to speak – on a daily basis.[5]

By the middle of the sixteenth century, Vasari himself had amassed a very substantial and distinguished collection of

David Ekserdjian

Georg Baselitz and the Collecting of Prints

HGoltzius Inue.

drawings, to which he makes repeated reference in his *Lives*. In his case, however, and for all that he cannot have been immune to their potential influence upon his own artistic endeavours, the prime motivation appears to have been connected with his art-historical project. At the same time, the elaborate mounts he designed for the drawings make it plain that he also appreciated them as works of art, and not merely as tools of either of his twin trades.[6] What is more – and this can hardly fail to be of interest in the present context, regardless of the necessarily different motivations – a major recent study has been devoted to the question of Vasari's engagement with prints.[7]

This is not the place to offer a full chronicle of artist-collectors and their activities down the ages, but it does seem worth underlining both the distinction and the diversity of the most prominent. In the first half of the seventeenth century Peter Paul Rubens is the outstanding figure, not simply because of the quality of what he owned, but also because of what he made of it. In his case – and to an unrivalled degree – activity as a collector and as a student of the art of the past were fruitfully combined.[8] Even more remarkably, and in a way that anticipates by centuries certain kinds of contemporary reworkings, he was ruthless in his willingness to transform what he evidently took to be inferior copies of important inventions by artists of earlier generations by amending them. We must hope he was right, since his visual glosses in the form of washes and heightenings have effectively buried the originals.[9] Rubens's superstar protégé Anthony van Dyck was still in a position to own such masterpieces by Titian as his paintings of the Vendramin Family (National Gallery, London) and Perseus and Andromeda (Wallace Collection, London), but thereafter many of the finest collections of Old Masters assembled by artists were of drawings.[10] The names of Sir Peter Lely, Jonathan Richardson (both senior and junior), Sir Joshua Reynolds and Sir Thomas Lawrence represent a glorious tradition, with many works passing down from one to another. Thanks to the custom of stamping drawings with printed collectors' marks – a practice all but invented by Lely's executors, as one of them, Roger North, recounts in his autobiography – the ownership of individual items down the generations is often gratifyingly and graphically apparent.[11] Intriguingly, and with the singular exception of Reynolds, these artist-collectors hardly ever seem to have plundered their holdings for inspiration.[12]

Many of the greatest artist-collectors of the nineteenth century, like the two Richardsons before them, were notably more distinguished as collectors than as artists. In consequence, only the best-informed visitors to such superlative collections as those of the Musée Fabre at Montpellier or the Musée Bonnat at Bayonne are likely to be aware of the fact that their founding collections, which to this day represent the best part of their holdings, were formed by artists.[13] Conversely, in the twentieth century such major figures as Picasso and Lucian Freud, whose painting of *l'Italienne* by Corot recently passed to the National Gallery, London, were true – if eclectic – collectors.[14]

Georg Baselitz's collecting differs radically in kind from all these precedents, both in the intensity of its focus and in its seriousness of purpose. From the outset, Baselitz has concentrated on prints to the virtual exclusion of all other media, and on the late fifteenth, sixteenth and early seventeenth centuries. There have been countless brilliant printmakers since then, of course, but they do not interest him in the same way. Even when it comes to chiaroscuro woodcuts, the productions of Anton Maria Zanetti in the eighteenth century leave him cold, in spite of the fact that they are often reproductions of drawings by Parmigianino: for him, they are too late in the day and feel dead. In the main, the prints he has chosen to collect are either by Italians or by artists in the Netherlands, France and the German-speaking lands who qualify to a greater or lesser extent as honorary Italians, and only in recent years have a select few, more characteristically German printmakers been added to their number. The group of prints from Baselitz's collection included in the present publication and the exhibition it accompanies is necessarily restricted to chiaroscuro woodcuts, but in this essay it makes no sense to cordon them off from other types of prints in the collection, especially since they were not among the first he collected.

To begin at the beginning, in 1965 Georg Baselitz, who was not yet thirty, was awarded a grant to spend six months in Florence at the Villa Romana. Unsurprisingly, the entire experience was a revelation, not least since Florence, whose fabric had been virtually untouched by the Second World War, represented a striking contrast to the still ravaged and scarred Berlin, where Baselitz had been studying and working since 1956. Already married and with a young son, the artist made the most of his time in the warm south, whose magical appeal for northerners was immortalised by Goethe in his poem 'Kennst du das Land?'[15]

One of Baselitz's preoccupations during his time in Florence was with the artistic style widely, if not entirely felicitously, termed 'Mannerism'. However, even before his arrival in Italy he had been steeping himself in Gustav René Hocke's *Die Welt als Labyrinth*.[16] This volume, in which the works of artists such as Parmigianino and Pontormo are juxtaposed with those of Salvador Dalí and René Magritte, was available in a paperback edition published by Rowohlt for a couple of marks and enjoyed considerable success in Germany, if not elsewhere.[17] Its profoundly different, but also much-read equivalent in English was John Shearman's *Mannerism*, issued by Penguin, a work whose existence may well have quashed any idea of a translation of Hocke's book.[18]

In Florence, Baselitz naturally sought out the paintings of such home-grown artists as Rosso Fiorentino, Pontormo and Bronzino, and was also able to study a number of major pictures by Parmigianino, above all his *Madonna of the Long Neck* in the Uffizi (fig. 4).[19] At the same time, he made pilgrimages by bus in order to see such Mannerist masterpieces as Rosso's *Deposition* at Volterra (fig. 3) and Pontormo's *Visitation* at Carmignano (fig. 5).[20] At the same time, and although all of this had nothing to do with painting, he frequented the Kunsthistorisches Institut, the German art history institute, in Florence with the help of Antje Kosegarten, daughter-in-law of its celebrated director, Ulrich Middeldorf. There, in the photographic archive, Baselitz began to look at reproductions of Italian Renaissance prints by such a master as Marcantonio Raimondi, of whom he had never heard, and learned

Fig. 3 Rosso Fiorentino, *The Deposition from the Cross*, 1521. Oil on wood, 341 × 201 cm.

Pinacoteca Comunale, Volterra

Fig. 4 Parmigianino, *Madonna of the Long Neck*, *c.* 1534–35. Oil on wood, 219 × 135 cm.

Galleria degli Uffizi, Florence

Fig. 5 Pontormo, *The Visitation*, *c.* 1528–29. Oil on wood, 202 × 156 cm.

San Michele, Carmignano

about his translations into engravings of the woodcuts in Albrecht Dürer's *Life of the Virgin*. The superb collection of works on paper in the Uffizi's Gabinetto dei Disegni e Stampe was near at hand and might well have proved even more revelatory, but sadly he was afflicted by what he refers to as 'Schwellenangst' (literally, 'fear of crossing the threshold') and would not have dreamt of trying to visit that holy of holies at this stage in his career.

Baselitz's experiences in Florence resulted not just in an abiding passion for prints, but also, and more importantly, in a concentration on his first love in the medium: the prints of the Italian Renaissance. It might have seemed more natural for his interest to be ignited by the printmakers of the Blaue Reiter or the Brücke, or indeed of the German Renaissance, but nothing could have been further from the truth. The other crucial point to bear in mind is that Renaissance prints have virtually never been a source of artistic inspiration for Baselitz: on the contrary, from the outset it was their refined otherness that appealed to him.

Almost immediately, Baselitz determined to acquire prints, but was not able to do so until after his return to Berlin. What he remembers as his first purchase was a work by Antonio Fantuzzi, one of the leading printmakers of the school of Fontainebleau, which was languishing at the Berlin auction house Rittershofer when he picked it up for forty marks. That was not much, but for him it was a serious outlay, representing about a third of his monthly income. Over the next two to three years – in the way of all true collectors – he assiduously hunted his prey and built up a good collection of Fontainebleau school prints, which then seemed to be of no particular interest to anybody else.[21]

Around the same time, in 1966 and 1967, he himself was experimenting with woodcut and chiaroscuro and had begun to study the works of such German Renaissance masters as Lucas Cranach and Hans Baldung Grien. In spite of the fact that he thought of himself as an avant-garde artist, he was often branded anachronistic, which at least encouraged him not to feel any obligation to repudiate the achievements of his artistic forebears. Looking back, Baselitz is keen to stress the existence of unwritten rules that every artist purporting to belong to the avant-garde was expected to follow, a state of affairs hard to imagine from today's perspective.

This exploration of woodcut in his own artistic practice was the only episode of what Baselitz refers to as a 'cynical' exploitation of his print collection as a source of inspiration through virtual quotation. The phase lasted for about a year before coming to an end as abruptly as it had begun. In a sense, it was complemented by a broadening of his collecting activity. Around this time he acquired his first woodcut (not a chiaroscuro), a work by Luca Cambiaso.[22] The bookseller he purchased it from – for in those days bookshops often had holdings of prints and drawings – thought it was a drawing, but it was still blessedly cheap.

Baselitz is eager to underline the fact that his early career was not without its setbacks. In 1966, for example, he and his family – by now there were two children – left Berlin and moved to the village of Osthofen, near Worms, where his wife became the breadwinner. A year or two later, financial hardship led to the sale of the artist's entire print collection, which by this time numbered

Fig. 6 Georg Baselitz, 2013

around forty or fifty items, to the Parisian dealer Prouté. Baselitz's only request, to which Prouté agreed, naturally enough, was that he should be given the opportunity to buy back any works remaining in stock if his situation improved reasonably soon. In the event, the corner was turned, and Prouté kept his word.

The next step, as his career began to take off, was to start collecting prints from the circle of Parmigianino, not least chiaroscuro woodcuts. At this stage, Parmigianino etchings, which were in any event few and far between on the market, were well beyond his means, but instead he was able to start acquiring etchings by Andrea Schiavone. Even today, Baselitz rates Schiavone – whom he describes trenchantly, but not unfairly, as 'a bad painter' – above Parmigianino as an etcher, principally because of his astonishing technical boldness. Schiavone is certainly not a household name, but he does have something of a cult following, and Baselitz smilingly recalls coming across one of his prints in the downstairs loo of the great critic David Sylvester. Decades later, his love affair with the prints of Parmigianino and his circle reached its apotheosis in the acquisition of the 'Spencer Album' from the Spencer family at Althorp House, Northamptonshire, which was the subject of a remarkable exhibition curated by Achim Gnann and shown at the Graphische Sammlung in Munich in 2007–08 and the Städel Museum in Frankfurt in 2008.[23] The Spencer Album boasts a number of superlative prints, including differently coloured versions of a single chiaroscuro woodcut and some remarkable rarities, such as an apparently unique impression of Parmigianino's celebrated etching of the *Entombment* on a golden-yellow ground.[24] In the case of this last item, Baselitz initially felt it was almost too good to be true, but was reassured after a transatlantic telephone call to the late Konrad Oberhuber, the sometime director of the Albertina in Vienna, whom he understandably reveres as arguably the greatest expert of all time in this field.

Baselitz's early purchases were made in Berlin, especially at the auction house Bassenge: he was not to engage with the international art market as a buyer for some years. When he eventually did so, however, he was prepared to act at the highest levels, as was dramatically demonstrated at the major sale of prints from the collection of the Duke of Devonshire at Chatsworth, which took place at Christie's in 1985.[25] The sale consisted of no fewer than one hundred and eighty-three lots. While a number of them, including the first forty-six, which were all German prints, and a stunning group of etchings by Rembrandt at the end, fell outside Baselitz's collecting focus, all too many were heartbreakingly and potentially bankruptingly to his taste. Like many another collector confronted by an *embarras de richesses* and possessing limited means, he was obliged to take some difficult decisions. With the notable exception of Jacopo Caraglio's *Fury* after Rosso Fiorentino (lot 77), he actually managed to keep his powder dry until almost the end of the sale. He then bought two successive lots – 171 and 172 – which are both spectacular examples of the northern response to Italian Mannerism around 1600. The former is Bartholomäus Spranger's etching of St Sebastian (listed in Christie's catalogue as 'a brilliant impression of this very rare print'), the latter Hendrik Goltzius's chiaroscuro woodcut of *Hercules Killing Cacus*, which its proud possessor regards as the finest copy of this print in existence (cat. 103).

Over the years since the Chatsworth sale, Baselitz has been fortunate enough to acquire a number of what might be described as 'ones that got away'. They include the entire series of chiaroscuro woodcuts of the *Triumphs of Caesar* by Andrea Andreani after the canvases that Mantegna painted for the Gonzaga of Mantua (now Hampton Court, London; cat. 138) and, most recently, Domenico Beccafumi's *Three Reclining Nudes in a Landscape* from the Breinin Collection.[26] This engraving was one of only a handful of prints that did not feature in the price list that accompanied the dealer's catalogue on its re-emergence, the reason being that it had already been sold. One of the advantages enjoyed by leading collectors is that their tastes are known to all the top dealers and they are thus given first refusal on works that seem destined for their collections. It is in this way that in recent years Baselitz has been able to add exceptional runs of prints by Mantegna and Bellange to his collection. In consequence, the riches that were revealed to the world by a substantial publication in 1994 and by an exhibition in Geneva in 2002 have been added to very considerably of late.[27] In the same vein, the present publication and exhibition include all sorts of thrilling surprises in the shape of items not to be found in the earlier selections.

W. H. Auden was fond of slightly misquoting Paul Valéry to the effect that no poem was ever truly finished, it was only abandoned, and the same sense of dissatisfaction gnaws at the vitals of all true collectors.[28] When asked to name the most tormenting gaps in his collection, Baselitz restricts himself to the wry and potentially rather misleading observation that, at least as far as chiaroscuro woodcuts are concerned, the works from the Albertina included here represent a pretty good guide to what he is missing.

Two fundamental and intimately related questions concerning Baselitz's collecting remain to be discussed: why he concentrates on prints to the virtual exclusion of all other media, and which aspects of the study and collecting of prints matter most to him. Unsurprisingly, perhaps, his responses are highly individual and remind one that, for all his profound knowledge of the material, he does not approach it in the way an academic art historian or museum curator would.

At the outset, collecting prints could have been a pragmatic solution to lack of funds, since prints are generally less expensive than paintings or drawings. Yet that was never Baselitz's motivation. He emphasises almost obsessively that his fascination with prints lies in their directness, in the sense that nothing comes between the viewer and their creator.

A similar impulse almost invariably inspires collectors of Old Master drawings, who love the feeling that they are in the presence of the artist's spontaneous and unmediated first thoughts. Those of us willing to speak up for paintings as last words would beg to differ, but can half understand why 'drawings people' are sometimes disappointed by what they regard as the laborious wholeness of finished paintings (it is no coincidence that many of them also admire the brio and dash of oil sketches). They also worry about the physical impairment almost always suffered by paintings over the centuries and lament the gulf that tends to separate what we see now from the pristine condition of the panel or canvas as it left the artist's easel.

Baselitz feels exactly the same way about Old Master paintings, but in addition he is convinced that remarkably few Renaissance drawings have reached us in a flawless state – and it is true that awareness of tampering has increased, at least in isolated instances.[29] Since the beginnings of his professional success, he has certainly had every opportunity to buy drawings, but has never really wished to, even in the case of an artist as dear to his heart as Parmigianino. He nevertheless agrees entirely with the widely accepted notion that many artists, perhaps especially those of the second rank, are at their best in drawings, instancing two remarkable life-size nude self-portrait drawings by Stanley Spencer, whose work he does not as a rule esteem very highly.[30] In fact, as in the case of Schiavone referred to above, and also that of Giovanni Pietro Possenti, who in effect is exclusively known for his etchings, he believes a similar principle can also on occasion be applied to printmakers.[31]

For Baselitz, the physical condition of prints is of fundamental importance, and the benign neglect to which they have tended to be consigned over the centuries has been crucial to their preservation. He has no interest in the fact that a print belonged to a duke or an earl, but is delightedly aware of the fact that prints from stately homes like Chatsworth and Althorp were never framed and exposed to the light – as some Renaissance drawings have been – but have instead benefited from the artistic equivalent of a state of suspended animation in their respective libraries. Because they were 'only' prints, in all probability they were virtually never shown to visitors. Perhaps the real point is that although old prints are by their nature multiples, in another and deeper sense they are all subtly different originals.

A similar paradox arguably defines the seeming narrowness of focus of Baselitz's collecting. When he talks about the sinuous elegance and exquisite refinement of the works of Parmigianino, he is responding to one aspect of what Mannerism has to offer. The other side of the coin is made manifest in what he terms the crudity, rawness and sheer muscular force of Goltzius's *Hercules Killing Cacus*. At the same time, he has never forgotten what *Die Welt als Labyrinth* taught him at the outset – that many of the major figures of the style were both resolutely anti-classical in their art and at the same time profoundly disturbed psychologically. Vasari relates that Parmigianino was imprisoned for failing to complete his frescoed decoration of the church of the Steccata in Parma, that on his release he jumped bail, fled the city and died at the age of thirty-seven 'as a wild man'.[32] Even more drastically, Rosso Fiorentino committed suicide in France.[33]

Two further observations concerning Baselitz's passion for prints should be made. The first relates to his absolute indifference to subject-matter. It scarcely crosses his mind that one particular print represents an episode from the New Testament while another is based on a Greek myth. Similarly, his interest in, say, Antonio da Trento's so-called *Narcissus* chiaroscuro after Parmigianino (cats 53–5) is purely formal, in spite of the fact that he is extremely well read in the scholarly literature and is therefore perfectly aware of the debates surrounding its subject.[34]

The second observation is arguably even more crucial, and concerns his repeated insistence – alluded to above – that his art and his art collecting are two absolutely distinct pursuits, almost like the two hemispheres of a single brain. He understands the well-nigh irresistible urge to imagine there must be links between them, but he repudiates the notion utterly. As he puts it, only slightly exaggerating the problem for comic effect, there are certain categories of material he feels himself virtually forbidden to collect, simply because it would be unbearable to have to listen to an unending litany of explanations of the influence of such works upon his own artistic practice.

One reason why Baselitz is enthusiastic about the idea of his collection playing a major part in a publication and exhibition devoted to chiaroscuro woodcuts is that he feels their merits have yet to be properly recognised, even within the already somewhat specialised field of Renaissance prints. It certainly does not seem unrealistic to assume that the present amalgamation of the cream of two very different, but exceptionally distinguished collections of chiaroscuro woodcuts will prove to be both a transformational experience and a pure joy for many viewers. It is to be hoped that they will never again think of these or any other master prints as the poor relations of their better-known cousins from the worlds of painting and drawing.

I am profoundly grateful to Georg Baselitz, and to his son Daniel Blau, for having given me the opportunity to conduct an interview with him in London on 19 June 2013. The transcript of that interview forms the basis of this text.

Editorial Note

Dates are those at which the woodblocks were cut or can be presumed to have been cut. Impressions may naturally have been taken at later points in time.

Measurements are given in centimetres, height before width. Image or block sizes are noted as such when they differ from the sheet size.

Inscriptions are printed unless otherwise stated.

Watermarks are given in the few cases where this has been possible.

Bibliographies for each work appear in the list of works on pp. 205–18. These aim not to be complete, but to offer a conspectus of opinion ranging from the earliest studies of the subject to the most recent. Where the cited literature differs in matters of attribution from the present publication this is noted in parentheses. References to the standard print catalogues produced by Adam Bartsch ('B.'), Friedrich W. H. Hollstein ('H.'), Charles Le Blanc ('Le Blanc') and Johann David Passavant ('P.') appear separately in the list of works, between the lender credit and the bibliography proper. Full details of these and all other publications will be found in the general bibliography (pp. 221–6).

Catalogue

Beginnings: Lucas Cranach in Wittenberg and Hans Burgkmair in Augsburg

I

The decisive steps in the development of the chiaroscuro woodcut were taken in the early sixteenth century. In a letter of 24 September 1508 the Augsburg jurist, humanist and antiquary Conrad Peutinger, a close adviser of Emperor Maximilian I and much involved in his artistic projects, mentions receiving some printed 'cuirassiers' by Cranach the year before that were 'made with gold and silver'.[1] This refers to the artist's woodcuts of St George. One example of these is in the British Museum (fig. 7). Printed on blue prepared paper from two line blocks, first black, then gold, it recalls a chiaroscuro drawing. The effect of gold printing was achieved by sprinkling gold dust onto the impression of the line block while the ink was wet: the gold adhered only to the ink and could easily be dusted off the rest of the paper.[2] Receipt of Cranach's *St George* in 1507 prompted Peutinger to have Hans Burgkmair produce trial prints of similar 'cuirassiers' and send them for approval to the court of Saxony, where Cranach was active. The woodcuts in question, both dated 1508, are *St George and the Dragon* and *Emperor Maximilian on Horseback* (cats 1, 2). In the earliest impressions of the former the gold line block was printed after the black one.[3] For *Emperor Maximilian on Horseback* a partly gold, partly silver line block was printed first, then the black block,[4] a sequence approximating more closely to that employed in chiaroscuro woodcuts.

The two prints produced at Peutinger's instigation are related in composition and subject-matter and must be seen as pendants. *Emperor Maximilian on Horseback* was produced in connection with Maximilian's acceptance of the imperial title in Trent in 1508. He was particularly devoted to St George, whom he chose as patron saint of the battle against Islam and the champion of Christians engaged in it. In 1493 he had established the Brotherhood of St George, and in 1503 the Society of St George; later he joined the Order of St George founded by his father, Emperor Friedrich III.[5] Burgkmair's image of the saint was presumably also created in association with the festivities surrounding Maximilian's coronation. In later impressions of both prints, such as those included here, a tone block with the white highlights cut away replaced the gold line block and the gold and silver line block respectively. This represented a step in the direction of the chiaroscuro woodcut proper. The name Jost de Neger, printed with movable type, appears in these later copies, which suggests that he was responsible for introducing the tone block in each case. De Negker, a woodcutter from Antwerp, probably settled in Augsburg in 1509–10. He collaborated closely with Burgkmair and was appointed supervisor of all the woodcutters involved in the major publications instigated by Maximilian and furthered by Peutinger, among them the *Weisskunig*, the *Freydal*, the *Theuerdank* and the emperor's genealogy.[6] He prepared the woodcuts for his assistants and went over their work in order to give the prints a unified appearance. Artistically, the introduction of the tone block represented an improvement over Burgkmair's original woodcuts. It substituted pure white for coloured paper, unifying pictorial space, filling it with light and air and lending it greater depth. In *Emperor Maximilian on Horseback* the white areas largely follow the

Fig. 7 Lucas Cranach the Elder, *St George and the Dragon*, *c.* 1507. Chiaroscuro woodcut printed from two line blocks, in black and gold, on prepared paper, 23.3 × 15.9 cm.
British Museum, London, 1895,122.264

givens established by the line block, whereas rigorous linearity is abandoned in *St George and the Dragon*: the addition of colour aids textural differentiation among the individual elements, the volumes acquire greater three-dimensionality and the architectural elements gain in structural firmness. All this suggests that the tone block was added to this print slightly later than to the image of Maximilian.

Around this time Cranach added a tone block to his woodcuts *St Christopher* and *Venus and Cupid* (cat. 3; fig. 8).[7] The impression of *St Christopher* included here is later, however, with the date removed and another tone block substituted for the first. Earlier copies bear the date 1506, but, as Eduard Flechsig demonstrated, this cannot be correct.[8] Cranach did not begin using the signature featuring two winged serpents until 1508 and first employed the coat of arms with the two electoral swords of Saxony in this form in 1509.[9] Stylistic comparisons also suggest a date around this time. It has rightly been assumed that Cranach deliberately predated *St Christopher* and *Venus and Cupid* to 1506 in order to claim precedence over Burgkmair and de Negker in the use of tone blocks and therefore appear as the inventor of the chiaroscuro woodcut. Burgkmair's *St George and the Dragon* and *Emperor Maximilian on Horseback* are dated 1508 in the line block, but that permits no conclusions to be drawn about the date of de Negker's tone block, which could have been printed with the line block at a later point in time. A date of *c.* 1509–10 seems reasonable because Burgkmair's *Lovers Surprised by Death* of *c.* 1510 and *Hans Paumgartner* of 1512, both also cut by de Negker, show greater skill and sophistication in the use of the technique (cats 4, 6).

A *St Christopher* signed by de Negker may have some bearing on the question of which artist was the first to use tone blocks.[10] The landscape is influenced by that in Cranach's chiaroscuro woodcut of the same subject, while the figure seems to have been based on a work by an Antwerp artist, suggesting that the print was produced in that city. That would mean that de Negker could not have settled in Augsburg before 1508–09, which, in turn, would mean that Cranach must have experimented with tone blocks before him (unless it is assumed that Cranach first printed *St Christopher* as a pure line woodcut and added a tone block only later). On the other hand, the development of the tone block from plain linearity towards subtler, more painterly forms can be traced step by step in Burgkmair's *St George and the Dragon* and *Emperor Maximilian on Horseback*, which tells in favour of the invention having been made by him.

The discovery of the chiaroscuro woodcut technique seems not to have occurred in an exclusively artistic context; rather, the essential impulses appear to have come from princely courts and subject-matter associated with them. Cranach's 1507 *St George* forms part of a group of woodcuts produced around this time that depict knights, hunters and jousts, testifying to the brilliance of the Saxon Elector's court and his love of display. Whereas the gold in this print evinces a decorative richness typical of Late Gothic art, Burgkmair's woodcuts feature antique-style inscriptions and classical architecture, lending them a markedly 'modern', Renaissance aspect intended to glorify an emperor

Fig. 8 Lucas Cranach the Elder, *Venus and Cupid*, '1506'. Chiaroscuro woodcut printed from two blocks, the tone block in yellowish brown, 27.6 × 18.7 cm.

British Museum, London, 1895,0122.268

concerned with his posthumous reputation. Significantly, too, a man like Peutinger, a humanist and an antiquary, promoted the development and perfection of the chiaroscuro woodcut, encouraging competitive rivalry between the two artists.

Burgkmair created a masterwork in the new technique in his allegory on the transience of life, *Lovers Surprised by Death* (cat. 4). The subject originated in northern Europe, yet the composition betrays the influence of Italian art, notably that of Venice, a city the artist may have visited on the journey he is thought to have undertaken in 1506–07.[11] Burgkmair's woodcut is the first to feature printing from three blocks. The subtly matched colours grant the image a unified, self-contained quality. Just as the line block no longer defines the image as a whole, but is used only for emphasis, so each block is incomplete without the addition of the others. Although de Negker's name appears only in later impressions, he probably cut the blocks from the outset, since the various states exhibit improvements, but not stylistic divergences.

Writing to Emperor Maximilian in October 1512, de Negker stated that he himself produced the portrait of the Augsburg patrician and imperial councillor Hans Paumgartner (cat. 6).[12] This is the first chiaroscuro woodcut to dispense with a (black) line block. Printing from three tone blocks in varying shades of a single colour, de Negker achieved unprecedented subtlety in the rendering of texture and delicacy in the depiction of detail. Light becomes an independent artistic tool, blurring the transition from one colour to the next, softening the outlines and defining the sitter's position in space in painterly fashion. This outstanding work, based on a drawing (now lost) by Burgkmair, had no immediate successors in the German-speaking world. Astonishingly, Burgkmair and de Negker never returned to the technique.[13] One reason for this may be that Emperor Maximilian accused de Negker of fulfilling commissions other than his own, an allegation against which the woodcutter defended himself in the letter of 1512 by pointing out the portrait of Paumgartner had been the only case of this.

DIVVS·GEORGIVS
CHRISTIANORVM·
MILITVM·PRO-
PVGNATOR
IHS
·H·BVRGKMAIR·
Jost de Negker.

1 **Hans Burgkmair the Elder**
St George and the Dragon
1508 and *c.* 1509–10

Chiaroscuro woodcut printed from two blocks, the tone block in beige,
31.9 × 22.5 cm
Inscribed (upper left): *DIVUS·GEORGIUS / CHRISTIANORUM· / MILITUM· PRO= / PUGNATOR*; (lower left): *H· BURGKMAIR*; (lower right): *Jost de Negker.*
Watermark: Ox head with staff ending in a flower; similar to Briquet 14734
Collection of Georg Baselitz

2 **Hans Burgkmair the Elder**
Emperor Maximilian on Horseback
1508 and 1518

Chiaroscuro woodcut printed from two blocks, the tone block in greenish beige,
32.3 × 22.6 cm
Inscribed (above): *IMP·CAES·MAXIMIL·AUG*; (lower right): *1518 / H·BURGKMAIR·*
Albertina, Vienna, DG1934/65

3 **Lucas Cranach the Elder**
St Christopher
1509 and second half of the sixteenth century

Chiaroscuro woodcut printed from two blocks, the tone block in yellowish brown, 28 × 19.6 cm
Inscribed (upper left, on tablet): *LC*; two coats of arms also hanging from the tree
Collection of Georg Baselitz

4 **Hans Burgkmair the Elder**
Lovers Surprised by Death
c. 1510

Chiaroscuro woodcut printed from three blocks, the tone blocks in blue, 21.3 × 15.2 cm
Inscribed (lower left edge, top to bottom): *Jost de Negker.*; (lower left): *H·/ BURGKMAIR*
Albertina, Vienna, DG1934/75

H
BVRGKMAIR
Joſt de Negker.

5 **Lucas Cranach the Elder**
The Rest on the Flight into Egypt
1509

Chiaroscuro woodcut printed from two blocks, the tone block in reddish brown, 28.5 × 18.6 cm
Inscribed (lower right, on tablet): *L C* [above winged serpent] / *1509*
Albertina, Vienna, DG1929/119

6 **Hans Burgkmair the Elder**
Hans Paumgartner
1512

Chiaroscuro woodcut printed from three blocks, the tone blocks in violet, 29.1 × 24.1 cm
Inscribed (upper right, on tablet): *ANN·SAL·MDXII / IOANNES·PAUNGARTNER· CI* [I within C] *AUGU / STA*^{N} [N retraced in pen and ink] *AETAT·SUAE·ANN·LVII*; (at centre left edge, top to bottom on the architecture): *·H·BURGKMAIR*
Albertina, Vienna, DG1934/69

ANN·SAL·M·D·XII
IOANNES·PAVNGARTNER·C·AVGV
STA·AETAT·SVAE·AN·LVII
H·BVRGKMAIR

Strasbourg: Hans Wechtlin and Hans Baldung Grien

II

In Strasbourg Hans Wechtlin soon followed the example set by Cranach and Burgkmair and adopted the new technique. His twelve chiaroscuro woodcuts, printed from two blocks and now extremely rare, can be dated *c.* 1510–12.[1] Some of them depict unusual subjects from classical mythology and were doubtless aimed at a sophisticated circle of humanist art lovers. These prints include *Orpheus* and *Alcon Rescuing His Son from the Serpent* (figs 9, 10). Wechtlin also represented religious subjects, among them three conceived as a group: a *St Sebastian*, a *Virgin and Child* and a *Christ on the Cross* (fig. 12; cats 9, 10). For these he created separate border frames featuring Late Gothic floral decoration or Renaissance motifs that could be printed with the images in any desired combination. Wechtlin's prints are notable for their consistently fine and subtle execution. They reveal a penchant for luxuriant natural forms with variegated light playing on them. The same forms occur in his chiaroscuro drawings (fig. 11). Despite the short period in which the chiaroscuro woodcuts were produced, they show a stylistic development, from hard-edged, slightly schematic shapes and additive compositions, as in *Orpheus* and *Knight and Lasquenet* (cat. 11), to the less densely, more spaciously structured religious scenes. The latter feature a more sparing use of highlights and more harmoniously orchestrated colours. Movements are more fluid, bodies have become rounder and appear more as self-contained volumes.

Wechtlin's woodcuts reveal the influence both of Italian Renaissance art and of Albrecht Dürer's prints of the late 1490s. In addition, the half-length figure in the *Virgin and Child* takes its

Fig. 9

Fig. 9 (Page 38)
Hans Wechtlin, *Orpheus*, *c.* 1510–12. Chiaroscuro woodcut printed from two blocks, the tone block in blue, 26.6 × 18 cm.
Albertina, Vienna, DG1949/649

Fig. 10 Hans Wechtlin, *Alcon Rescuing His Son from the Serpent*, *c.* 1510–12. Chiaroscuro woodcut printed from two blocks, the tone block in beige, 27.4 × 18.5 cm.
Albertina, Vienna, DG 1949/651

Fig. 11 Hans Wechtlin, *Adam and Eve*, *c.* 1505–15. Pen and ink and wash, heightened with white, 23.3 × 16 cm.
Musée du Louvre, Paris, Collection Rothschild, 48 DR

Fig. 12 Hans Wechtlin, *St Sebastian*, *c.* 1510–12. Chiaroscuro woodcut printed from two blocks, the tone block in greyish green, 23.2 × 18.3 cm.
Albertina, Vienna, DG 1949/648

cue from Dürer's *Haller Madonna* (National Gallery, Washington). The two artists may have been personally acquainted. It has not been established how Wechtlin came to know Cranach's and Burgkmair's chiaroscuro woodcuts. A letter written by Peutinger to Emperor Maximilian in 1510 suggests that relations existed between woodcutters in Augsburg and Strasbourg. Peutinger reports that the departure of a qualified cutter from Augsburg has created a bottleneck in the production of the series of prints depicting the emperor's ancestors and, in a deleted passage, that he is considering replacing the cutter by one from Strasbourg.[2]

Hans Baldung Grien turned to the chiaroscuro woodcut at the same time and in the same place as Wechtlin. He became a member of the painters' guild in Strasbourg in 1510, established a workshop there and created his first independent woodcuts since his apprenticeship in Dürer's workshop in Nuremberg. His image of witches preparing their Sabbath announced his presence in the city with the force of a thunderbolt (cat. 12). Amid bones and skulls witches are brewing a sinister concoction in a pot from which steam escapes bearing a selection of uncanny creatures. The terrifying, demonic aspect of the image is softened by the frank eroticism of the women in their lascivious poses. Such subject-matter was of special interest in Strasbourg.[3]

In his other chiaroscuro woodcuts Baldung depicted similar religious subjects to Wechtlin. *The Virgin and Child with Angels in a Landscape*, for example, belongs to the same type of outdoor image of the Madonna as Wechtlin's *Virgin and Child* (cats 7, 8). Both prints also resemble each other in formal terms and were based on the same engraving by Dürer (B. 44). In comparison with Wechtlin, whose meticulously detailed woodcuts recall miniatures, Baldung opts for areas of colour that are larger and more self-contained, reduces the highlighting and follows more closely the example of Cranach. His figures are more expressive and more monumental, and they testify to the idiosyncratic nature of an artist who delighted in such scurrilous motifs as the putto presenting his buttocks in the foreground of *The Virgin and Child with Angels in a Landscape*. Eroticism often features strongly in his work. His *Adam and Eve*, for instance, stresses Eve's seductive beauty and Adam's sexual urge (cat. 14). The chiaroscuro woodcuts are even more compelling and unusual than his paintings of this period. All the dramatic aspects of the Crucifixion, for example, are emphasised (cat. 13). Shafts of lightning flash through the night sky and the quaking earth billows upwards, no longer offering a firm footing for the figures. Angular drapery folds give visible expression to the mourners' lamentations. The towering cross, seemingly rising from nowhere, dominates everything, although Christ himself is smaller than the figures standing on either side. Despite the stylistic differences between Wechtlin's and Baldung's chiaroscuro woodcuts, there can be little doubt that the two artists engaged with each other's work in a spirit of rivalry.

7 **Hans Wechtlin**
Virgin and Child
c. 1510–12

Chiaroscuro woodcut printed from two blocks, the tone block in blue-grey; blue wash added to the sky, 26.5 × 17.8 cm
Inscribed (lower left, on tablet): *Io[annes] V[echtlin]* [with two crossed pilgrim's staffs]
Albertina, Vienna, DG1949/644

8 **Hans Baldung Grien**
Virgin and Child with Angels in a Landscape
c. 1511

Chiaroscuro woodcut printed from two blocks, the tone block in greyish brown, 37.3 × 26 cm; cut down at the lower edge
Inscribed (lower right, on tablet): *HB* [monogrammed]
Albertina, Vienna, DG1931/94

9 **Hans Wechtlin**
Christ on the Cross
c. 1510–12

Chiaroscuro woodcut printed from two blocks, the tone block in greyish blue; ornamental frame printed from four blocks, 27.7 × 19.2 cm
Inscribed (lower left, on tablet): *Io[annes] V[echtlin]* [with two crossed pilgrim's staffs]
Albertina, Vienna, DG1949/643

10 **Hans Wechtlin**
Virgin and Child
c. 1510–12

Chiaroscuro woodcut printed from two blocks, the tone block in greyish green, 27 × 18.5 cm
Inscribed (upper left, on foreshortened tablet resting on the cornice): *Io[annes] V[echtlin]* [with two crossed pilgrim's staffs]
Albertina, Vienna, DG1949/645

11 **Hans Wechtlin**
Knight and Lansquenet
c. 1510–12

Chiaroscuro woodcut printed from two blocks, the tone block in blue, 26.9 × 18.1 cm
Inscribed (lower left, on tablet): *Io[annes] V[echtlin]* [with a flower and two crossed pilgrim's staffs]; (upper left): *P*[?] *mariette 1665* [in pen and ink]
Albertina, Vienna, DG1949/653

12 **Hans Baldung Grien**
Witches' Sabbath
1510

Chiaroscuro woodcut printed from two blocks, the tone block in greyish beige, 37 × 25.5 cm
Inscribed (at centre right edge, on tablet hanging from a branch): *HGB* [monogrammed]; (on the tree trunk): *1510* [below a vine leaf, his journeyman's mark]; area of loss at centre left
Albertina, Vienna, DG1931/87

I·N·R·I
HB·

13 **Hans Baldung Grien**
Christ on the Cross, with the Virgin and SS. John the Evangelist and Mary Magdalene
c. 1511–12

Chiaroscuro woodcut printed from two blocks, the tone block in orange-brown, 37 × 25.8 cm
Inscribed (lower right corner, on tablet): *HGB* [monogrammed, in pen and ink]; (lower centre edge): *AD* [monogram of Albrecht Dürer, in pen and ink, not autograph]
Albertina, Vienna, DG1931/104

14 **Hans Baldung Grien**
Adam and Eve
1511

Chiaroscuro woodcut printed from two blocks, the tone block in greyish brown, 37.5 × 25.6 cm
Inscribed (upper centre, on tablet): *LAPSUS HUMA / NI GENERIS*; (lower left, on tablet): *HGB* [monogrammed, below a vine leaf, his journeyman's mark] / *1511*; outlines of the figures pricked with holes
Albertina, Vienna, DG1931/50

The Chiaroscuro Woodcut Elsewhere in the German-speaking World

III

The chiaroscuro woodcuts created by Cranach in Wittenberg, by Burgkmair and de Negker in Augsburg and by Wechtlin and Baldung in Strasbourg date from the years 1507 to 1512.[1] Within this short period the technique developed from experimental beginnings to the point at which out-and-out masterpieces were being created in it. This level of achievement was not maintained in the German-speaking world in succeeding years. Albrecht Altdorfer, for example, used six blocks to create *The 'Beautiful Virgin' of Regensburg* – the largest number in any German colour print – but this woodcut, produced for pilgrims, is notable more for its variegated, eye-catching colours than for the sophistication of their arrangement (fig. 13).

A coloured tone block was often added to later impressions of line woodcuts, either to lend them a different, more attractive appearance, as with Hans Weiditz's *Man of Sorrows* and *Man of Sorrows Seated* (cats 15, 16), or to distract attention from damage to blocks caused by frequent printing, as was presumably the case with Cranach's *St John the Baptist Preaching* of 1516 (cat. 20). Such prints were originally conceived in monochrome terms, the lines creating an entirely self-sufficient image without the addition of colour.

Dürer never concerned himself with the chiaroscuro technique. Not until *c.* 1620 – that is, some hundred years after their creation – were tone blocks used in printing two of his woodcuts. The Amsterdam publisher Willem Janssen added one tone block to the artist's print of the Indian rhinoceros presented to King Manuel I of Portugal, which Dürer knew only from a drawing, and two blocks to his portrait of a Swiss friend, Ulrich Varnbühler, imperial councillor and chancellor to Archduke Ferdinand I, King of Bohemia and Hungary (cats 17, 18). Exceptionally fine and varied lines characterise Dürer's woodcuts. Curving gently, curling or uniting to form different kinds of hatching, they combine with the white of the paper to differentiate between a wide range of textures in the objects represented. They weave light and atmosphere into pictorial space, grant movements dynamism and fill the figures with inner life. By generating subtle gradations of tone in this way, Dürer invests the images with a maximum of painterly richness. At the same time, the black of the lines creates unity. Given the almost limitless expressive power of these lines it is understandable that the artist felt no need to use colour. Erasmus wrote an unsurpassable description of the phenomenon in his Latin eulogy of Dürer, published in Basle in 1528, the year of the artist's death: 'Dürer, though admirable also in other respects, what does he not express in monochromes, that is, in black lines. Light, shade, splendour, eminences, depressions; and, though derived from the position of one single thing, more than one aspect offers itself to the eye of the beholder. He observes accurately proportions and harmonies. Nay, he even depicts that which cannot be depicted: fire, rays of light, thunder, sheet lightning, or, as they say, the "clouds on the wall"; all the sensations and emotions; in fine, the whole mind of man as it reflects itself in the behaviour of the body, and almost the voice itself. These things he places before the eye in the most pertinent lines – black ones, yet so that if you should spread on pigments

Fig. 13 Albrecht Altdorfer, *The 'Beautiful Virgin' of Regensburg*, *c.* 1519–20. Chiaroscuro woodcut printed from six blocks, the tone blocks in yellow, red, pale brown, brown and blue, 36.8 × 26 cm (sheet).
Albertina, Vienna, DG 1926/1847

Fig. 14 Hans Sebald Beham, *The Unequal Lovers*, after 1533. Woodcut, 24 × 25 cm.
Albertina, Vienna, Sekt. Dt. I/21, S. 13

you would injure the work. And is it not more wonderful to accomplish without the blandishments of colour what Apelles accomplished with their aid?'[2]

Dürer's lack of engagement with the colour woodcut did not deter artists who were strongly influenced by him from adopting the technique. The chiaroscuro prints of Wechtlin and Baldung, for instance, have been discussed earlier (pp. 38–41). Another such artist was Hans Sebald Beham, whose compelling devotional image of the head of Christ crowned with thorns exists in its first state both as a line woodcut and as a chiaroscuro print (cat. 19). The addition of a brown tone block does not increase the evocative power of the head appreciably and was perhaps undertaken because it brought the print closer to images of Christ on St Veronica's sudarium, which are always brownish in colour. A chiaroscuro woodcut of Adam and Eve, inspired by Dürer's engraving (B. 1), addresses Eve's double nature as both tempted and tempting: on the one hand, because she is a victim of the serpent; on the other, because she offers Adam the apple (cat. 22). The skull that appears threateningly above the couple alludes to the fact that eating fruit from the tree of knowledge brought death into the world. This print, not executed by Beham himself, is a copy of his woodcut *Adam and Eve*,[3] which was produced without the addition of a tone block. Another chiaroscuro woodcut included here, *Unequal Lovers*, is attributed to Beham and has a pendant featuring a young man beside an old woman, both again shown as half-length figures, beneath a window arch (cat. 21; fig. 14). The subject, extremely popular in German literature and art since the late fifteenth century, pillories relationships between people of vastly differing ages: entered into solely for financial reasons, they are destined to fail and arouse the mockery of others. Both images illustrate the Nuremberg poet Hans Sachs's satirical 'Zweierlei ungleiche Ehen' (Two Unequal Marriages), written on 1 May 1533 and printed at the foot of the sheet in the first state.[4] Colour was added to the present woodcut in the later state, presumably to disguise damage that had occurred in the line block. In terms of quality it cannot withstand comparison with the chiaroscuro woodcuts by Cranach and Burgkmair.

15 **Hans Weiditz**

Man of Sorrows Seated

c. 1522

Chiaroscuro woodcut printed from two blocks, the tone block in brownish orange, 28.2 × 19.8 cm
Inscribed (centre right): *ECCE HOMO*
Albertina, Vienna, DG1949/417

16 **Hans Weiditz**

Man of Sorrows

1522

Chiaroscuro woodcut printed from two blocks, the tone block in brownish red, 29.4 × 22.1 cm; cut down slightly at left and right edges
Inscribed (upper right): *1522*; (lower left): *ECCE HOMO*
Collection of Georg Baselitz

1522
ECCE HOMO

17 **Albrecht Dürer**

Ulrich Varnbühler

1522 and *c.* 1620

Chiaroscuro woodcut printed from three blocks, the tone blocks in yellowish brown and brown, 43.5 × 32.8 cm
Inscribed (at upper edge): *VLRICHVS VARNBULER ZC M.D.XXII.*; (in the cartouche): *Albertus Durer Noric[u]s, / hac imagine Vlrichum cognom[en] to / Varnbuler Ro[mani] Caesarei Regimin[i]s / in Imperio, a Secretis, simul[ar]chi / gramateum, vt quem amet / vnice, etiam posteritati [vul]t / cognitum reddere c[olere] que / conatur.* [restorations from Thausing 1884, vol. 2, p. 268, n. 3]
Collection of Georg Baselitz

18 **Albrecht Dürer**

Rhinoceros

1515 and *c.* 1620

Chiaroscuro woodcut printed from two blocks, the tone block in green
Inscribed (upper right): *1515 / RHINOCERVS / AD* [monogrammed], 21.1 × 29.9 cm
Albertina, Vienna, DG1934/512

1515
RHINOCERVS

19 **Hans Sebald Beham**
Head of Christ Crowned with Thorns
c. 1520–21

Chiaroscuro woodcut printed from two blocks, the tone block in brown,
45.3 × 20.2 cm
Watermark: Eagle with coat of arms shield in the centre
Albertina, Vienna, DG1936/1080

20 **Lucas Cranach the Elder**
St John the Baptist Preaching
1516

Chiaroscuro woodcut printed from two blocks, the tone block in reddish brown,
34 × 23.7 cm
Inscribed (lower right, on tablet): *1516* [with winged serpent];
the coat of arms of the Elector of Saxony hanging from the tree at upper right
Collection of Georg Baselitz

21 **Hans Sebald Beham**

The Unequal Lovers

after 1533

Chiaroscuro woodcut printed from two blocks, the tone block in olive green,
24.6 × 24.9 cm
Watermark: P below a shield with the imperial orb and with an H on either side; cf. Piccard Online no. 11514
Collection of Georg Baselitz

22 **After Hans Sebald Beham**

Adam and Eve

c. 1530–40

Chiaroscuro woodcut printed from two blocks, the tone block in yellow ochre,
35.4 × 25.7 cm
Damage at the left, right and lower edges and in the upper right corner has been made up
Collection of Georg Baselitz

Beginnings in Italy: Ugo da Carpi

IV

In July 1516 Ugo da Carpi applied to the Venetian Senate for a 'privilege' for publishing chiaroscuro woodcuts, making the production of imitations punishable by law. The application includes the false claim that he had invented the technique,[1] but he did introduce it into Italy, develop it in key ways and create outstanding works in it. Ugo was a painter as well as a type-founder and woodcutter, which helps to explain the remarkable use of colour in his chiaroscuro woodcuts. Unlike the German artists, he cut his own blocks. By 1511 he had moved from his native Carpi to Venice, the centre of the Italian publishing industry. He produced his first chiaroscuro woodcut, a *St Jerome*, in 1516 (cat. 23). It resembles the early German examples in its use of one tone block in combination with a line block reproducing the entire composition. Ugo will certainly have known the colour illustrations in the books that Erhard Ratdolt published in Venice in the 1480s and must also have been familiar with Cranach's and Burgkmair's chiaroscuro woodcuts, perhaps brought to Venice by artists on their travels or by merchants (traders from Augsburg and Nuremberg maintained an exchange, the Fondaco dei Tedeschi, in the city).[2]

Fig. 15

Ugo's style is characterised by extremely vibrant, dynamic lines, which curl forcefully, alternate with long, emphatically curving lines and form complex groups of hatchings. The lines model limbs boldly while binding together the body in a coherent whole. They also echo the style of the artist who provided the design – in the case of *St Jerome* Titian, who may have drawn the composition directly onto the woodblock. Ugo built up his later chiaroscuro prints from three or more tone blocks, their carefully gradated colours step by step rendering the line block superfluous. His achievement was to free the chiaroscuro woodcut from its attachment to line, modelling images by colour and light alone to attain the effect of painting to an extraordinary degree.

Ugo moved to Rome at some point in 1516–18 and, about the same time as the engravers Marco Dente and Agostino Veneziano, joined the great Bolognese artist Marcantonio Raimondi in the workshop that produced prints after Raphael. Rome now became the 'print capital' of Italy. Ugo's first work there was probably *Hercules Chasing Avarice from the Temple of the Muses*, after Baldassare Peruzzi (cats 24, 25), followed by two other scenes

Fig. 15 (Page 62)
Raphael, *The Miraculous Draught of Fishes*, 1515. Pen and ink heightened with white, and chalk, 20 × 33.9 cm.
Royal Collection Trust, RL 12749

Fig. 16 Ugo da Carpi, *David and Goliath*, c. 1518–20. Chiaroscuro woodcut printed from three blocks, the tone blocks in ochre and brown, 26.3 × 39.2 cm.
Albertina, Vienna, DG2002/272

Fig. 17 Ugo da Carpi, *Hercules and the Nemean Lion*, c. 1516–18. Chiaroscuro woodcut printed from two blocks, the tone block in light brown, 30 × 22.5 cm.
Albertina, Vienna, DG2002/312

featuring Hercules that already show a reduction in linearity, an increase in clarity and spatial depth and a more organic feeling for figures' movements (cat. 26; fig. 17). The preliminary drawings for these were doubtless by Raphael, but have not survived. Raphael mostly provided Ugo with designs for paintings subsequently executed in an altered form. The large woodcut *Aeneas and Anchises*, after a design for *The Fire in the Borgo* in the Vatican Stanze, dispenses with the line block and was printed entirely from four tone blocks consisting of large, irregular areas of colour (cat. 27). This print, like *The Death of Ananias* (cat. 28), after a design by Raphael for a series of tapestries in the Sistine Chapel, bears an inscription including the date of 1518 and a 'privilege' awarded by the pope and the Venetian Senate, which states that the work is protected by copyright. The *Archimedes*, which dates from the same period or a little later, was probably based on a design executed by Raphael around the time he was producing studies for his *Transfiguration* and is known to survive only in the impression included here (cat. 30). In these woodcuts the areas of colour are sharp-edged and overlap additively, but in *David and Goliath*, based on a *modello*, now lost, for a scene in the Vatican Loggia, the colour areas and the highlights interact more harmoniously, rendering the movements more supple and the bodies rounder (fig. 16). This marks the beginning of a freer, more painterly style, as represented by *The Miraculous Draught of Fishes* (cat. 29). The fact that Ugo was now receiving more summarily executed drawings, with the addition of wash and

Fig. 18 Parmigianino, *Nymphs Bathing*, *c.* 1526–27. Pen and ink and wash heightened with white, 29.5 × 21.1 cm.

Galleria degli Uffizi, Florence, Gabinetto dei Disegni e delle Stampe, 751 E

Fig. 19 Parmigianino, *Man Surprised*, *c.* 1526–27. Pen and ink and wash and black chalk, 22.8 × 15 cm.

Musée du Louvre, Paris, D.A.G., 6433r

white heightening, instead of pen-and-ink studies, as the basis for his woodcuts contributed to this development. In *The Miraculous Draught of Fishes*, based on a preliminary drawing by Raphael at Windsor Castle (fig. 15) and probably made after the latter's death, in 1520, Ugo focuses principally on optical effects, with one tone block printed over the entire picture plane, the areas of colour arranged broadly and fluidly, the highlights flashing brightly. This does not impair the solidity of the figures, however: colours and light are used sparingly to model their bodies, establish their position in space and indicate foreshortening.

In 1524 Ugo began a fruitful collaboration with Parmigianino, who had just arrived in Rome. In *Olympus*, *Nymphs Bathing* and other works after Parmigianino he skilfully translated the painter's elegantly elongated forms into the woodcut medium (cats 35, 36; figs 18, 19). *Diogenes*, Ugo's masterpiece, probably dates from *c.* 1527 (cats 37–9). It impresses by reason of the monumentality of the figure, the expressiveness of the movements and the almost explosive dynamism of the colour and light, which dissolve into areas that add up to a convincing image only when printed together, creating an effect closely approximate to that of a painting. With Parmigianino, who was much interested in disseminating his artistic ideas in the form of prints and was the first Italian to recognise the expressive potential of etching, which he practised himself, the chiaroscuro woodcut acquired a significance greater than with any other Italian artist.

23 **Ugo da Carpi, after Titian**
St Jerome
1516

Chiaroscuro woodcut printed from two blocks, the tone block in grey,
16 × 9.9 cm
Inscribed (centre): *TICIANUS*; (lower edge, centre right): *UGO*
Albertina, Vienna, DG2002/324

24 **Ugo da Carpi, after Baldassare Peruzzi**
Hercules Chasing Avarice from the Temple of the Muses
c. 1516–17

Chiaroscuro woodcut printed from two blocks, the tone block in green, 29.9 × 22.6 cm; damaged lower corners have been made up
Inscribed (lower left corner): *BAL·S·EN*; (lower right corner): *PER UGO*; verso inscribed: *J. Storck a Milan 1797 / In. No. 548* [in pen and ink]
Watermark: Crossbow within a circle beneath a star
Albertina, Vienna, DG2002/913

BAL·SEN·
PERVGG

25 **Ugo da Carpi,**
after Baldassare Peruzzi

Hercules Chasing Avarice from the Temple of the Muses

c. 1517–20

Chiaroscuro woodcut printed from two blocks, the tone block in beige,
29.7 × 22.5 cm
Inscribed (lower left corner): *BAL·S·EN*; (lower right corner): *PER UGO*
Watermark: Circle enclosing an indecipherable motif
Collection of Georg Baselitz

26 **Ugo da Carpi, after Raphael**

Hercules and Antheus

c. 1516–18

Chiaroscuro woodcut printed from two blocks, the tone block in greyish blue
Inscribed (upper left, in the frieze): *RAPHAEL / URBINAS*; (lower right): *UGO*,
30.1 × 22.2 cm; small holes in the centre
Collection of Georg Baselitz

27 **Ugo da Carpi, after Raphael**
Aeneas and Anchises
1518
Chiaroscuro woodcut printed from four tone blocks, in beige and grey,
51 × 37.4 cm
Inscribed (lower right, in cartouche): *RAPHAEL / URBINAS / QUISQUIS. HAS.TABELLAS / INVITO. AUTORE.INPRIMET. / EX.DIVI. LEONIS·X·AC ILL[USTRIS]. / PRI[N]CIPIS. VENETIARUM.DE / CRETIS.EXCOMINICATIO. / NIS. SENTE[N]TIA[M].ET.ALIAS. / PENAS.INCURRET. / ROME.APUD. UGUM. DE DARPI. I[M]PRESA[M] / M.DXVIII.*; (lower right edge): *[F?] Mariette 1728* [in pen and ink]
Collection of Georg Baselitz

28 **Ugo da Carpi, after Raphael**
The Death of Ananias
1518

Chiaroscuro woodcut printed from four blocks, the tone blocks in brown,
27 × 38.1 cm; lower left corner has been made up
Inscribed (below): *RAPHAEL. URBINAS. / QUISQUIS. HAS. TABELLAS. INVITO. AUTORE. INPRIMET. EX. DIVI. LEONIS. X. / AC. ILL. PRINCIPIS. ET. SENATUS. VENETIARUM. DECRETIS. EXCOMVNICATI / ONIS. SENTENTIAM. ET. ALIAS. PENAS. INCURRET. / ROME. APUD. UGUM. DE DARPI. INMPRESSAM. M.D.XVIII.*; (lower left): *P. mariette 1668* [in pen and ink]
Albertina, Vienna, DG2002/290

29 **Ugo da Carpi, after Raphael**
The Miraculous Draught of Fishes
c. 1523–27

Chiaroscuro woodcut printed from three blocks, the tone blocks in red,
23.4 × 35.7 cm
Watermark: Anchor within a circle, below a star; similar to Briquet 478, 484, 485, 490, 493
Albertina, Vienna, DG2002/282

.RAPHAEL.VRBINAS.
QVISQVIS.HAS.TABELLAS.INVITO.AVTORE.INPRIMET.EX.DIVI.LEONIS.X.
AC.IIL.PRINCIPIS.ET.SENATVS.VENETIARVM.DECRETIS.EXCOMVNICATI
ONIS.SENTENTIAM.ET.ALIAS.PENAS.INCVRRET.
ROME.APVD.VGVM.DE.CARPI.INPRESSAM.M.D.XVIII.

30 **Ugo da Carpi, after Raphael**
Archimedes (?)
c. 1518–20

Chiaroscuro woodcut printed from five blocks, the tone blocks in beige, pale brown, brown and blackish brown, 44.5 × 34.7 cm
Watermark: Sailing boat within a circle, above a star
Albertina, Vienna, DG2002/524

31 **Ugo da Carpi, after Raphael**
The Deposition from the Cross
c. 1520–23

Chiaroscuro woodcut printed from three blocks, the tone blocks in pale and dark green, 32.9 × 26.9 cm; cut down at the sides and top
Inscribed (lower centre edge): *·RAPHAEL· URBINAS +*; (lower right corner, on the tablet): *UGO / DA / CAR / PI*; (lower right edge): *J. Mariette 1730* [in pen and ink]
Albertina, Vienna, DG 2002/287

32 **Ugo da Carpi, after Parmigianino**

Circe and the Companions of Ulysses

c. 1524–27

Chiaroscuro woodcut printed from four blocks, the tone blocks in beige, pale blue and blue, 20.9 × 18.8 cm; cut down on all sides
Collection of Georg Baselitz

33 **Ugo da Carpi, after Parmigianino (?)**

Saturn

c. 1524–27

Chiaroscuro woodcut printed from four blocks, the tone blocks in green and brown, 31.6 × 43.3 cm
Inscribed (lower left): *P. Mariette 1661* [in pen and ink]
Albertina, Vienna, DG2013/13

34 **Ugo da Carpi, after Parmigianino (?)**

Saturn

c. 1524–27 and 1604

Chiaroscuro woodcut printed from four blocks, the tone blocks in greyish brown, 32.3 × 43.4 cm
Inscribed (lower right edge): *A[ndrea] A[ndreani]* [monogrammed] *in mantoua 1604*
Collection of Georg Baselitz

in mantoua 1604

35 **Ugo da Carpi, after Parmigianino**

Olympus

c. 1526–27

Chiaroscuro woodcut printed from three blocks, the tone blocks in olive green and yellow, 27 × 19.2 cm

Verso inscribed: *no. 3637 / N: 325* [in pencil]

Collection of Georg Baselitz

36 **Ugo da Carpi, after Parmigianino**

Nymphs Bathing

c. 1526–27

Chiaroscuro woodcut printed from three blocks, the tone blocks in brownish orange and brown, 30.6 × 21.1 cm (sheet)

Collection of Georg Baselitz

P. mariette 1679

37 **Ugo da Carpi, after Parmigianino**
Diogenes
c. 1527

Chiaroscuro woodcut printed from four blocks, the tone blocks in green and blue, 47.8 × 34.3 cm; crease mark across the centre
Inscribed (lower left corner, on book page): *FRANCISCUS / PARMEN. / PER UGO CARP*; (lower centre edge): *P. Mariette 1679* [in pen and ink]
Albertina, Vienna, DG2003/3031

38 **Ugo da Carpi, after Parmigianino**
Diogenes
c. 1527

Chiaroscuro woodcut printed from four blocks, the tone blocks in green, 48.5 × 35 cm; crease mark across centre
Inscribed (lower left corner, on book page): *FRANCISCUS / PARMEN. / PER UGO CARP*; (lower centre edge): *P. mariette 1690* [in pen and ink]
Collection of Georg Baselitz

39 **Ugo da Carpi, after Parmigianino**
Diogenes
c. 1527

Chiaroscuro woodcut printed from four blocks, the tone blocks in brown, 47.6 × 34 cm
Inscribed (lower left corner, on book page): *FRANCISCUS / PARMEN· / PER UGO CARP*
Watermark: Coat of arms with two crossed axes, beneath a lily (?)
Collection of Georg Baselitz

40 **Circle of Parmigianino**

SS. Peter and John Healing the Lame Man

c. 1525–30

Etching and woodcut tone block in greyish brown, 28 × 40.8 cm
Inscribed (lower left corner): *20 go* [?] [in pen and ink];
verso inscribed: *P. m.*
[in pen and ink]; traces of black and red chalk at the left edge on verso
Collection of Georg Baselitz

41 **Circle of Parmigianino**

SS. Peter and John Healing the Lame Man

c. 1525–30

Etching, 26.9 × 40.6 cm
Inscribed (lower left corner, on base of column): *I ·V· R·*
Watermark: Triple mountain
Collection of Georg Baselitz

42 **Circle of Parmigianino**

SS. Peter and John Healing the Lame Man

c. 1525–30

Etching and two woodcut tone blocks in ochre and brown, 27.9 × 40.9 cm
Inscribed (lower left corner, on base of column): *I·V·R·*
Collection of Georg Baselitz

43 **Circle of Parmigianino**

SS. Peter and John Healing the Lame Man

c. 1525–30

Etching and two woodcut tone blocks in reddish brown, 26.9 × 40.7 cm; damaged lower corners have been made up
Inscribed (lower left corner, on base of column): *I·V·R·*
Collection of Georg Baselitz

Ugo da Carpi's Pupils and Followers

V

All surviving prints by the woodcutter Antonio da Trento – according to Eduard Kolloff, a total of thirty-six woodcuts – are based on drawings by Parmigianino.[1] One of the earliest and finest, *The Martyrdom of SS. Peter and Paul*, was printed from three blocks (cat. 44). Otherwise Antonio generally restricted himself to a line block and one tone block, echoing closely the linear style evident in the early work of Ugo da Carpi, who most probably taught Antonio in Rome. Ugo's networks of lines are finer and subtler, however, modelling the details of volumes by means of complex hatching, whereas Antonio's lines are freer and more fluid. They generate an almost autonomous rhythm, conveying in an individual way the elegance of Parmigianino's figures. Vasari listed *Sibyl Reading* (cat. 45) among Ugo's works,[2] but the free-flowing, almost calligraphic nature of the lines, and the highlights seemingly flitting across the picture plane, reveal the characteristic style of Antonio, as encountered in *St Cecilia* and two versions of *Circe and the Companions of Ulysses* (fig. 22; cats 47, 48). Parmigianino doubtless produced the drawings for these prints during his Roman period, from 1524 to 1527,[3] and Antonio's faithful reproductions of them may date from this time. By contrast, his graceful oval-shaped image of the Virgin and Child with the infant St John the Baptist is based on an earlier design, created by Parmigianino *c.* 1523 and perhaps brought to Rome from his native Parma (cat. 51). Antonio followed Parmigianino to Bologna after the sack of Rome in 1527. There he produced *The Lute Player* and its pendant, *St John the Baptist in the Wilderness* – the only woodcuts by him to bear his monogrammed initials, AT (cats 50, 52) – and the rear-view nude that probably depicts Narcissus gazing at his reflection in the water of a spring (cats 53–5). These works tend to portray figures in a more planar manner and to compose backgrounds with greater density. In his latest woodcut, *Augustus and the Tiburtine Sibyl*, Antonio reduces the prominence of the lines, concentrates on the modelling of the figures and increases the extent of pictorial space (cats 57, 58). Parmigianino produced various studies for this image in 1529–30, before returning to Parma without Antonio.[4] According to Vasari, Antonio had lived in Parmigianino's house and, one morning when the latter was still in bed, had made off with a chest containing all his woodcuts, engravings and drawings. The prints, deposited with a friend, were recovered, but Parmigianino never set eyes on the drawings again.[5]

Niccolò Vicentino, too, reproduced compositions by Parmigianino, but this woodcutter also based chiaroscuro prints on works by other artists, including Polidoro da Caravaggio, Francesco Salviati and Perino del Vaga. He mostly used three or four blocks for his woodcuts, which take their cue from Ugo's late, painterly style. A passage in Vasari has led to the assumption that Niccolò did not become active until the death of Parmigianino, in 1540,[6] but his chiaroscuro prints reproduce preliminary drawings by the painter datable to the 1520s with such subtlety that they may well have been made under his supervision. Like Antonio da Trento, Niccolò probably trained under Ugo in Rome and joined Parmigianino in Bologna in the

Fig. 20 Niccolò Vicentino, *Augustus and the Tiburtine Sibyl*, *c.* 1529–30. Chiaroscuro woodcut printed from four blocks, the tone blocks in beige and brown, 34.4 × 26.4 cm.

Museum of Fine Arts, Boston, Helen and Alice Colburn Fund, M28192

Fig. 21 Niccolò Vicentino, *Virgin and Child with Saints*, *c.* 1533–40. Chiaroscuro woodcut printed from three blocks, the tone blocks in green, 28.9 × 22.9 cm.

Collection of Georg Baselitz

Fig. 22 Antonio da Trento, *St Cecilia*, *c.* 1524–27. Chiaroscuro woodcut printed from two blocks, the tone block in orange-brown, 24.9 × 24.8 cm.

Albertina, Vienna, DG1130

period 1527 to 1530–31. Various arguments may be adduced in favour of this hypothesis. In his early work Niccolò follows Ugo's style so closely that prints such as the latter's *Miraculous Draught of Fishes* and *Olympus* have been attributed to him (cats 29, 35). There is nevertheless a clear stylistic difference between *Olympus* and Niccolò's *Christ Healing the Lepers* (cat. 68). The areas of colour are similarly fluid in both, but in Niccolò's print they do not perform the modelling function with which Ugo invests them. Niccolò lays them over one another in planar fashion and strews the highlights across the image in streaks, without giving the volumes notable solidity or foreshortening them. The figures appear extremely loose-limbed, almost as though made from some flexible or malleable substance. Their motions are dynamic, but they do not move freely in the self-determining manner of Ugo's figures. In *Olympus*, for example, the figure is animated from within; it dominates the surrounding space, while touches of colour and light articulate each part of the body and convey a feeling of solidity. With Niccolò, on the other hand, graphic elements outline the figures, binding them together in a network of rhythmic curves and anchoring them to the picture plane. *Olympus* and *Nymphs Bathing* (cat. 36) are important stages on the road to the masterly *Diogenes*, which can surely not have been the only collaboration between Parmigianino and Ugo. The fact that neither *Olympus* nor *The Miraculous Draught of Fishes* bears Ugo's signature does not tell against him as their creator, not least because his *Archimedes* also lacks a signature.[7]

Niccolò produced a version of Parmigianino's *Augustus*

Fig. 23 Niccolò Vicentino, *The Flight of Cloelia*, *c.* 1539–45. Chiaroscuro woodcut printed from three blocks, the tone blocks in brown, 28.1 × 42.1 cm.

Albertina, Vienna, DG 2002/363

Fig. 24 Niccolò Vicentino, *Christ Healing a Lame Man*, *c.* 1539–45. Chiaroscuro woodcut printed from four blocks, the tone blocks in grey and greyish blue, 26.6 × 20.5 cm.

Albertina, Vienna, DG 2002/424

Fig. 25 Niccolò Vicentino, *Homage to Psyche*, *c.* 1539–40. Chiaroscuro woodcut printed from three blocks, the tone blocks in red, 27.5 × 26.3 cm.

Albertina, Vienna, DG 2002/556

and the Tiburtine Sibyl slightly different from Antonio's (cat. 56). There is every reason to believe that the painter deliberately gave the same drawing to both woodcutters, the one recording it in his characteristic linear style, the other in his typically painterly manner. Impressions exist showing the tone block from Antonio's print used in Niccolò's version (fig. 20),[8] a process that naturally demanded identical dimensions and similar compositions in both cases. The two prints thus probably originated at the same time, *c.* 1529–30, in Bologna. Like Antonio, Niccolò did not accompany Parmigianino on his return to Parma in 1530–31. Henceforth he reproduced designs by artists strongly influenced by Parmigianino. *Virgin and Child with Saints*, for example, is based on a design by Camillo Boccaccino for an altarpiece in Cremona cathedral, while *Homage to Psyche* was done from a depiction of a ceiling painting, rediscovered a few years ago, by Francesco Salviati in the Palazzo Grimani, Venice (figs 21, 25). The two prints reveal a stylistic development towards a more sparing use of line and highlights, a stronger modelling of volumes, clearer distinctions between figures and an increase in spatial depth. Niccolò's latest known prints record two works now destroyed: a façade fresco painted in Rome by Maturino and a mural of *c.* 1539 by Perino del Vaga in the Massimi chapel in SS. Trinità dei Monti, also in Rome (figs 23, 24). Possibly, then, Niccolò returned to Rome in the late 1530s or early 1540s.

44 **Antonio da Trento, after Parmigianino**
The Martyrdom of SS. Peter and Paul
c. 1524–25

Chiaroscuro woodcut printed from three blocks, the tone blocks in reddish brown and brown, 29 × 48.6 cm
Collection of Georg Baselitz

45 **Attributed to Antonio da Trento, after Parmigianino**
Sibyl Reading
c. 1524–27

Chiaroscuro woodcut printed from two blocks, the tone block in brown,
27.8 × 22.1 cm; fragment inserted into the area of the sibyl's knees
Inscribed (upper right): *•R/R•V•I•*
Collection of Georg Baselitz

46 **Antonio da Trento, after Parmigianino**
Virgin and Child with Saints
c. 1527–30 and *c.* 1602–10

Chiaroscuro woodcut printed from two blocks, the tone block in brown,
31 × 21.4 cm
Inscribed (lower left): *A[ndrea] A[ndreani]* [monogrammed]
Collection of Georg Baselitz

47 **Antonio da Trento, after Parmigianino**

Circe and the Companions of Ulysses

c. 1524–27 and *c.* 1602–10

Chiaroscuro woodcut printed from three blocks, the tone blocks in beige and brown, 22.5 × 21.2 cm (sheet)
Inscribed (lower left corner): *A[ndrea] A[ndreani]* [monogrammed, in the block]; (lower left): *K·g*; [in pen and ink]; figure sketch and various inscriptions on verso
Collection of Georg Baselitz

48 **Antonio da Trento, after Parmigianino**

Circe and the Companions of Ulysses

c. 1524–27

Chiaroscuro woodcut printed from two blocks, the tone blocks in orange brown, 24.9 × 21.6 cm; cut down at both sides
Collection of Georg Baselitz

49 **Antonio da Trento, after Parmigianino**
The Lute Player
c. 1527–30

Chiaroscuro woodcut printed from two blocks, the tone block in greyish green,
11.9 × 10.9 cm
Watermark: Circle enclosing a V and an I (?)
Collection of Georg Baselitz

50 **Antonio da Trento, after Parmigianino**
The Lute Player
c. 1527–30

Chiaroscuro woodcut printed from two blocks, the tone block in brownish green,
14 × 13.8 cm
Inscribed (on frame, below): *AT* [monogrammed]
Collection of Georg Baselitz

51 **Antonio da Trento, after Parmigianino**
The Madonna of the Roses
c. 1524–27

Chiaroscuro woodcut printed from two blocks, the tone block in green,
20.4 × 24.8 cm; damaged lower left corner has been made up
Inscribed (lower centre border): *669*·[in pen and ink]
Watermark: Circle enclosing an indecipherable motif
Collection of Georg Baselitz

52 **Antonio da Trento, after Parmigianino**
St John the Baptist in the Wilderness
c. 1527–30

Chiaroscuro woodcut printed from two blocks, the tone block in green,
13.9 × 13.9 cm
Inscribed (lower section of frame): *AT* [monogrammed]
Albertina, Vienna, DG2002/464

A

53 **Antonio da Trento, after Parmigianino**
Narcissus
c. 1527–30/1

Chiaroscuro woodcut printed from two blocks, the tone block in green,
28.5 × 18.1 cm
Collection of Georg Baselitz

54 **Antonio da Trento, after Parmigianino**
Narcissus
c. 1527–30/1

Chiaroscuro woodcut printed from two blocks, the tone block in brown,
28.9 × 18 cm
Collection of Georg Baselitz

55 **Antonio da Trento, after Parmigianino**
Narcissus
c. 1527–30/1

Chiaroscuro woodcut printed from two blocks, the tone block in reddish brown,
29 × 18.3 cm; crease mark across the centre
Several inscriptions on verso, including (lower left edge): *E[...] Mark* [perhaps a previous owner, in pencil]
Collection of Georg Baselitz

56 **Niccolò Vicentino, after Parmigianino**
Augustus and the Tiburtine Sibyl
c. 1529–30

Chiaroscuro woodcut printed from four blocks, the tone blocks in blue and greenish blue, 34.2 × 25.6 cm; traces of emendations in pen and brown ink; damaged upper right corner has been made up
Inscribed (lower left): *P. mariette 1670* [in pen and ink]
Collection of Georg Baselitz

57 **Antonio da Trento, after Parmigianino**
Augustus and the Tiburtine Sibyl
c. 1529–30

Chiaroscuro woodcut printed from two blocks, the tone block in brown, 34.9 × 26.6 cm (sheet); 34 × 26 cm (block)
Collection of Georg Baselitz

58 **Antonio da Trento, after Parmigianino**
Augustus and the Tiburtine Sibyl
c. 1529–30

Chiaroscuro woodcut printed from two blocks, the tone block in reddish brown, 36.6 × 28.2 cm
Collection of Georg Baselitz

59

60

61

62

59 **Antonio da Trento, after Parmigianino**
St Matthew
c. 1524–27
Chiaroscuro woodcut printed from three blocks, the tone block in brown, 15.5 × 10.6 cm
Albertina, Vienna, DG2002/443

60 **Antonio da Trento, after Parmigianino**
St Thomas
c. 1524–27
Chiaroscuro woodcut printed from three blocks, the tone block in brown, 15.1 × 10.5 cm
Albertina, Vienna, DG2002/449

61 **Antonio da Trento, after Parmigianino**
St Simon
c. 1524–27
Chiaroscuro woodcut printed from three blocks, the tone blocks in brown, 15.5 × 10.6 cm
Albertina, Vienna, DG2002/445

62 **Antonio da Trento, after Parmigianino**
St Paul
c. 1524–27
Chiaroscuro woodcut printed from three blocks, the tone blocks in brown, 15.1 × 10.8 cm
Albertina, Vienna, DG2002/447

63 **Antonio da Trento, after Parmigianino**
St John the Evangelist
c. 1524–27
Chiaroscuro woodcut printed from three blocks, the tone blocks in beige and brown, 13.1 × 8.6 cm
Collection of Georg Baselitz

64 **Antonio da Trento, after Parmigianino**
St Peter
c. 1524–27
Chiaroscuro woodcut printed from three blocks, the tone blocks in ochre, 15.3 × 10.5 cm
Albertina, Vienna, DG2002/441

63

64

65

65 **Antonio da Trento, after Parmigianino**
St Jude
c. 1524–27
Chiaroscuro woodcut printed from three blocks, the tone blocks in brown,
12.4 × 7.4 cm
Albertina, Vienna, DG2002/444

66 **Antonio da Trento, after Parmigianino**
St Andrew
c. 1524–27
Chiaroscuro woodcut printed from three blocks, the tone blocks in green and brown,
14.5 × 9.9 cm
Albertina, Vienna, DG2002/439

67 **Antonio da Trento, after Parmigianino**
St Philip
c. 1524–27
Chiaroscuro woodcut printed from three blocks, the tone blocks in red,
12.4 × 7 cm
Albertina, Vienna, DG2002/460

66

67

68 **Niccolò Vicentino,**
after Parmigianino
Christ Healing the Lepers
c. 1527–29

Chiaroscuro woodcut printed from three blocks, the tone blocks in violet,
29.1 × 40.7 cm; small area of loss at lower right edge
Inscribed (lower right, barely legible):
IOSEPH·NICOLAUS VICENTINI
Collection of Georg Baselitz

PVLIDORO·CAR
IO·NIC·VICEN

POLIDORO DA CARAVAGIO.

69 **Niccolò Vicentino, after Polidoro da Caravaggio**
The Death of Ajax
c. 1525–27
Chiaroscuro woodcut printed from three blocks, the tone blocks in green,
31.4 × 41.6 cm
Inscribed (lower right corner): *PULIDORO · CAR / IOs · NIC· VICEN*; (lower left): *T Mariette 1725* [in pen and ink]
Albertina, Vienna, DG2002/342

70 **Niccolò Vicentino, after Polidoro da Caravaggio**
The Death of Ajax
c. 1525–27 and 1608
Chiaroscuro woodcut printed from three blocks, the tone blocks in beige and grey,
31.7 × 42.1 cm
Inscribed (lower right corner): *POLIDORO DA CARAVAGIO / INVENT[OR] A[ndrea] A[ndreani] in mantoua 1608*
Collection of Georg Baselitz

71 **Niccolò Vicentino, after Raphael (?)**
Hercules and the Nemean Lion
c. 1525–27 and 1602–10
Chiaroscuro woodcut printed from two blocks, the tone block in ochre,
25.3 × 19.7 cm
Inscribed (lower left corner): *RAPH[AEL] • UR[BINAS] / A[ndrea] A[ndreani]*
Collection of Georg Baselitz

72 **Niccolò Vicentino, after Parmigianino**
The Adoration of the Magi
c. 1527–29

Chiaroscuro woodcut printed from three blocks, the tone blocks in beige,
29.2 × 23.9 cm; cut down at the upper, lower and right edge
Inscribed (lower right corner): *F•[P]*; verso inscribed: *Mariette* [in pen and ink]
Collection of Georg Baselitz

73 **Niccolò Vicentino, after Parmigianino**
Virgin and Child with St Sebastian and a Bishop
c. 1527–29 and 1605

Chiaroscuro woodcut printed from four blocks, the tone blocks in beige,
39.8 × 30 cm
Inscribed (lower right corner): *A[ndrea] A[ndreani]* [monogrammed] *in mantoua 1605•*
Collection of Georg Baselitz

ÆA in mantoua 1605.

74

75

76

77

74 **Niccolò Vicentino, after Perino del Vaga (?)**
Faith
c. 1539–45

Chiaroscuro woodcut printed from three blocks, the tone blocks in grey and greyish blue, 14.1 × 9.4 cm
Collection of Georg Baselitz

75 **Niccolò Vicentino, after Perino del Vaga (?)**
Hope
c. 1539–45

Chiaroscuro woodcut printed from three blocks, the tone blocks in brown, 14.5 × 9.7 cm
Albertina, Vienna, DG2002/480

76 **Niccolò Vicentino, after Perino del Vaga (?)**
Charity
c. 1539–45

Chiaroscuro woodcut printed from three blocks, the tone blocks in brown, 14.5 × 10.1 cm
Collection of Georg Baselitz

77 **Niccolò Vicentino, after Perino del Vaga (?)**
Fortitude
c. 1539–45

Chiaroscuro woodcut printed from three blocks, the tone blocks in brown, 14.5 × 9.8 cm
Collection of Georg Baselitz

78 **Niccolò Vicentino, after Perino del Vaga (?)**
Temperance
c. 1539–45

Chiaroscuro woodcut printed from three blocks, the tone blocks in brown, 14.4 × 9.8 cm
Verso inscribed: *P. Mariette* 1689 [in pen and ink]
Albertina, Vienna, DG2002/482

79 **Niccolò Vicentino, after Perino del Vaga (?)**
Prudence
c. 1539–45

Chiaroscuro woodcut printed from three blocks, the tone blocks in yellow and blue-green, 14.2 × 9.8 cm
Collection of Georg Baselitz

78

79

Domenico Beccafumi

VI

With one exception all sixteenth-century Italian woodcutters came from northern Italy. The exception was Domenico Beccafumi of Siena. This exceptionally versatile artist, who was also active as a painter, sculptor and engraver, created some of the most idiosyncratic and compelling of all chiaroscuro woodcuts, presumably in the last decade of his life, in the 1540s. Prominent among them are prints for three series of apostles, none of which he finished. The figure of an apostle standing in front of the base of a temple and another of St Philip probably belong to the earliest, 'small' apostle series (cats 80, 81). With poses dominated by vibrant curves, their movement directed outwards, the apostles gaze keenly into the distance, apparently transfixed by a divine vision. Flickering light and shade anchors them in space. The way in which the painterly distribution of colour and light dissolves some areas into forms resembling scraps of cloth recalls such late chiaroscuro woodcuts by Ugo as *The Apostles Peter and John* and *Diogenes* (fig. 28; cats 37–9). The action of the cutting tool can be traced in the hard-edged shapes and the roughly etched lines. Like no other woodcutter, Beccafumi gives the wood a voice of its own.[1]

Also included here are images of SS. Peter and Philip, along with an unidentified apostle, that belong to a further, larger series (cats 82–5). Conceived more monumentally, they are more dignified and distinguished in appearance, more inward-looking and contemplative. At the same time, they are full of inner tension – a state expressed by the intense highlights, which seem to be releasing electric charges across the picture plane. The apostles dominate the surrounding space, seemingly invading it. Their Michelangelesque

Fig. 26

Fig. 26 (Page 112)
Domenico Beccafumi, *Woman Gazing at the Moon*, late 1540s. Chiaroscuro woodcut printed from three blocks, the tone blocks in grey, 21.5 × 15.6 cm.

Albertina, Vienna, DG 2002/545

Fig. 27 Domenico Beccafumi, *Sibyl*, late 1540s. Chiaroscuro woodcut printed from two blocks, the tone block in grey, 14.9 × 14.9 cm.

Albertina, Vienna, DG 2002/546

Fig. 28 Ugo da Carpi, *The Apostles Peter and John*, c. 1524–27. Chiaroscuro woodcut printed from three blocks, the tone blocks in green, 15.5 × 10.4 cm.

Albertina, Vienna, DG2002/456

bodies bring to mind the artist's apostles in the apse fresco of *c.* 1544 in Siena cathedral and his *Sacrifice of Isaac* of *c.* 1547 in the intarsia pavements there.[2] These resemblances suggest that the prints date from the mid-1540s.

A pair of apostles belonging to yet another series probably originated about the same time (cat. 86). Beccafumi here added a woodblock impression to an engraving, as he did in *Group of Men and Women* and elsewhere (cat. 87). The impetus for this complex combination of intaglio and relief printing may have come from an anonymous *SS. Peter and John Healing the Lame Man*, which records a drawing by Parmigianino after a design by Raphael for the Sistine Chapel tapestries (cats 40–3). This print, however, combines chiaroscuro woodcut with etching, not engraving. Beccafumi uses engraved lines in the shaded areas of the two apostles and the highlights match the engraving by taking on a finer, more linear character. This foreshadows his delicate, finely incisive late style, in which he sought to grant woodcut the precision of engraving. In *Woman Gazing at the Moon* and *Sibyl*, which are presumably his latest chiaroscuro woodcuts, produced in the late 1540s, the wood of the line block is cut back to form ridges so thin that they resemble engraved lines when printed (figs 26, 27). The highlights, no longer broad and irregular, cover the limbs like a gossamer net and the limbs evince greater volume and roundness. Technically, these are Beccafumi's most highly developed and subtlest chiaroscuro woodcuts. Stylistically, their increased linearity is indebted to chiaroscuro prints by Antonio da Trento, including *The Madonna of the Roses* (cat. 51).

80 **Domenico Beccafumi**

An Apostle

c. 1540–45

Chiaroscuro woodcut printed from three blocks, the tone blocks in grey and grey-blue, 28.9 × 17.7 cm

Inscribed (lower right edge): *Du Beccafumi.* [in pen and ink]; verso inscribed: *Mariette* [in pen and ink]

Collection of Georg Baselitz

81 **Domenico Beccafumi**

St Philip

c. 1540–45

Chiaroscuro woodcut printed from three blocks, the tone blocks in brown,
28.5 × 17.3 cm
Albertina, Vienna, DG2002/391

82 **Domenico Beccafumi**

St Philip

c. 1544–47

Chiaroscuro woodcut printed from three blocks, the tone blocks in reddish brown,
41 × 21.2 cm
Inscribed (lower right):
P. Mariette 1689 [in pen and ink]
Albertina, Vienna, DG2013/17

83 **Domenico Beccafumi**

St Philip

c. 1544–47

Chiaroscuro woodcut printed from three blocks, the tone blocks in grey and blue, 39.6 × 20.9 cm

Inscribed (lower right): *P. mariette 1678* [in pen and ink]

Albertina, Vienna, DG2002/385

84 **Domenico Beccafumi**

St Peter

c. 1544–47

Chiaroscuro woodcut printed from four blocks, the tone blocks in green and grey, 41 × 21.1 cm
Inscribed (lower left corner): *P. mariette 1662* [in pen and ink]
Albertina, Vienna, DG2013/18

85 **Domenico Beccafumi**
An Apostle
c. 1544–47

Chiaroscuro woodcut printed from three blocks, the tone blocks in brown,
39.7 × 19 cm
Albertina, Vienna, DG2002/387

86 **Domenico Beccafumi**

Two Apostles

c. 1544–47

Engraving with woodcut tone block in ochre, 41.3 × 20.9 cm; traces of red paint on the right Albertina, Vienna, DG2002/388

87 **Domenico Beccafumi**
Group of Men and Women
c. 1545–47

Engraving with two woodcut tone blocks, in pale blue and blue, 14.3 × 22.2 cm; area of loss in the back of the rear-view figure
Albertina, Vienna, DG2002/395

Cremona and Bologna

VII

The five known prints by Antonio Campi of Cremona, all chiaroscuro woodcuts, date from around the same time as the later works by Beccafumi discussed in the previous section.[1] Produced between 1547 and 1553, they show that the impact of Parmigianino's art continued unabated after his death, in 1540. In fact, in a line woodcut Campi copied a drawing by Parmigianino, now lost,[2] that in the eighteenth century was reproduced in a chiaroscuro woodcut by Anton Maria Zanetti (B. XII, p. 193, no. 57). In Campi's *The Holy Family with St Catherine of Alexandria*, dated 1547, the influence of Parmigianino is evident in the graceful elegance of the figures, their dense and essentially planar arrangement in space and their rhythmical animation (cat. 88). The limitation to a line block and one tone block, together with the linear treatment of the highlights, can be related to the chiaroscuro woodcuts of Antonio da Trento, whereas later prints by Campi, including a *Holy Family* of 1550, disclose a freer, more painterly approach that brings to mind Niccolò's prints (cf. fig. 29 and cat. 72). In the *Holy Family* he makes no use of the line block to render outlines, but dissolves the forms into areas of colour juxtaposed and superimposed in the manner of flowing brush strokes.

Bologna became a centre of chiaroscuro woodcut production when Parmigianino, Antonio da Trento and Niccolò Vicentino moved to the city. The technique was also practised there by Alessandro Gandini, resident in Bologna by the mid-1540s.[3] His *Virgin and Child with Saints*, relating to an altarpiece by Girolamo da Treviso in the church of San Domenico, was probably based on a preliminary drawing that differed slightly from the painting (cat. 89; fig. 30).[4] Gandini's *Feast in the House of Simon the Pharisee* (cat. 90), a rare work printed from three blocks, records a fresco from a series of scenes from the life of Mary Magdalene (now destroyed) painted by Giulio Romano and Giovanni Francesco Penni in the Massimi chapel in SS. Trinità dei Monti, Rome, after designs by Raphael. Gandini modelled his print on a drawing by Parmigianino that was presumably a copy of a design by Raphael that has not survived. The woodcut is unusual in that it rejects colour in favour of black and shades of grey, accentuating the highlights and giving the whole the effect of a white line print. A drawing of the same subject by Parmigianino is listed in an inventory as heightened with silver,[5] so perhaps Gandini was attempting to imitate this in his woodcut. On the other hand, the inventory may be incorrect and the drawing identical with one now in a private collection (fig. 31).[6] In 1609 Andrea Andreani reissued the *Feast in the House of Simon the Pharisee*, apparently using Gandini's blocks (cat. 91).[7]

Also active in Bologna was an anonymous woodcutter who signed five of his chiaroscuro prints with the initials 'NDB' and dated two of these '1544'. Caroline Karpinski has totalled his surviving oeuvre at eleven woodcuts.[8] His *Massacre of the Innocents* reproduces one of twelve tapestries in the Vatican with scenes from the life of Christ woven in the workshop of Pieter van Aelst in Brussels (cats 93, 94). Raphael was probably responsible for the original designs, as the inscription on the woodcut states, but they seem to have been worked up by assistants. Master NDB's style typically shows figures with thin outlines printed from the

Fig. 29 Antonio Campi, *The Holy Family*, 1550. Chiaroscuro woodcut printed from three blocks, the tone blocks in pale green and grey, 14.9 × 11 cm.

Albertina, Vienna, DG 2002/558

Fig. 30 Girolamo da Treviso, *The Madonna and Child with Angels, Saints and a Donor*, *c.* 1529–32. Oil on panel, 225.4 × 147.3 cm.

National Gallery, London, NG623

line block and hard-edged shadows, both features that can be linked to chiaroscuro woodcuts by Ugo da Carpi, including the *Deposition from the Cross* (cat. 31). Impressions of the *Massacre of the Innocents* taken from the line block alone must be of later date because the outlines are broken in several places, indicating damage to the block through use. Two chiaroscuro woodcuts of putti at play are connected with another series of tapestries designed by Raphael, the *Giochi di Putti* displayed along the bottom of the walls in the Sala di Costantino in the Vatican (fig. 32 and B. XII, pp. 108–9, no. 4). Various motifs from the tapestries appear in Master NDB's prints, one of which names Raphael as the inventor – important documentary evidence pointing to him as the creator of the compositions.

Catherine Jenkins has established that Master NDB's woodcuts are printed on paper bearing French watermarks and concludes that they were produced in Fontainebleau.[9] At the same time Dominique Cordellier made the significant discovery that in the 1540s members of the school of Fontainebleau were creating chiaroscuro woodcuts in addition to etchings. According to Cordellier, a chiaroscuro woodcut by an unknown artist showing the Holy Family with the infant St John the Baptist was printed in Fontainebleau after a design by Luca Penni, who was active there (B. XII, p. 59, no. 16).[10] Another chiaroscuro woodcut by Master NDB records a drawing of the Holy Family, now lost, by Rosso Fiorentino that the artist made shortly before his death in France, in 1540 (B. XII, p. 59, no. 17).[11] Master NDB here reproduced a model that was already in France, but in the case of the Raphael

Fig. 31 Parmigianino, *Feast in the House of Simon the Pharisee*, *c.* 1526. Pen and ink and wash heightened with white, 18.7 × 32.4 cm.
Private collection

Fig. 32 Master NDB, *Putti at Play*, 1544. Chiaroscuro woodcut printed from three blocks, the tone blocks in brown, 28.4 × 39.3 cm.
Albertina, Vienna, DG 2002/310

LVICKES·BEN·
D·R·ANNA·
INVENTVR·

Fig. 33 Georg Matheus, *Diana and Actaeon*, *c.* 1540–60. Chiaroscuro woodcut printed from three blocks, the tone blocks in beige and pale brown, 34.3 × 47.9 cm.

Albertina, Vienna, DG 2002/350

Fig. 34 Georg Matheus, *The Flight into Egypt*, *c.* 1540–60. Chiaroscuro woodcut printed from three blocks, the tone blocks in green, 34.5 × 47.7 cm.

Albertina, Vienna, DG1984/173

Fig. 35 Luca Penni, *Diana and Actaeon*, *c.* 1540–60. Pen and ink and wash, 11.1 × 18 cm.

The Print Room of the University of Warsaw Library, 7481

Fig. 36 Master NDB, *Virgin and Child with Saints*, *c.* 1540–50. Chiaroscuro woodcut printed from three blocks, the tone blocks in brown, 23.8 × 18 cm.

Albertina, Vienna, DG 2002/436

designs it is not known whether he took the painter's preliminary drawings to Fontainebleau or whether they were provided by artists working there. Similarly, Master NDB could have taken the design for the *Virgin and Child with Saints* to France (fig. 36). This drawing by Parmigianino, also now lost, was later reproduced frequently in drawings and prints made in France. Further research on the basis of Jenkins's and Cordellier's discoveries is required to establish how important the chiaroscuro woodcut was in sixteenth-century France in general and in the school of Fontainebleau in particular.

The prints produced by the Augsburg woodcutter Georg Matheus must be mentioned in this context. His *Diana and Actaeon* records a composition by Luca Penni for which a study has survived in the University Library in Warsaw (figs 33, 35). The woodcut, printed from three blocks, reveals skilful cutting that renders every detail precisely. This also applies to Matheus's *Flight into Egypt* (fig. 34). Here the Raphaelesque figures, the composition featuring ruins in the background and the resemblance to an *Adoration of the Magi* etched by Jean Mignon after Penni[12] suggest that the latter again provided the model. It has not been established whether Matheus received the drawings from Penni in France or whether they came from Italy, provided by the painter's son Laurent, who travelled there in 1559, or by another artist in Italy. Matheus's *Martha Leading Mary Magdalene to Christ* reproduces another scene from the frescoes in the Massimi chapel in SS. Trinità dei Monti, though based not on a drawing by Raphael,[13] but on an engraving after it by Marcantonio Raimondi (cat. 92; B. XIV, pp. 51–2, no. 45).

88 **Antonio Campi, after Parmigianino**

The Holy Family with St Catherine of Alexandria

1547

Chiaroscuro woodcut printed from two blocks, the tone block in reddish brown, 19 × 12.8 cm (sheet), 18 × 12.2 cm (image)
Inscribed (upper left): *ANTONIUS / CREMONENSIS / 1547*
Collection of Georg Baselitz

89 **Alessandro Gandini, after Girolamo da Treviso**

Virgin and Child with Saints

c. 1540–50 and 1610

Chiaroscuro woodcut printed from three blocks, the tone blocks in ochre and brown, 35.9 × 24.2 cm
Inscribed (on the step of the throne): *Taglio d'Alex'. ghandinj* [in the darker tone block]; (lower centre): *A[ndrea] A[ndreani]* [monogrammed] */ IN MANTOVA / MDCX*; [in the line block]; verso inscribed: *Fraca*[?] [in pen and ink]
Collection of Georg Baselitz

IN MANTOVA
MDCX

90 **Alessandro Gandini, after Parmigianino**

Feast in the House of Simon the Pharisee

c. 1540–50

Chiaroscuro woodcut printed from three blocks, the tone blocks in grey and black, 24.6 × 37.5 cm

Inscribed (lower right, on the base of the seat): *Taglio d'Alex.*^{ro} *Ghandinj*

Albertina, Vienna, DG2002/285

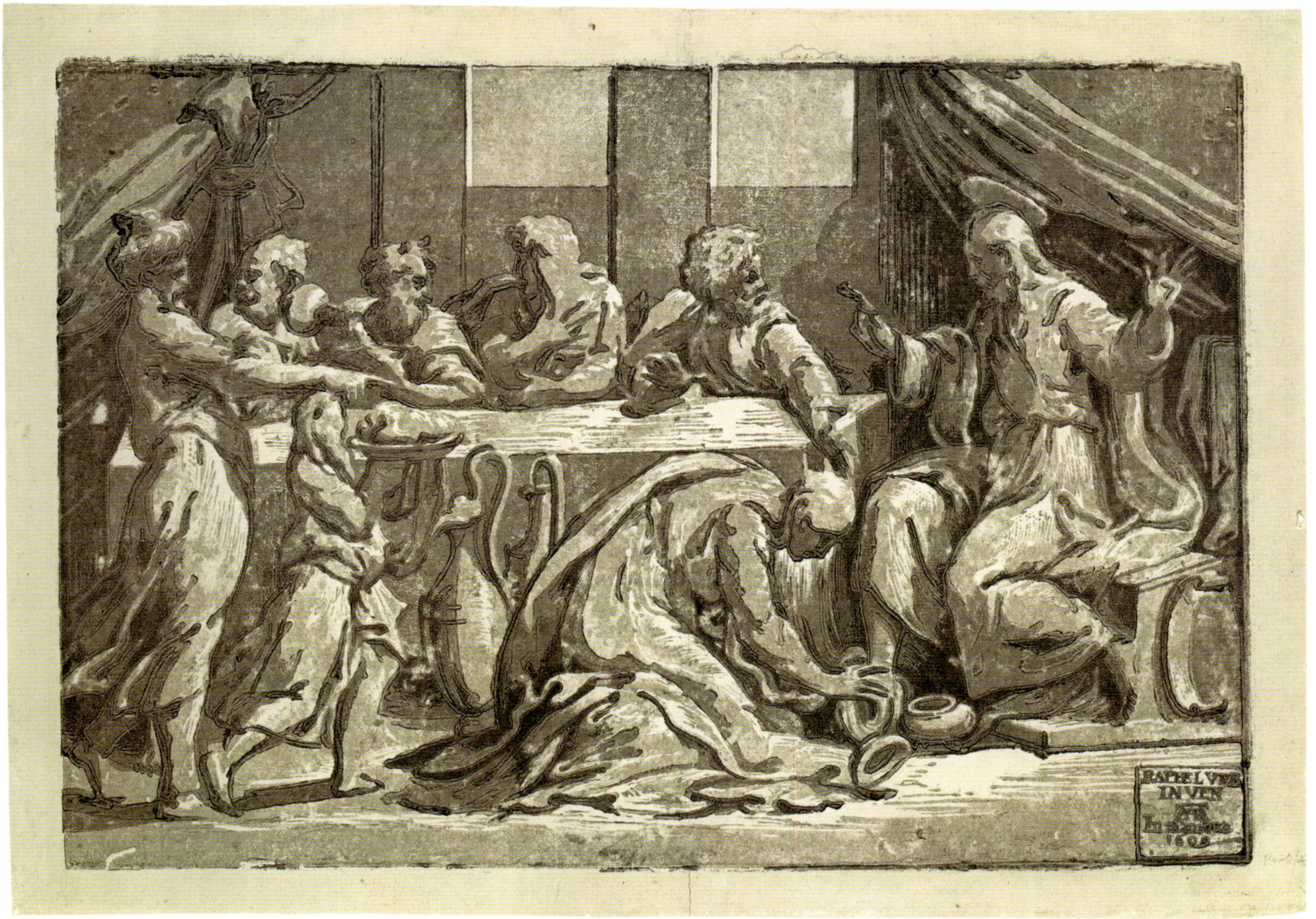

91 **Alessandro Gandini, after Parmigianino**
Feast in the House of Simon the Pharisee
c. 1540–50 and 1609

Chiaroscuro woodcut printed from four blocks, the tone blocks in grey, 28.5 × 40.3 cm (sheet), 25.3 × 37 cm (image)
Inscribed (lower right corner): *RAPH[A]EL VRB[INAS] / IN VEN[IT] / A[ndrea] A[ndreani]* [monogrammed] */ In mantoua / 1609*; verso inscribed: *Lisa & Leonard / L [pomegranate] L Baskin / 1965* [in pen and ink]
Collection of Georg Baselitz

92 **Georg Matheus**

Martha Leading Mary Magdalene to Christ

c. 1540–60

Chiaroscuro woodcut printed from two blocks, the tone block in brown,
24.5 × 35 cm
Inscribed (lower centre): *·M·* [in the tone block]; verso inscribed: *F[?]a[?]co Mazzuoli* [in pen and ink]
Collection of Georg Baselitz

93 **Master NDB, after Raphael (?)**

The Massacre of the Innocents

c. 1540–50

Chiaroscuro woodcut printed from three blocks, the tone blocks in pale brown and brown,
29.3 × 50.7 cm; area of loss at upper right corner
Inscribed (lower edge, centre): *RAPH[AEL]. URB[INAS]. INVEN[IT].*; (lower right corner, on the block of stone): *NDB / 1544*
Collection of Georg Baselitz

94 **Master NDB, after Raphael (?)**

The Massacre of the Innocents

c. 1540–50

Woodcut; small areas of loss at right edge and upper right corner,
31.1 × 52 cm
Collection of Georg Baselitz

RAPH. VRB. INVEN.

Germany and the Netherlands in the Second Half of the Sixteenth Century

VIII

The woodcutter Erasmus Loy was active in Regensburg, not far from Augsburg, the native city of Georg Matheus, whose work was described in the previous section. In a variety of formats Loy's perspective views of architecture imaginatively combine Renaissance buildings (loggias, porticoes, towers and so forth), often grouping them around a square (cats 95, 96). Their purpose explains their schematic rendering of form and their limitation to black and brown, juxtaposed abruptly with one another. For Loy's prints constitute a unique form of the chiaroscuro woodcut: they were intended to be pasted onto wood as cheap substitutes for intarsia decoration. On items of furniture, doors or wall panelling, they were generally pasted over paper printed with woodcut patterns imitating the grain of wood veneers, which showed through in the white areas of the design. Loy also produced such woodcuts with ornamental motifs. This 'printed wallpaper' could be cut out and arranged in strips of any desired length to form border decoration. The architectural prints were particularly well suited to the fronts of chests, which were often articulated with blind arcading.[1] Loy's chiaroscuro woodcuts, the first colour-printed 'wallpaper', are extremely rare and sometimes survive in only one impression, as with the print from the Baselitz collection included here. Their architectural motifs resemble those in prints produced by artists in Augsburg and Nuremberg, such as Peter Flötner, Erhard Schoen, Virgil Solis and Lorenz Stoer,[2] but no specific models have been identified. Neither have drawings for Loy's woodcuts come to light.[3]

The first artist in the Netherlands to produce chiaroscuro woodcuts may have been the Amsterdam painter, woodcutter, etcher and mapmaker Cornelis Anthonisz. (*c.* 1505–1553). A tone block was certainly added to the second state of his *Last Supper*, yet it cannot be established when exactly this was done.[4] The first to exploit the full potential of the new technique was the Antwerp painter and etcher Frans Floris. On a trip to Italy in the early 1540s he made a close study of antique sculpture in Rome and of the work of contemporary artists. Hence his *David Playing the Harp before Saul*, for example, betrays the influence of Polidoro da Caravaggio and Michelangelo (cat. 97). The inscription on this print includes the date '1555' and names the woodcutter as Jodocus de Curia, who is probably identical with Joos Gietleughen, born in Courtrai in the Southern Netherlands.[5] Certain features – the broad, painterly arrangement of the colour areas, the highlights strewn across the surface like blots and the outlining of details with thin lines printed from the line block – indicate that Gietleughen took his cue not from woodcuts by German artists, but from Niccolò Vicentino's prints after Parmigianino (for instance, cats 68, 72). A print attributed to Floris depicting an antique statue of Venus Felix and Cupid, dated 1555 and hitherto unpublished, is the first chiaroscuro woodcut to reproduce a sculpture (fig. 37). His *Ceres*, in which the vibrant strips of colour are distributed even more freely and in an even more painterly manner, and in which no use is made of the line block, was doubtless produced later (cat. 98). The print may belong to an unfinished series devoted to the abduction of Proserpina.[6]

The two woodcuts of *c.* 1570–80 by Adriaen Thomasz. Key also

show Italian influence (cats 99, 100). Apparent in the *all'antica* figures and in the relief-like composition, it was presumably transmitted by prints. *Joab Killing Absalom* may have been inspired by the battle-scene engravings of Gian Giacomo Caraglio and Marco Dente (B. XV, p. 93, no. 59; B. XIV, p. 316, no. 420), while *Nebuchadnezzar Casting Daniel's Companions into the Fiery Furnace* betrays knowledge of Raphael's tapestries – *The Death of Ananias*, for instance – and Dente's engraving after Baccio Bandinelli's *Massacre of the Innocents* (B. XIV, pp. 24–5, no. 21). The impression of the Nebuchadnezzar woodcut included here is the only known copy printed on cloth, which creates the illusion of a tempera painting on canvas. Stylistically, both prints are closely related to Floris's, but acquire a more linear character through the smaller scale both of the highlights and of the elements printed from the darker tone block and the line block.

Crispin van den Broeck's prints are notable for the addition of blue printed from a tone block to an etched image. Experiments combining an intaglio print with tone blocks had been undertaken in Italy by the unknown woodcutter who etched Parmigianino's *SS. Peter and John Healing the Lame Man* and by Beccafumi, who used engravings rather than etchings (cats 40–3, 86, 87). In the Netherlands Hubert Goltzius had had impressions from two tone blocks added to the portraits within medallions with which he illustrated *Vivae Omnium Fere Imperatorum Imagines*, a volume first published in Antwerp in 1557.[7] Crispin signed a *Visitation* of 1571 and other prints in this series devoted to the childhood of Christ with his monogram (fig. 38). The attribution to him

Fig. 37 Attributed to Frans Floris, *Venus Felix and Cupid*, 1555. Chiaroscuro woodcut printed from four blocks, the tone blocks in ochre and green, 43.3 × 22.3 cm (sheet), 42.3 × 21.5 cm (image). Albertina, Vienna, DG2013/20

Fig. 38 Crispin van den Broeck, *The Visitation*, 1571. Etching with tone woodblock in blue, 23.7 × 23.7 cm.
Albertina, Vienna, DG2013/21

of a *Feast in the House of Simon the Pharisee*, from a sequence after designs by Floris showing the four feasts attended by Christ, is disputed (cat. 101). Yet the delicate lines of the etching, finely executed and densely juxtaposed, and the thin highlights, which combine with the greyish blue of the tone block to generate a silvery glow, exhibit the same style as the Childhood of Christ prints. Crispin may possibly have seen etchings by Parmigianino and, as Konrad Oberhuber conjectured, Andrea Schiavone, who occasionally printed his etchings on paper covered with coloured wash, producing an effect similar to Crispin's prints.[8]

The most important exponent of the chiaroscuro woodcut in the Netherlands was the engraver, etcher and painter Hendrick Goltzius, who produced some of the finest of all essays in the technique. He engaged with it for several years from *c.* 1588, but it has not been established for how many of the prints, which he generally signed, he cut the blocks himself. His largest and most compelling chiaroscuro woodcut, *Hercules Killing Cacus*, is the only one to bear a date – 1588 (cats 102, 103). The powerful lines, arranged closely together and sometimes swelling in the middle, closely echo the technique of his engravings, including the *Great Hercules* of 1589. In using the line block to create a self-sufficient image in *Hercules Killing Cacus*, Goltzius follows the practice of Antonio da Trento in *Narcissus* and other works (cats 53–5). Nonetheless, the Hercules woodcut is completely satisfying only with the addition of the two tone blocks, which bind together the lines and create strong chiaroscuro contrasts that lend the image a dramatic quality.

Allegory of Time, Nature and Eternity, also known as *The Demiurge*, probably dates from the same time (cats 104, 105). It shows an old man recording events on a tablet. On either side of him hover a snake biting its own tail (a symbol of eternity) and, in a soap bubble (a symbol of transience), the goddess of nature in the shape of the many-breasted Artemis, who is blowing plants, fruits and animals into the air from a huge syringe. The print formed a kind of frontispiece for a particularly fine, slightly later (*c.* 1589–90) series of images of gods inscribed within ovals (cats 106–11). Grouped in pairs, the gods embody in complex fashion such opposites as day and night (Helios and Nyx), death and life (Pluto and Proserpina), summer and winter (Pluto and Proserpina again) and old age and youth (Oceanus and Thetis). They also represent the contrast between strength and beauty, the male gods exhibiting an almost brute physical force and the goddesses a suave elegance. The prints are technically subtler than their predecessors: the line block alone does not ensure complete 'legibility' of the image. Lines are less prominent, restricted to modelling shaded body parts and depicting foreground detail. The background is rendered exclusively by the two tone blocks, the colours forming dynamically swaying areas or flowing alongside each other in curving strips. Contrasting with the firmly modelled figures, the forms in the backgrounds dissolve atmospherically to produce a marked increase in pictorial depth.

The development towards a more painterly approach apparent in these prints, already noted by Anton Reichel,[9] may have been encouraged by familiarity with the chiaroscuro woodcuts of

Fig. 39 Niccolò Boldrini, *Shepherd Boy with Young Bull*, 1566. Chiaroscuro woodcut printed from two blocks, the tone block in brown, 14.3 × 18.6 cm.

Albertina, Vienna, DG 2002/327

Fig. 40 Niccolò Boldrini, *Rabbit Hunter on Horseback*, 1566. Chiaroscuro woodcut printed from two blocks, the tone block in brown, 14.2 × 18.6 cm.

Albertina, Vienna, DG 2002/328

Fig. 41 Hendrick Goltzius, *Landscape with Trees and a Shepherd Couple*, *c.* 1593–98. Woodcut, 12 × 15 cm.

Albertina, Vienna, Sekt. Holl. I/32, p. 114, no. 243

Antonio Gallo. In *Perseus with the Head of Medusa*, for example, Gallo likewise uses the line block for rendering only the figure and the sections around him and employs the tone blocks to create comparable painterly features in the background (cat. 124). Goltzius probably produced *Mars* and *Bacchus* around the same time as the pairs of deities (cats 117, 118). The two Olympic gods, identified by their signs of the zodiac (Aries and Scorpio respectively) and astrological symbols ('V' and 'm'), would seem to belong to a series of months of the year that was never continued.

Goltzius's remarkably attractive series of four landscapes is notable for the vitality and diversity of its lines, for its varied depiction of nature and for its pervasive atmospheric freshness (cats 112–15). According to Winslow Ames, the landscapes may allude to the four seasons in combination with the four temperaments and elements.[10] In them the artist united his own studies from nature with features derived from the work of Pieter Breughel the Elder and the Brill brothers, along with aspects of landscape depictions by Titian, Domenico Campagnola and Girolamo Muziano, which he could have seen on his trip to Italy in 1590–91. Niccolò Boldrini's genre-like depictions of country life may also have provided a model (figs 39, 40). Goltzius's landscapes focus on single motifs that have a determining effect on the activity of the figures: an angler fishing by a water mill, a couple sheltering beneath a magnificent tree, peasants at work on their farm and a man praying in front of a towering rock with ships in a storm out at sea. The artist began by printing the line block on blue prepared paper (fig. 41), then applied white highlighting with the brush, as he did in early impressions of his portrait of the painter and engraver Gillis van Breen (cat. 116).[11] In their first states, then, the landscapes are pure line woodcuts. The addition of two tone blocks helped to emphasise the main compositional elements, to differentiate more clearly between the textures of the natural objects and to unify the whole in chromatic terms. Possibly dating from *c.* 1593–98, the prints are characteristic of Goltzius's late chiaroscuro woodcuts, in which the areas of colour, arranged broadly and fluidly, serve principally to generate atmospheric effects, rather than to model individual forms.

Mit Rö: Kay: vnd Khü: May: &c
Freyhait: nit Nachzudruckhen

95 **Erasmus Loy**

Courtyard with Renaissance Architecture

c. 1550

Chiaroscuro woodcut printed from two blocks, the tone block in reddish brown, 44.2 × 36.1 cm (sheet), 42.4 × 35.6 cm (image)
Inscribed (lower centre edge): *Mit Kö: Kaÿ: und Khü Maÿ / freÿhait: nit Nachzudruckhen*
Watermark: R above two crossed keys (watermark of the city of Regensburg), similar to Briquet 1139
Collection of Georg Baselitz

96 **Erasmus Loy**

View of Architecture with a Figure in the Background

c. 1550

Chiaroscuro woodcut printed from two blocks, the tone block in reddish brown, 39.2 × 30.2 cm (sheet), 34.7 × 28.8 cm (image)
Inscribed (lower centre edge): *Mit Kö: Kaÿ: und Khü Maÿ / freÿhait: nit Nachzudruckhen*
Watermark: R above two crossed keys (watermark of the city of Regensburg), similar to Briquet 1139
Albertina, Vienna, DG1984/102

97 **Frans Floris**
David Playing the Harp before Saul
1555

Chiaroscuro woodcut printed from four blocks, the tone blocks in pale red and reddish brown, on brownish paper,
33.4 × 48.1 cm; various tears, small areas have been made up
Inscribed (on the base of the throne): *SAVL· ·I· REG·CA·XVI*; (on the step): *FRĀ[N]CISCVS·FLORIS INVĒ[N]TOR · IVDOCE DE CVRIA· EXCVDEBAT: 1555.*
Collection of Georg Baselitz

98 **Frans Floris**
Ceres
c. 1560–70

Chiaroscuro woodcut printed from three blocks, the tone blocks in pink and red,
43 × 29.5 cm
Verso inscribed: *Mariette 1752* [in pen and ink]
Albertina, Vienna, DG85339

99 **Adriaen Thomasz. Key**
Joab Killing Absalom
c. 1570–80

Chiaroscuro woodcut printed from three blocks, the tone blocks in green, 30.1 × 47.6 cm
Inscribed (lower right, on a stone): *ATK* [monogrammed]
Watermark: Coat of arms shield with linked letters, the first a P, above the inscription *P PRICARD*; cf. Briquet 9613
Albertina, Vienna, DG2013/23

100 **Adriaen Thomasz. Key**
Nebuchadnezzar Casting Daniel's Companions into the Fiery Furnace
c. 1570–80

Chiaroscuro woodcut printed from three blocks, the tone blocks in pale green and blue-green, on cloth, 24.4 × 31.5 cm; browning lower left
Inscribed (upper right, on tablet hanging on the wall): *ATK* [monogrammed]; verso inscribed (upper left): *Of / König Vienna 1849 / rare 30*[?] [in pen and ink]
Collection of Georg Baselitz

101 **Crispin van den Broeck (?)**
Feast in the House of Simon the Pharisee
c. 1570

Etching with tone woodcut block in greyish blue, 23.2 × 23.5 cm
Albertina, Vienna, DG2013/22

102 **Hendrick Goltzius**
Hercules Killing Cacus
1588

Woodcut,
41.2 × 32.9 cm
Indecipherable watermark
Collection of Georg Baselitz

103 **Hendrick Goltzius**
Hercules Killing Cacus
1588

Chiaroscuro woodcut printed from three blocks, the tone blocks in yellow and green,
41.1 × 33.3 cm
Inscribed (left centre, top to bottom on the rock): *A° .88 / H Goltzius inve:*
Collection of Georg Baselitz

HGoltzius Inue.

104 **Hendrick Goltzius**
Allegory of Time, Nature and Eternity (The Demiurge)
c. 1588

Chiaroscuro woodcut printed from three blocks, the tone blocks in beige and grey, 36.8 × 27 cm (sheet), 34.8 × 26.3 cm (image); crease mark across centre
Inscribed (lower centre): *HG* [monogrammed]. *f* [both in tone block]
Collection of Georg Baselitz

105 **Hendrick Goltzius**

Allegory of Time, Nature and Eternity (The Demiurge)

c. 1588

Chiaroscuro woodcut printed from three blocks, the tone blocks in ochre and blue-green,
35.3 × 26.1 cm (sheet),
35 × 26.4 cm (image)
Inscribed (lower centre):
HG [monogrammed]. *f*
[both in tone block]
Collection of Georg Baselitz

106 **Hendrick Goltzius**
Oceanus
c. 1589–90

Chiaroscuro woodcut printed from three blocks, the tone blocks in beige and green, 35 × 26.5 cm
Inscribed (lower centre edge): *HG* [monogrammed]. *F*
Collection of Georg Baselitz

107 **Hendrick Goltzius**

Thetis

c. 1589–90

Chiaroscuro woodcut printed from three blocks, the tone blocks in beige and green, 38.3 × 29.5 cm (sheet), 35 × 26.5 cm (image)
Inscribed (lower centre edge): *HG* [monogrammed]. *fe*
Collection of Georg Baselitz

108 **Hendrick Goltzius**

Pluto

c. 1589–90

Chiaroscuro woodcut printed from three blocks, the tone blocks in beige and green, 34.5 × 25.9 cm (image); area of loss at lower edge has been made up

Inscribed (lower centre): *HG* [monogrammed]. *fe*

Collection of Georg Baselitz

109 **Hendrick Goltzius**

Proserpina

c. 1589–90

Chiaroscuro woodcut printed from three blocks, the tone blocks in brown,
34.4 × 25.8 cm (image);
crease marks across centre
Inscribed (centre left edge, at the foot of the tree): *HG* [monogrammed, in the lighter tone block]
Collection of Georg Baselitz

110 **Hendrick Goltzius**
Day (Helios)
c. 1589–90

Chiaroscuro woodcut printed from three blocks, the tone blocks in beige and green, 38.3 × 29.5 cm (sheet), 27 × 35 cm (image)
Inscribed (lower centre): *HG* [monogrammed]. *fe.*
Indecipherable watermark
Collection of Georg Baselitz

111 **Hendrick Goltzius**

Night (Nyx)

c. 1589–90

Chiaroscuro woodcut printed from three blocks, the tone blocks in beige and green, 34.8 × 26.2 cm
Inscribed (lower centre): *HG* [monogrammed] *fe.*
Collection of Georg Baselitz

112 **Hendrick Goltzius**
Landscape with Watermill
c. 1593–98

Chiaroscuro woodcut printed from three blocks, the tone blocks in light green and green, 13.8 × 17.4 cm (sheet), 11.6 × 15.1 cm (image)
Inscribed (lower left): *HG.* [monogrammed]
Collection of Georg Baselitz

113 **Hendrick Goltzius**
Landscape with Trees and a Shepherd Couple
c. 1593–98
Chiaroscuro woodcut printed from three blocks, the tone blocks in pale green and green,
14 × 17.6 cm (sheet),
11.7 × 15.3 cm (image)
Inscribed (lower centre edge):
HG [monogrammed]
Collection of Georg Baselitz

114 **Hendrick Goltzius**

Landscape with Farm

c. 1593–98

Chiaroscuro woodcut printed from three blocks, the tone blocks in pale green and green, 17.6 × 14.2 cm (sheet), 11.5 × 14.8 cm (image)
Inscribed (lower centre): *HG* [monogrammed]
Collection of Georg Baselitz

115 **Hendrick Goltzius**
Coastal Scene with a Large Rock
c. 1593–98

Chiaroscuro woodcut printed from three blocks, the tone blocks in pale green and green, 11.5 × 14.7 cm
Inscribed (lower centre, on a rock): *HG* [monogrammed]
Collection of Georg Baselitz

116 **Hendrick Goltzius**
Gillis van Breen
c. 1588

Chiaroscuro woodcut printed from three blocks, the tone blocks in ochre and brown, 20.5 × 14.1 cm
Inscribed (upper right corner): *HG* [monogrammed] *fe*
Collection of Georg Baselitz

117 **Hendrick Goltzius**

Mars

c. 1589-90

Chiaroscuro woodcut printed from three blocks, the tone blocks in orange-brown and brown
24.4 × 14.7 cm
Inscribed (upper left):
HG [monogrammed]
Collection of Georg Baselitz

118 **Hendrick Goltzius**

Bacchus

c. 1589–90

Chiaroscuro woodcut printed from two blocks, the tone block in light brown,
23.8 × 14.3 cm
Inscribed (lower right):
H Goltzius [?] [in pen and ink, in an early hand]
Collection of Georg Baselitz

Developments in Italy

IX

By the mid-sixteenth century Venice was developing into an important centre in the production of chiaroscuro woodcuts. Niccolò Boldrini, born in Vicenza, may already have been making woodcuts after compositions by Titian in Venice by the mid-1530s, but collaboration between the two is first documented in 1566 – the date inscribed on Boldrini's chiaroscuro woodcut *Venus and Cupid* (fig. 43). Along with the unknown woodcutter (perhaps Domenico Campagnola) who produced the magnificent image of a tree (cat. 119), Boldrini continued the chiaroscuro technique introduced into Venice by Ugo da Carpi, employing a line block and a single tone block.[1] Some of his prints were once attributed erroneously to Ugo. The latter's lines, however, are finer and more subtly used. Alternating between the short and emphatic and the longer and flowing, they appear in various superimposed combinations to generate powerfully modelled figures with an intense life of their own. With Boldrini, on the other hand, the lines, though powerful and vibrant, do not come together to form complex structures, but appear side by side at regular intervals and can occasionally induce a sense of monotony. Ugo opens up the outlines of his motifs towards the light, whereas Boldrini encloses his figures in unbroken contours. He generally uses a brown tone block, in which he cuts the highlights in such a way that they seem to spread an even glow over the figures.

Chiaroscuro woodcuts can be ascribed to Boldrini on the basis of two signed examples, the *Venus and Cupid* mentioned above and a leaping horse and rider after Pordenone (fig. 42). Attributions include a *St John the Baptist* recording a design by Raphael, now lost, for the painting of *c.* 1516–18 housed in the Uffizi (cat. 120).[2] This print shows a comparably meticulous, almost pedantic execution and a similar, closed contour around the figure, which binds it to the picture plane. The same style occurs in three prints after designs by Giulio Romano for works he produced in Mantua in the early 1530s: *Harvest, The Nativity of the Virgin* and *The Presentation of the Virgin* (figs 44–6). It has yet to be established whether Boldrini received the designs from Giulio himself (who died in 1546) in Mantua or whether he acquired them later. Indeed, the date of many chiaroscuro woodcuts by Boldrini is a subject requiring further research.

Andrea Zezza has surmised that Giovanni Gallo is identical with a 'Joannes Gallo, painter from Antwerp' documented in Naples in 1595.[3] Certainly, most of Gallo's prints reproduce works created by the Siena-born artist Marco Pino (1521–1583) in Naples in the 1570s and later. Pino fashioned an individual style, notable for its subtle use of colour and narrative variety, from influences derived from such major artists as Beccafumi, Michelangelo, Perino del Vaga and Daniele da Volterra. Gallo's prints, including *Perseus with the Head of Medusa* and *The Lamentation of Christ*, are characterised by strong, luminous colour and a free, painterly approach in the manner of Ugo da Carpi and Niccolò Vicentino (cats 124, 125). Their fluid areas of colour and their highlights seem to have been applied with a brush, prompting the viewer to forget the relative intractability of the material from which they are cut. In illuminated sections, colours and the black lines printed from the line block trail off into lines that appear to have been lightly

Fig. 42 Niccolò Boldrini, *Leaping Horse and Rider*, *c.* 1560–70. Chiaroscuro woodcut printed from two blocks, the tone block in brown, 23.2 × 19 cm.
Albertina, Vienna, DG 2002/351

Fig. 43 Niccolò Boldrini, *Venus and Cupid*, 1566. Chiaroscuro woodcut printed from two blocks, the tone block in brown, 31.2 × 23.4 cm.
Albertina, Vienna, DG2002/331

sketched in pen and ink, combining with the highlights to grant volumes fullness and roundness. Gallo succeeds masterfully in conveying the *modello*-like style of Pino's designs in the medium of the chiaroscuro woodcut.

The oeuvre of the woodcutter and publisher Andrea Andreani, Italy's leading woodcutter in the later sixteenth century, includes thirty-eight prints for which he cut the blocks himself and twenty-nine cut by others and published by him. Most are chiaroscuro woodcuts. Andreani produced his earliest dated prints in Florence, where he is first documented in 1584. They show three views of Giambologna's recently unveiled sculpture *Rape of a Sabine Woman*. In what is probably the earliest of the prints Andreani used only one tone block, creating from the line block a dense network of parallel lines and cross-hatching that shows certain similarities with the woodcuts of Boldrini (cat. 127). The remaining woodcuts of *Rape of a Sabine Woman* were both originally printed from four blocks, their perfect registration already demonstrating superb command of the chiaroscuro technique (cats 128, 129). Two woodcuts dated 1585 that record bronze reliefs by Giambologna – a *Rape of the Sabine Women* and a *Christ before Pilate* – were printed from three and two sets of four blocks respectively (cats 130, 131). Put together from more than one sheet of paper, these works display a comparable technical mastery in large formats.

Andreani's prints often bear dedications – to the rulers of Tuscany and Mantua, for example, to other members of the aristocracy or to art lovers of high rank who doubtless supported his work. In Florence he became friends with the Tuscan Grand Ducal court painter Jacopo Ligozzi, whose drawings, with their rich contrasts of light and dark and their delicate highlighting, occasionally in gold, he translated expertly into the medium of the chiaroscuro woodcut. Products of their collaboration included an ingenious allegory of the type favoured in the Mannerist period and a print of the Virgin and Child with saints (cats 126, 132). The former shows Love (*Amore*), Error (*Errore*), Ignorance (*Ignoranza*) and Opinion (*Opinione*) assailing Virtue (*Virtù*), the initial letters of the Italian words listing all five vowels in alphabetical order and also evoking the Habsburg motto A.E.I.O.U. (Austria Est Imperare Orbi Universo: 'It is the duty of Austria to rule over the whole world') when the V is read as a U (which was commonly printed as V). This may allude in turn to the strained relations between the Habsburg dynasty and Grand Duke Francesco de' Medici at this time.[4]

In 1586 Andreani moved to Siena, following in the footsteps of Beccafumi, the first to practise the chiaroscuro woodcut technique in the city. His prints after Beccafumi's marble intarsia pavements in Siena cathedral include the monumental *Sacrifice of Isaac*, printed from five sets of four blocks and extremely complex in detail (cat. 135). During his five-year stay in Siena, Andreani collaborated with the most important artists in the city, who provided him with their designs for paintings, usually on religious subjects, for dissemination as chiaroscuro woodcuts. Several prints record works by his friend Alessandro Casolani. They include one of Andreani's finest achievements – an image

TITIANVS INV
Nicolans Boldrinus
Vincentinus inci-
debat 1560.

Fig. 44 Attributed to Niccolò Boldrini, *The Harvest*, second third of the sixteenth century. Chiaroscuro woodcut printed from two blocks, the tone block in brown, 20.8 × 23.6 cm.

Albertina, Vienna, DG 2002/333

Fig. 45 Attributed to Niccolò Boldrini, *The Nativity of the Virgin*, second third of the sixteenth century. Chiaroscuro woodcut printed from two blocks, the tone block in brown, 34.5 × 37 cm.

Albertina, Vienna, DG2002/332

Fig. 46 Attributed to Niccolò Boldrini, *The Presentation of the Virgin*, second third of the sixteenth century. Chiaroscuro woodcut printed from two blocks, the tone block in brown, 35.5 × 37.6 cm.

Albertina, Vienna, DG 2002/335

of a woman contemplating a skull resting between her hands (cat. 136). This woodcut is indicative of a change in his style. Prints from his Florentine period, among them an *Entombment of Christ* after Raffaellino da Reggio, had shown large, strongly contrasting areas of colour and boldly modelled figures (cat. 133). In Siena the colours become less emphatic and the gradations of tone gentler and richer in nuances. *Woman Contemplating a Skull* recalls in some respects Burgkmair's portrait of Hans Paumgartner (cat. 6). Modelling by means of black lines occurs here only in the figure and the skull, facilitating the creation of a rapt stillness in the room and the harmonious integration into it of these two principal elements. The print points forward to Andreani's late style, as embodied in *The Triumphs of Caesar* after Mantegna (cat. 138). The lines here are flowing, as though sketched swiftly, and the areas of colour applied fluidly, not so as to stress the three-dimensional presence of the volumes, but to increase the illusion of figures in a light- and air-filled space.

Andreani's largest single-scene woodcut is a *Lamentation of Christ* after a painting by Casolani in SS. Quirico e Giulitta, Siena (cat. 137). The print, which probably served as a substitute painting, was doubtless based on Casolani's cartoon, which has not survived. Chiaroscuro woodcuts on such a huge scale all but exceeded the limits of the technique. Returning to his native Mantua in 1593, Andreani was commissioned by Duke Vincenzo Gonzaga I to make chiaroscuro woodcuts of the well-known paintings by Andrea Mantegna of *The Triumphs of Caesar* (now at Hampton Court Palace, London). Work on the woodcuts, printed from over forty blocks, occupied Andreani for seven years. Pasted together with a title page and pilasters separating each of the nine scenes, the prints formed a frieze over four metres in length that must have been used as wall decoration.

In subsequent years – from 1602 to 1610 – Andreani limited his activity almost exclusively to the reissue of chiaroscuro woodcuts by earlier artists, sometimes re-cutting blocks he had acquired, occasionally in damaged condition, or adding new ones. In doing so, he often showed little regard for the original woodcutters, removing their names and substituting his monogrammed initials (one A enclosed in another) so as to mark himself out as the owner and printer of the blocks.

119 **Unknown woodcutter (Domenico Campagnola?), after Titian**

Tree with Two Goats

c. 1530–40

Chiaroscuro woodcut printed from two blocks, the tone block in grey, 49.2 × 21.7 cm
Inscribed (lower right edge): *T[iziano]* [in pen and ink]; buckling mark across centre, border line retraced in pen and ink at upper left corner
Albertina, Vienna, DG2002/329

120 **Attributed to Niccolò Boldrini, after Raphael**
St John the Baptist
second third of the sixteenth century
Chiaroscuro woodcut printed from two blocks, the tone block in brown,
38.8 × 27.6 cm
Inscribed (lower left edge):
RAPHA[EL]·UR[BINAS]·IN[VENTOR]
Watermark: Coat of arms shield bearing a plant (?)
Collection of Georg Baselitz

121 **Niccolò Boldrini, after Pordenone**
Marcus Curtius on Horseback
second third of the sixteenth century
Chiaroscuro woodcut printed from three blocks, the tone blocks in ochre and brown,
39.5 × 25.9 cm
cut down at the left, right and lower edges
Albertina, Vienna, DG2002/353

122 **Unknown woodcutter, after Federico Barocci**
The Holy Family Resting on the Return from Egypt
last third of the sixteenth century
Chiaroscuro woodcut printed from two blocks, the tone block in brown,
35.6 × 28.7 cm
Inscribed (lower left edge):
•F[edericus]•B[arotius]•V[rbinas]•I[nvenit]
Collection of Georg Baselitz

123 **Giovanni Gallo, after Marco Pino**
Cain and Abel
c. 1570–80

Chiaroscuro woodcut printed from four blocks, the tone blocks in beige and blue,
40 × 26.1 cm
Inscribed (lower edge): *Marcus Senensis invē / Ioanes Gallus incid.* [cropped]
Albertina, Vienna, DG2002/583

124 **Giovanni Gallo, after Marco Pino**
Perseus with the Head of Medusa
c. 1570–80

Chiaroscuro woodcut printed from four blocks, the tone blocks in orange and reddish brown,
35.9 × 22.7 cm
Inscribed (lower right, in the border): *Marcus Senensis invē[nit] / Ioānes Gallus incid[it].*; verso inscribed: *Mariette 1728 / Desneux* [in pen and ink]
Albertina, Vienna, DG2002/587

125 **Giovanni Gallo, after Marco Pino**

The Lamentation of Christ

c. 1570–80

Chiaroscuro woodcut printed from four blocks, the tone blocks in green, 44 × 28.4 cm
Inscribed (lower right, in the border): *Marcus Senensis invē[nit] / Ioanes Gallus incid[it].*; verso inscribed: *P. mariette 1668 / Desneux* [in pen and ink]
Albertina, Vienna, DG2002/586

126 **Andrea Andreani, after Jacopo Ligozzi**

Virtue Assailed by Love, Error, Ignorance and Opinion

1585

Chiaroscuro woodcut printed from four blocks, in brown, 46.2 × 32.1 cm; area of loss at lower right corner has been made up
Inscribed (lower left corner): *FRANCISCO / MEDICI / Sereniss.^{o} Magno / Ethrurie Duci. / Andreas Andreanus / incisit ac dicavit Iacobus Ligotius Veronenš / invenit / ac / Pinxit*; (lower right corner): *In / Firenze / 1585 / Lettere Vocale / figurate ·A·Amore ·E·Errore / I· Ignora:^{za} O·Opinio^{e} / ·V· Virtu*
Collection of Georg Baselitz

FRANCISCO
MEDICI
Sereniss:° Magno
Ethruriç Duci
Andreas Andreanus
incisit ac Dicauit
Iacobus
Ligotius
Veronens:
inuenit
ac
Pinxit
In
firenze
1585
Lettere Vocale
figurate
A· Amore· E· Errore
I· Ignorã· O·
V·

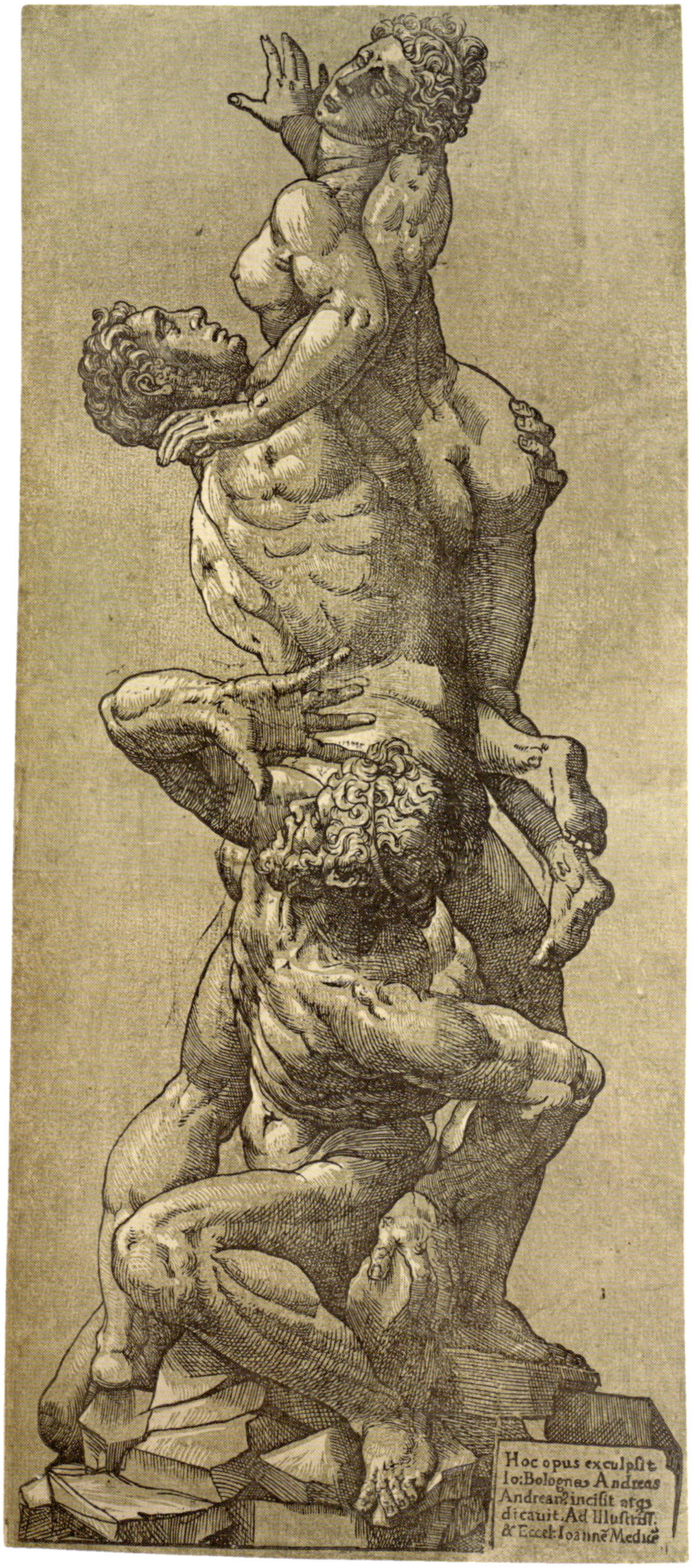

127 **Andrea Andreani, after Giambologna**

Rape of a Sabine Woman

1584

Chiaroscuro woodcut printed from two blocks, the tone block in greyish green,
45.3 × 20.2 cm
Inscribed (lower right):
Hoc opus exculpsit / Io:Bologna Andreas / Andreani incisit atq' / dicavit. Ad Illustriss. / & Eccel: Ioannē Medicē
Watermark: Eagle (?) within a circle
Albertina, Vienna, DG2002/572

128 **Andrea Andreani, after Giambologna**

Rape of a Sabine Woman

1584

Chiaroscuro woodcut printed from four blocks, the tone blocks in brown,
44.7 × 20.9 cm; areas of loss at upper left, upper right and lower right corners have been made up
Inscribed (lower left corner):
Raptā Sabinā à Ioa: / Bolog: marm: exculptā / Andreas Andrean' Mant. Īci: / atqu' Equiti Nicc: Gaddio / dicavit M.D.LXXXIIII. Flor.
Collection of Georg Baselitz

129 **Andrea Andreani, after Giambologna**

Rape of a Sabine Woman

1584

Chiaroscuro woodcut printed from four blocks, the tone blocks in ochre and brown,
44.4 × 20.5 cm
Inscribed (lower right): *Raptā Sabinam, à / Io: Bolog·marm:excul·/ Andreas Andrean' Māt: / incisit, atq. Bernard / Vechiett dicavit año/ M·D·LXXXIIII*; *P. mariette 1652* [?] and *P. mariette 1674 [?]* [both in pen and ink]
Albertina, Vienna, DG2002/570

Raptā Sabinā à Ioa:
Bolog: marm: exculptā
Andreas Andrean⁹ Mant. ici:
Equiti Nicc: Gaddio
M·D·LXXXIIII. Flor.

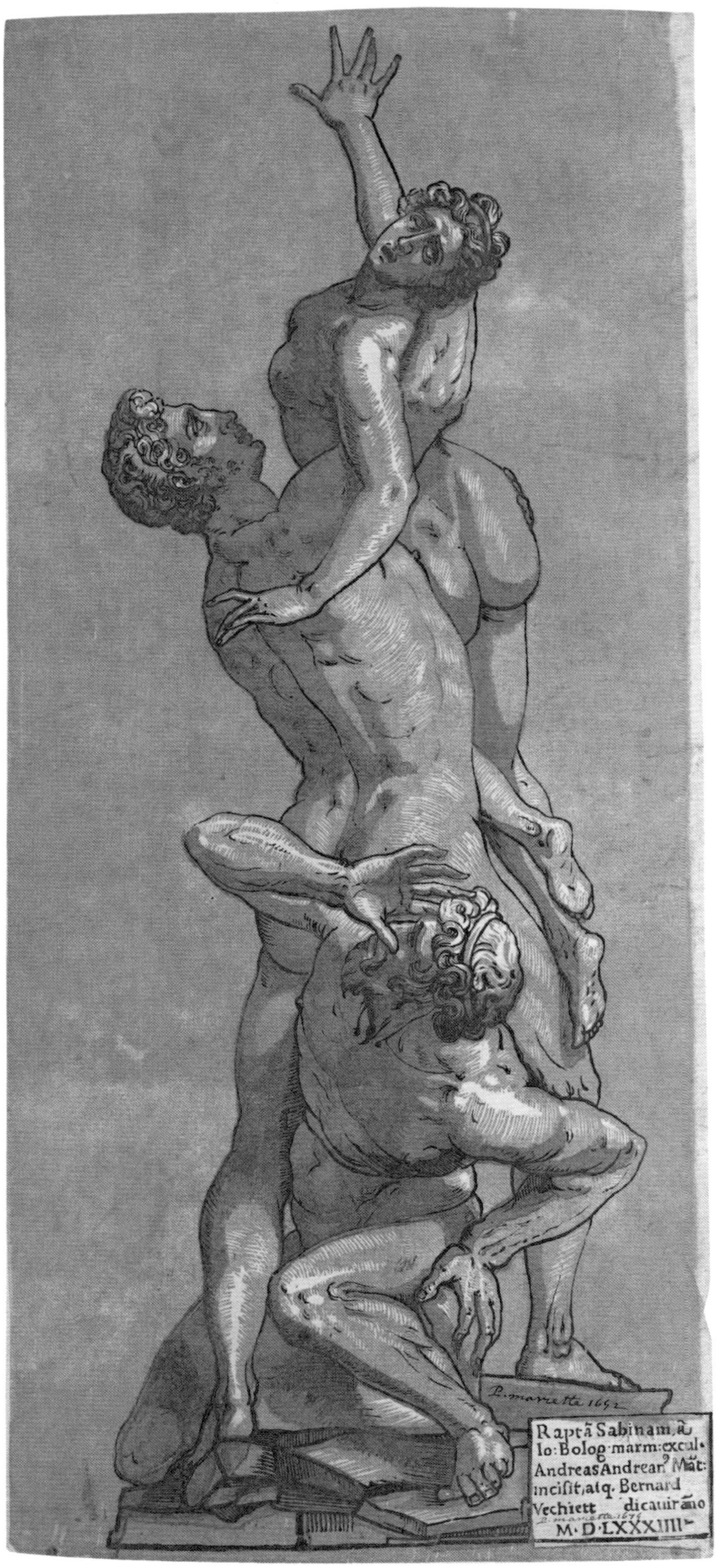
P. mariette 1692
Raptā Sabinam, à
Io: Bolog: marm: excul.
Andreas Andrean⁹ Māt:
incisit, atq. Bernard
Vechiett dicauit āno
M·D·LXXXIIII.

Andreas Andrean. Mantuan.
eam incisit, impressit.
Anno Domini.
M·D·LXXXV.
Haec est hystoria raptus Sabinarum in aere sculpta
Io: Bologna Serenissi: Magni Etr. Ducis sculpt

130 **Andrea Andreani, after Giambologna**
Rape of the Sabine Women
1585

Chiaroscuro woodcut printed from three sets of four blocks, the tone blocks in ochre and brown, on six sheets of paper,
75.2 × 94.5 cm
Verso inscribed: *F. Rechberger 1800*; (lower left): *Andreas Andrean' Mantuan' / eam incisit, impressit· / Anno Domini· / M·D·LXXXV ·/ Florentiae; Hec est hystoria raptar[um] Sabinar[um] in are scupltar[um] per Doūm / Io: Bolognam Sereniss: Magni Etre Ducis scupltorē celeberr*
Albertina, Vienna, DG2002/574

131 **Andrea Andreani, after Giambologna**

Christ before Pilate

1585

Chiaroscuro woodcut printed from two sets of four blocks, the tone blocks in brownish red, on two sheets of paper, 44.8 × 65.1 cm

Inscribed (on the throne plinth): *MD L XXXV*; (on the shield of the soldier on the right): *Gianbologna 'scolpi-/ Andrea Andriano= / lo'ntagliatore, / A.Giovambatista. Deti gen= / til'huomo Fiorentino*

Collection of Georg Baselitz

132 **Andrea Andreani, after Jacopo Ligozzi**

Virgin and Child with the Infant John the Baptist and SS. Catherine of Siena and Francis

1585

Chiaroscuro woodcut printed from three blocks, the tone blocks in ochre and brown,
46.2 × 37.4 cm
Inscribed (upper left corner): *Iacopo Ligozia Veronese Pictor'del / Sereniss: Gran Duca. d. Tosc. Inven[tor]· / Andrea Andriano / Mant.° Intagliator^{e} / All Ill^{o} Signor / Nicolo Gaddi / in Fiorenza / ·1585·*
Collection of Georg Baselitz

133 **Andrea Andreani, after Raffaellino da Reggio**
The Entombment of Christ
1585

Chiaroscuro woodcut printed from four blocks, the tone blocks in orange-red and reddish brown, 41.8 × 32.7 cm
Inscribed (lower left): *Raff. da Reggio Inuent: Andrea Andriano / Mant^{o}: Intagliatore / All Illmo et l'ec:^{mo} sig.^{r} Don Giovañ Medici / 1585*
Collection of Georg Baselitz

134 **Andrea Andreani, after Alessandro Casolani**
Christ Carrying the Cross
1591

Chiaroscuro woodcut printed from three blocks, the tone blocks in reddish brown and brown, 36.9 × 26.4 cm; foxing at upper left edge
Inscribed (lower margin): *CALI* [monogrammed] / *A^{l} Sig.^{r} Fabio Buonsignori Nobile senese / Andrea Andreani Intagliatore in Siena 1591.*
Collection of Georg Baselitz

135 **Andrea Andreani, after Beccafumi**

The Sacrifice of Isaac

1586

Chiaroscuro woodcut printed from five sets of four blocks, the tone blocks in grey, on ten sheets of paper, 73.5 × 169.5 cm
Inscribed (lower left): *Al Ser.mo S.re il S.r Franc.o M.a della Rovere / Duca d'Vrb.o etc. / Fra le nobiliss.e pitture di chiaroscuro ch'adornano il marmo / reo Pavim.to del Duomo di Siena, v'ha quella del figlio d'Abra.o / offerto in sacrificio: inventione di D.nico Beccafumi pittore / Sanese: la qle Andrea Andriani da Mantoua ha ridotto / in q.a breve forma: riponendo intorno ad essa tutte le forze del suo / ingegno: cosi come con tutto l'affetto del cuore la dona, e dedi / ca al chiariss.o nome di V.A. che per l'egregie sue virtù viverà / glorioso, mentre havrà vita il mondo. In Siena a di xij di / Novembre. M.D.Lxxxvj.*
Albertina, Vienna, DG24089–90

136 **Andrea Andreani, after Alessandro Casolani**
Woman Contemplating a Skull
c. 1591

Chiaroscuro woodcut printed from four blocks, the tone blocks in reddish brown and brown, 28.4 × 21.2 cm
Inscribed (lower left corner): *P. Vischer* [in pen and ink]
Collection of Georg Baselitz

137 **Andrea Andreani, after Alessandro Casolani**
The Lamentation of Christ
1593

Chiaroscuro woodcut printed from four sets of four blocks, the tone blocks in brown, on thirteen sheets of paper, 174.8 × 119.8 cm
Inscribed (lower left corner): *Vincentio Gonzagae Mantuae, et / Montisferrati duci Sereníßimo etc / Ab Alexandro Casulano Senensi lineis co / loribusq. Ductum opus, domi Octavij Prenati / Canonici ab Andrea vero Andriano / Mantuano varijs novisq. Ligneis formis in= / cisum ac intimo cordis affectu dicatum. / Senis M·D·XCIII·*; labels on verso inscribed: *F. Gawet 1822* [in pen and ink]
Vienna, Albertina, DG24096–97

Andrea Andreani,
after Mantegna
The Triumphs of Caesar
1599

138.0 **Title page with a portrait of Mantegna and dedication**

Chiaroscuro woodcut printed from four blocks, the tone blocks in yellow ochre and brown, 39.4 × 37.2 cm
Inscribed: *SER.mo PRINCIPI VINCĒTIO GŌZAGÆ.D.G / MANTVÆ AC MONTIS FERRATI OPTIMO DVCI / TABVLÆ TRVNPHI CÆSARIS. OLIM NVTV ECCELSI FRANCISCI GONZAGÆ INCLITÆ / VRBIS MANTVÆ TVNC MARCHIONIS. IIIJ. PROPE D.SEBASTIANI ÆDES, IN MAIORI EIVS / AVLA, AB ANDREA MANTINEA MANTVANO EA.DILIGENTIA PICTÆ, VT IAM PER ANNOS / SVPRA CENTVM, NON SOLVM INCOLARVM, VERVMETIĀ EX VARIIS ORBIS PARTIBVS, / ADVENARVM OCVLOS TANQUĀM MIRABILE QVODDAM AD SVI INSPECTIONEM ATTRA- / HANT, QVEMADMODVM NON SOLVM OPVS IPSŪ ADHVC OSTENDIT, VERŪETIAM GEOR- / GII VASARII HISTORICI IN VITIS PICTORVM TESTIMONIO COMPROBATVR. / ANDREAS ANDRIANVS PARITER MANTVANVS, QVO ABSENTIVM VOLVNTATI, MELIO- / RI QVA POSSET RATIONE SATISFACERET, ET MVNICIPIS TANTI VIRI FAMA LATVIS PER / ORA VIRVM ET COMMODIVS VOLITARET. IDCIRCO HIS TYPIS LIGNEIS NOVA SVAR / FORMAR ADŪBRATIŌE INCISIT, TVÆQ CELSITVDINIS INVICTO NOMINI OMNIVM VIR- / TVTIS AMATORVM AVGVSTO MECÆNATI, QVOD IPSVM A SENARVM ETIAM SI CARA / SIBI VRBE, AD PATRIĀ BENIGNE REVOCAVERIS, QVOD ET AD OPVS PERFICIENDVM ET AD / VICTVM NECESSARIA, SPONTE, ATQ ABVNDANTISSIME SVPPEDITAVERIS MAXIMA / HVMILITATE DICAVIT. / VTINĀ NOVVS HAC ÆTATE VIRIBVS, ET ANIMO CÆSAR, SICVTI PAR EST, / IMPERIO NOVO, NOVISQ POTIARE TRIVMPHIS. / BERNAR. MALPITIVS PICT. MANT. F. MANTVAE. M.DXCVIIII.*
Collection of Georg Baselitz

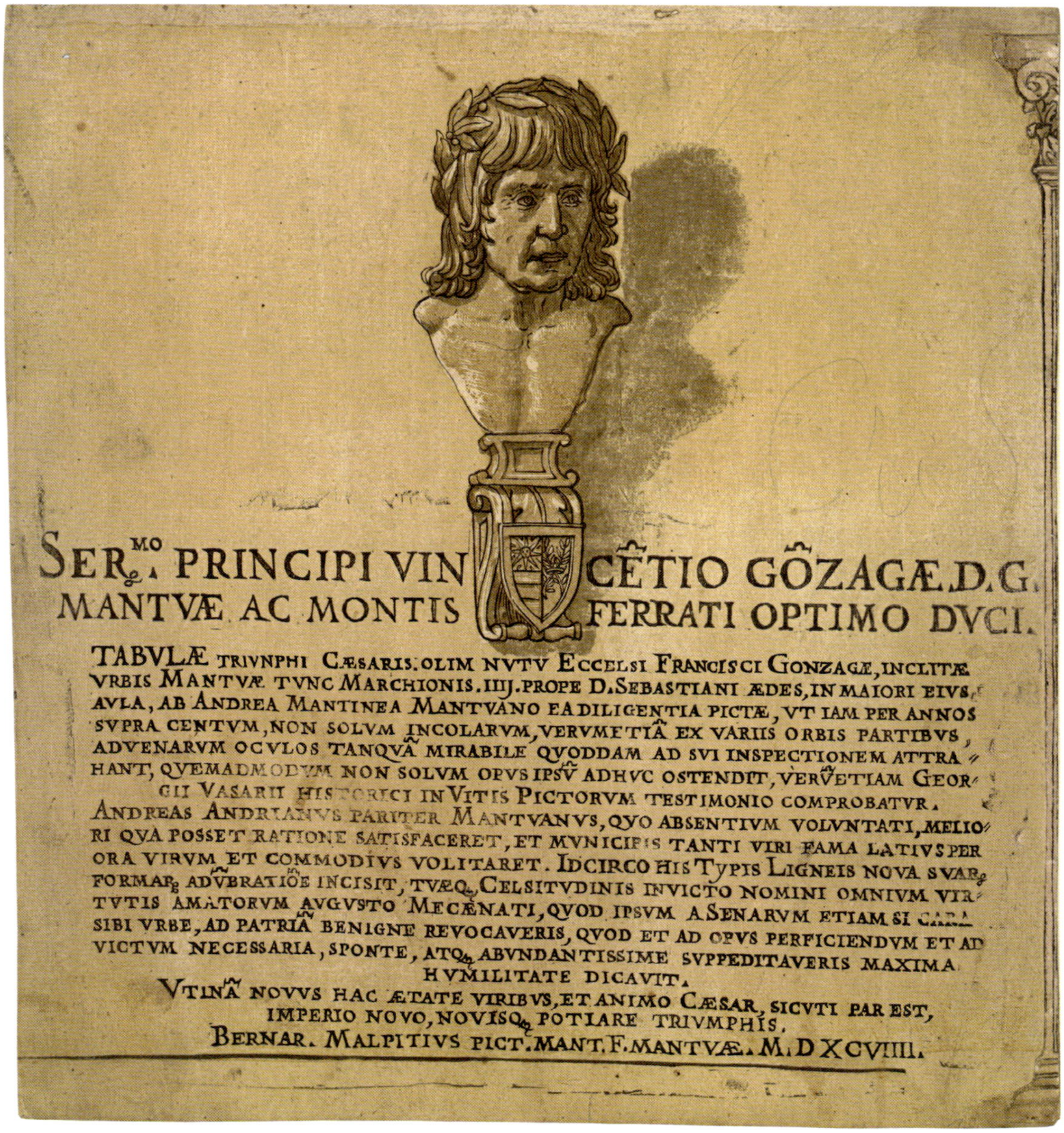

138.1 **Andrea Andreani, after Mantegna**

Trumpeters, bearers of standards and banners ('The Trumpeters')

Chiaroscuro woodcut printed from four blocks, the tone blocks in yellowish brown and brown,
39.8 × 38.7 cm
Collection of Georg Baselitz

138.2 **Andrea Andreani, after Mantegna**

Captured statues and siege equipment, a representation of a captured city and inscriptions ('The Triumphal Carts')

Chiaroscuro woodcut printed from four blocks, the tone blocks in yellowish brown and brown, 38.7 × 39.9 cm
Collection of Georg Baselitz

138.3 **Andrea Andreani, after Mantegna**
Trophies and bearers of coins and vases ('The Trophy Bearers')
Chiaroscuro woodcut printed from four blocks, the tone blocks in yellowish brown and brown,
39.5 × 38.5 cm
Collection of Georg Baselitz

138.4 **Andrea Andreani, after Mantegna**

Bearers of coins and vases, youths leading oxen, trumpeters ('The Vase Bearers')

Chiaroscuro woodcut printed from four blocks, the tone blocks in yellowish brown and brown,
38.9 × 38.3 cm
Collection of Georg Baselitz

138.5 **Andrea Andreani, after Mantegna**
Trumpeters, youths leading oxen, elephants with attendants ('The Elephants')

Chiaroscuro woodcut printed from four blocks, the tone blocks in yellowish brown and brown, 39.3 × 38.3 cm
Collection of Georg Baselitz

138.6 **Andrea Andreani, after Mantegna**
Bearers of coins and plate, trophies of royal armour ('The Corselet Bearers')

Chiaroscuro woodcut printed from four blocks, the tone blocks in yellowish brown and brown, 39.6 × 38.5 cm
Collection of Georg Baselitz

138.7 **Andrea Andreani, after Mantegna**
Captives, musicians ('The Captives')

Chiaroscuro woodcut printed from four blocks, the tone blocks in yellowish brown and brown, 39.2 × 38.5 cm; same image on verso, printed from the line block and one tone block
Collection of Georg Baselitz

138.8 **Andrea Andreani, after Mantegna**
Musicians and standard bearers ('The Musicians')
Chiaroscuro woodcut printed from four blocks, the tone blocks in yellowish brown and brown, 39.2 × 38.3 cm
Collection of Georg Baselitz

138.9 **Andrea Andreani, after Mantegna**
Julius Caesar on his chariot

Chiaroscuro woodcut printed from four blocks, the tone blocks in yellowish brown and brown, 39 × 38.3 cm
Collection of Georg Baselitz

138.10 **Andrea Andreani, after Mantegna**
Seven cut-out pilasters for *The Triumphs of Caesar*
1598

Chiaroscuro woodcut printed from two blocks, the tone block in brown (five central pilasters), and from three blocks, the tone blocks in yellow and brown (two outer pilasters); Andreani's view of Mantua, 1607, on versos of the two outer pilasters, each approx. 37.5 × 80 cm
Collection of Georg Baselitz

The Artists

Compiled by Michael Foster and Achim Gnann

Information and literature on some artists/woodcutters is scarce. However, wherever possible each entry is followed by two bibliographical references of relatively recent date. Further references will be found in the list of works exhibited (pp. 205–18).

Andrea Andreani

Born in Mantua in 1558–59, Andreani was the most prolific cutter and printer of chiaroscuro woodcuts in Italy in the later sixteenth century. He is documented in Florence in 1584 and in Siena from 1586, but by 1593 was active in his native city, where he set up a workshop and where he died in 1629. One work by him, a copy of Titian's *The Triumph of Faith*, was published in Rome. Along with drawings by Jacopo Ligozzi, Raffaellino da Reggio and others, his woodcuts reproduce intarsia pavements (by BECCAFUMI, in Siena cathedral) and sculptures (among them works by Giambologna; cats 127–31, 135). Andreani's oeuvre includes many large prints comprising several sheets, while some of his most enterprising works, notably his copies of drawings based on Andrea Mantegna's cartoons for *The Triumphs of Caesar* (Hampton Court Palace, London; cat. 138), required more than forty blocks. The remarkable accuracy of his copies in these and other prints was aided by a subtle use of very fine, unbroken outlines and by the generally outstanding quality of the printing. Perhaps owing to lack of commissions, from 1602 to 1610 Andreani also reprinted and re-cut chiaroscuro woodblocks by UGO DA CARPI, ANTONIO DA TRENTO and NICCOLÒ VICENTINO dating from decades earlier (for example, cats 34, 46, 47, 70, 73).

● Bibliography: Goldfarb 1981; Van Gastel 2007.

Hans Baldung Grien

Hans Baldung (the addition 'Grien' to his name probably refers to his penchant for that colour) was born in 1484 or 1485, probably in Schwäbisch Gmünd. Unusually for an artist, he came not from the artisan class but from a family of physicians, lawyers and scholars who, in the 1490s, settled in Strasbourg, where he will have received his first training. In 1503 he entered DÜRER'S workshop in Nuremberg, which he headed during that artist's second trip to Venice (1505–07). On Dürer's return, Baldung moved to Halle to fulfil two commissions for religious paintings. In Strasbourg again by 1509, he became a member of the artists' guild and established a workshop the following year. From 1512 to 1517 he was in nearby Freiburg im Breisgau, working on the cathedral high altarpiece and other, smaller commissions. As with most artists in Germany, his work was affected by the Reformation and, after his return to Strasbourg from Freiburg in 1517, he came to embrace more mythological and historical subjects and to adapt his manner in the direction of greater stylisation. He died in Strasbourg in 1545.

Baldung, like Grünewald, possessed a highly individual, notably 'expressive' style. He seems to have designed his first woodcuts while in Dürer's workshop and they reflect the fact that much of his output was aimed at a sophisticated clientele. Baldung's chiaroscuro woodcuts are among the finest of all essays in the technique and include one of the most striking images in German Renaissance art, *Witches' Sabbath* (cat. 12).

● Bibliography: Washington and New Haven 1981; von der Osten 1983.

Domenico Beccafumi

Born at Cortine in Valdibiana Montaperti, Tuscany, in 1486, the artist became the protégé of a wealthy Sienese citizen, Lorenzo Beccafumi, at an early age and adopted his benefactor's name. Active as a painter, sculptor, draughtsman, printmaker and illuminator, Beccafumi ranks among the most original artists of his time, an inveterate experimenter and a leading exponent of Tuscan Mannerism who worked in an intensely personal, imaginative style characterised by vibrant compositions and a delight in dramatic effects of light. That style was based on the formal vocabulary of High Renaissance art in Rome and Florence, enriching the initial influence of Sodoma (1477–1549) and Perugino (*c.* 1450–1523?) by study of Raphael and Michelangelo during a sojourn in Rome in 1510–12 and of Fra Bartolommeo (1472–1517) in Florence. Apart from brief periods at the Doria court in Genoa (*c.* 1533) and in Pisa (1536–38), Beccafumi spent most of the rest of his life in Siena, where he died in 1551.

Beccafumi's prints are among the finest and most distinctive of any produced in the sixteenth century. In his chiaroscuro woodcuts, for which he cut the blocks himself, he took his cue from UGO DA CARPI. He also employed the technique in his engravings, printing the engraved plate over an impression of the tone block (cats 86, 87).

● Bibliography: Siena 1990; Hartley 1991.

Hans Sebald Beham

Hans Sebald Beham, together with his brother Barthel, belonged to the third generation of a family of artists in Nuremberg, where he was born in 1500. He was probably trained in part by DÜRER and may have been running his own workshop by 1525. That year he and his brother were tried by Nuremberg city council for holding radical religious and political views and expelled from the city, though permitted to return later the same year. In 1528, found guilty of publishing a book that plagiarised a text by Dürer, he was again forced to leave Nuremberg. He seems to have been in Munich *c.* 1530, and around this time, despite his religious opinions, was commissioned by Cardinal Albrecht of Brandenburg to illustrate a prayerbook (Schloss Johannisburg, Aschaffenburg). In 1531 or thereabouts he apparently moved to Frankfurt am Main, where he died in 1550.

Alongside his activity as a painter and designer of stained glass, Beham produced a vast number of prints. Encompassing some 1,500 engravings, etchings and woodcuts, these are his chief claim to fame. Their content ranges widely, from traditional religious, historical and allegorical subjects to portraits, classical themes and scenes of peasant life. Stylistically, the artist took his cue in his early years from Dürer and from Albrecht Altdorfer (*c.* 1480–1538), but his work also reveals the influence of Italian models, including Raphael as transmitted by the engravings of Marcantonio Raimondi.

● Bibliography: Nuremberg 2011.

Niccolò Boldrini

Boldrini inscribed a signed chiaroscuro woodcut of *Venus and Cupid* with the name of the creator of the original motif, Titian, and the date '1566'. Yet he may have been active as a woodcutter in Venice as early as the mid-1530s, producing prints after works by Titian, and was probably born in Vicenza *c.* 1500. The *Venus and Cupid* is one of two chiaroscuro woodcuts among the four prints bearing Boldrini's signature. A total of about thirty woodcuts of varying style and quality have been linked with his name.

Boldrini, perhaps along with Domenico Campagnola (1500–1564), continued the practice of chiaroscuro woodcutting initiated in Venice by UGO DA CARPI. He favoured closed contours and he often simplified forms. His lines, notably regular, lack both the subtlety of Ugo's and the expressive quality of ANTONIO DA TRENTO'S. He employs a single tone block, using it to generate an overall atmosphere rather than to clarify detail.

● Bibliography: Washington, Dallas and Detroit 1976–77, pp. 176–84; Matile 2003, pp. 58–67.

Crispin van den Broeck

The Flemish painter and draughtsman Crispin van den Broeck was born in Mechelen in 1523, son of the painter Jan van den Broeck. His two brothers were also artists, Willem a sculptor, Hendrik a painter documented only in Italy. Crispin, too, may have visited Italy, but there is no documentary evidence to support this assumption. Probably trained by his father, he was still living in his hometown in 1557, though in 1555 the records of the artists' guild in Antwerp list him as a master. At first he probably worked there in the studio of FRANS FLORIS. Certainly, the two artists collaborated until Floris's death, in 1570, when van den Broeck completed some paintings the latter had left unfinished. In 1558 van den Broeck rented a house in Antwerp and became a citizen the following year. His work for the publisher and printer Christopher Plantin seems to have commenced in 1566. Especially from the 1570s onwards he produced a large number of drawings for engravings, including illustrations in works issued by Plantin. Van den Broeck died in Antwerp between 1589 and early 1591.

It has not been established whether the artist engraved prints himself or merely produced drawings for them. Some etchings by or attributed to him, among them that included here (cat. 101), were printed with the addition of a tone block, a technical challenge involving two different kinds of printing press that had already been tackled in Italy.

● Bibliography: Amsterdam and Cleveland 1992–93; Mielke 2011.

Hans Burgkmair the Elder

The elder Hans Burgkmair, among Germany's greatest artists of the late fifteenth and early sixteenth century, was born in Augsburg and probably received his initial training with his father, Thoman, who in 1488–89 sent him to work with Martin Schongauer (*c.* 1435/50–91), the leading painter in the Upper Rhine region and one of the finest printmakers north of the Alps. There are indications that in 1503 Burgkmair left Augsburg again and travelled to Cologne and the southern Netherlands. He seems to have visited northern Italy in 1506–07. Henceforth he followed DÜRER in introducing classical harmony and Renaissance motifs into his work, though he was more concerned with decorative and lighting effects than his more or less exact contemporary. Like CRANACH, Dürer and other major German artists of the day, he benefited from the patronage of Elector Friedrich the Wise of Saxony, but his most important patron was Emperor Maximilian I: he became a member of the illustrious circle of artists and humanists surrounding the emperor. Burgkmair died in his native city in 1531.

For most of his career, Burgkmair was a prolific designer of woodcuts. One of his most noteworthy contributions to pure woodcut was his part in *Maximilian's Triumphal Procession* (1516–18), a sequence of prints arranged to form a frieze fifty-four metres in length. From 1508 to 1512 he collaborated with the Antwerp woodcutter Jost de Negker on the development of new techniques, experimenting with printing in gold and silver before producing some of the earliest and finest essays in chiaroscuro woodcut (cats 1, 2). His *Lovers Surprised by Death*) may be termed the first masterwork in the new technique (cat. 4).

● Bibliography: Falk 1968; Berlin 1974.

Antonio Campi

Born in 1523 into a leading family of artists in Cremona, Antonio Campi probably trained with his brother Giulio (*c.* 1508–1573). He worked as a painter in his birthplace, in Brescia, Milan, Piacenza, Rome, Torre Pallavicina and elsewhere, sometimes collaborating, mainly on frescoes, with Giulio and his other brother,

Vincenzo (1530/35–1591). His style ranged widely in the course his career. Antonio was also active as a printmaker, a sculptor and an architect, attached in the latter capacity to the cathedral works in Cremona. He died in his native city in 1587.

Antonio may have learned woodcutting from his brother Giulio, who produced book illustrations for publishers in Cremona. Seven single-leaf woodcuts by Antonio are known, five of them pure chiaroscuros and all of them dating from 1547 to 1553. During this short period the young artist's painting style owed much to PARMIGIANINO and the local artist Camillo Boccaccino (1504/05–1546), and this is reflected in the prints. Technically and in their woodcut style, Antonio's chiaroscuros betray the influence of UGO DA CARPI, ANTONIO DA TRENTO and, especially, the mature NICCOLÒ VICENTINO.

● Bibliography: Cremona 1985; De Klerck 1999.

Ugo da Carpi

Born at Carpi in the modern-day province of Modena *c.* 1470–80, Ugo was the first and most important cutter of chiaroscuro woodcuts in Italy. He trained as a painter and type-founder, and by 1501 was creating illustrations and calligraphic letters for leading publishers in his native city. He is first documented in Venice, the centre of the Italian publishing industry, in 1511. In addition to mainly reproductive book illustrations, he produced a large print of the *Sacrifice of Isaac*, based on a design by Titian and printed from four blocks. Unusually, Ugo signed his blocks, and in 1516 he applied to the Venetian Senate for a 'privilege' relating to the chiaroscuro woodcut process, which he claimed to have invented, though he must have seen earlier German examples. Some time in 1516–18 he moved to Rome, where he joined the engraver Marcantonio Raimondi (*c.* 1470/82–1527/34) and other outstanding printmakers in Raphael's studio. His essays in the chiaroscuro technique gradually increased in technical and artistic sophistication: he regularly employed three to five blocks instead of the two-block method favoured by BURGKMAIR and CRANACH and in his own earlier work, reducing the importance of the line block and developing the use of tone blocks to replace cross-hatching as a way of generating contrasts and reproducing masses. By 1518 Ugo had set up on his own as a printer, and in 1525 he compiled, cut and published a treatise on writing, *Thesauro de' scrittori*. He fled Rome after the sack of the city, in 1527, and seems to have settled in Bologna, where he worked with PARMIGIANINO – a collaboration, begun in Rome in 1524–25, that had a major impact on his style.

● Bibliography: Johnson 1982; Carpi 2009.

Lucas Cranach the Elder

Lucas Müller, born in 1472, adopted the name of his birthplace, now spelled 'Kronach', some fifty-five miles north of Nuremberg. Next to nothing is known about his life and work before 1501–02, when he is documented in Vienna. His double portrait of Johannes Cuspinian and his wife (Oskar Reinhart Collection, Winterthur), a principal work of the Danube school of painting, testifies to his humanist connections in the city. In 1505 he was appointed court artist to Duke Friedrich the Wise of Saxony in Wittenberg. Here, too, he mixed in humanist circles, acquired considerable wealth, received a coat of arms from the duke in 1508 (the winged serpent that thenceforth formed part of his standard signature) and was mayor of the city on three occasions. In 1508 he travelled to the Netherlands at the duke's behest. His close links with Martin Luther and Reformation politics did not prevent him from also working for the Catholic Cardinal Albrecht of Brandenburg. When the Protestant armies were defeated in 1547 Cranach followed his captive patron, Johann Friedrich, Elector of Saxony, to Augsburg and Innsbruck, then, after the elector's release, to Weimar, where he died in 1553.

Cranach produced a large number of woodcuts throughout his career, both single-leaf prints and book illustrations. Like his painting, they ranged widely in subject-matter, portraits existing alongside religious, mythological and polemical images. His *St George and the Dragon* (fig. 7 p. 30), printed on blue prepared paper, played a key role in the development of the chiaroscuro woodcut: the coloured paper needed only to be replaced by colour printed from a tone block. Indeed, by inscribing two of his chiaroscuros with the false date '1506' he laid claim to invention of the technique.

● Bibliography: Wittenberg 1998; Brussels and Paris 2010–11.

Albrecht Dürer

Born in Nuremberg in 1471, Dürer was first apprenticed to his goldsmith father, then, from 1486 to 1489, to the local painter Michael Wolgemut (1434/37–1519). There are indications that, as a journeyman, he followed the example of many contemporary artists and travelled to the Netherlands. He certainly went to Colmar to visit Martin Schongauer (*c.* 1435/50–91), who had just died, however, and thence to Basle and Strasbourg, returning to Nuremberg in 1494. Later that year he travelled to Venice. On his return to Nuremberg the following year he established a workshop. He left Nuremberg on two more occasions, for Venice (1505–07) and the Netherlands (1520–21), before his death in his native city in 1528. His life and work, wide-ranging in technique, subject-matter and style, and augmented by theoretical writings on human proportion and other topics, can be seen as an attempt to synthesise the art of Italy with his northern heritage. Among other things, this entailed freeing the artist from the status of an artisan.

Dürer's prints, which encompass woodcuts, engravings, etchings and drypoints, are perhaps his most important contribution to the art of his time and played a pivotal role in introducing the art of the Italian Renaissance to Germany and elsewhere north of the Alps. The artist never employed the chiaroscuro woodcut technique – the graphic and painterly sophistication of his 'straight' woodcuts, which he cut himself, rendered it largely superfluous – and the examples shown here, which include the immensely popular rhinoceros (cat. 18), date from around a century after his death, when the Amsterdam publisher Willem Janssen added tone blocks to original blocks he had acquired from a fellow publisher in The Hague.

● Bibliography: Nuremberg 2000; Schoch, Mende and Scherbaum 2002.

Frans Floris

The Flemish painter, draughtsman and etcher Frans Floris was born in Antwerp in 1519–20, the son of the sculptor Cornelis Floris (1513/1575). He trained as a painter with Lambert Lombard (1505/06–1566) in Liège *c.* 1538–39, and in 1540–41 was accepted into the artists' guild in Antwerp as a master. Shortly thereafter he travelled to Italy, becoming a prominent member of the Netherlandish community in Rome, where he made drawings after antique sculptures and copied paintings by Raphael, Michelangelo, Polidoro da Caravaggio and others. He also visited other cities. In Mantua, for example, he studied Giulio Romano's frescoes in the Palazzo Ducale and the Palazzo del Te. By 1545 he had returned to Antwerp: that year he married a goldsmith's daughter and set up a workshop. The recipient of many important commissions, and an artist whose work was widely collected by affluent burghers, Floris acquired enough wealth to have a grand house and studio built in a new area of Antwerp. He died in the city in 1570.

Floris exerted enormous influence on art in Antwerp. He was a major representative of the distinctive synthesis of High Renaissance and Mannerist styles practised by Netherlandish artists who had visited Italy ('Romanists') and played an important part in introducing mythological subject-matter into Flemish art. In addition, many of the large number of assistants he employed ranked – or were to rank – among the city's leading artists. Floris began designing chiaroscuro woodcuts in the mid-1550s. About five examples are known. Some of them recall the manner of NICCOLÒ VICENTINO so strongly that it has been suggested that the Flemish artist who cut Floris's blocks had trained with the Italian.

● Bibliography: Van de Velde 1975; Wouk 2011.

Giovanni Gallo

Next to nothing is known about this woodblock cutter. He has been thought to come from France (once being identified as the painter and engraver Jean Salomon, active in Lyons) or from Lombardy, but a recent suggestion that he is the 'Joannes Gallo, painter from Antwerp' documented in 1595 as a witness at a wedding in Naples seems more plausible. Gallo based many of his chiaroscuro woodcuts on works by the painter Marco Pino (born in Siena in 1521), a prominent member of the younger generation of Mannerists who, apart from the years 1568–70, which he spent in Rome, was active in Naples from 1552 and died there in 1583. Pino, who at one time had been a member of BECCAFUMI's studio, is known to have employed printmakers in his own workshop. Only one print by Gallo, a 'pure' woodcut of the *Mystical Marriage of St Catherine* (British Museum, London, 1870,1008.1984), bears a date – 1578 – and he is now held to have produced his chiaroscuro woodcuts during Pino's late period in Naples. Notably painterly in style, they continue the manner initiated by UGO DA CARPI and NICCOLÒ VICENTINO and developed by ANTONIO CAMPI.

● Bibliography: Zezza 2003.

Alessandro Gandini

Very little is known about this woodcutter, but information recently brought to light shows that he was a resident of Bologna in 1546. He is recorded there again in 1555 and 1564, although in the latter instance he is described as a mathematician, an occupation he cannot otherwise be shown to have pursued. Gandini must therefore rank among the city's earliest exponents of the chiaroscuro woodcut, along with PARMIGIANINO's collaborators ANTONIO DA TRENTO and NICCOLÒ VICENTINO and the unidentified artist known as MASTER NDB.

Including attributions, Gandini's oeuvre encompasses six chiaroscuro woodcuts. In style and technique they resemble the early work of UGO DA CARPI, while also revealing links with the prints of Antonio da Trento. ANDREA ANDREANI later acquired some of the blocks, reprinting and occasionally reworking them (cats 89, 91).

● Bibliography: Rome, Weimar and Munich 2001–03; Johnson 2013.

Hendrick Goltzius

The finest Dutch engraver of his time, who was also active as a painter, draughtsman, etcher and print publisher, was born in Bracht, near Viersen, in 1558. From his father, Jan Goltz II, who moved to Duisburg when Hendrick was three, he learned glass painting, then, in 1574–75, trained as an engraver and etcher with Dirck Volkertsz. Coornhert in Xanten. In 1577 he followed Coornhert to Haarlem, where in 1579 he married a shipbuilder's widow and adopted her son, Jacob Matham, who also became an important engraver. In 1582 he established his own print publishing house. A member of humanist circles, he became friends the following year with Carel van Mander ('the Dutch Vasari') who showed him drawings by Bartholomäus Spranger that had a decisive influence on his work. In 1590–91 he visited Florence, Venice, Rome and Naples, meeting Giambologna, Federico Zuccari and other major artists. The principal objects of his study in Rome were the works of classical antiquity and those of the leading Renaissance artists. He had returned to Haarlem by the end of 1591. From *c.* 1600 he largely ceased producing prints and focused on painting. He died in Haarlem in 1617.

For at least ten years from *c.* 1588 Goltzius was the leading exponent of the chiaroscuro woodcut in the northern Netherlands. His essays in the technique, which include a number of landscapes (cats 112–15), belong among the finest anywhere. How many of them he cut himself is not known. Most show a distinctive technique: tone blocks were employed only after the line block had been printed on blue paper and the design heightened with white.

● Bibliography: Amsterdam and Cleveland 1992–93; Amsterdam, New York and Toledo 2003–04.

Adriaen Thomasz. Key

The Flemish painter and woodcutter Adriaen Thomasz. Key was in born in Antwerp *c.* 1544 into a family of artists. The register of the Antwerp artists' guild listed him in 1558 as a pupil of Jan Haeck, then, in 1568, as an independent master. The earliest known dated paintings by him originated in 1572. In 1585, after the capture of Antwerp by Catholic forces under the Duke of Parma, he was registered as a Calvinist, but stayed in the city. He is last mentioned in the guild records in 1589. Although he produced altarpieces for churches in his hometown, his principal claim to fame is as a painter of keenly observed portraits.

The two chiaroscuro woodcuts included here are attributed to Key on the basis of the monogram 'ATK', which also appears on the artist's paintings (cats 99, 100). Whether he cut the blocks himself is not known. Although the prints bear a certain stylistic resemblance to the work of FRANS FLORIS, they are more pronouncedly linear in character. Technically, they are closer to UGO DA CARPI than to NICCOLÒ VICENTINO, who clearly influenced Floris.

● Bibliography: Jonckheere 2007; Wouk 2011, vol. 1, p. LV.

Erasmus Loy

Biographical information about this German woodcutter is sparse, but he is documented in Regensburg and is thought to have been active there *c.* 1520 to *c.* 1570. He specialised in prints intended to be pasted onto furniture and other items of woodwork as inexpensive substitutes for intarsia decoration and grained woods. By 1557 he had been granted an imperial 'privilege' relating to this practice, which he claimed – probably correctly – as his invention. The chiaroscuro woodcuts were used in domestic and ecclesiastical contexts, affixed to clearly defined areas of cupboards, chests, doors, wall panelling, pulpits, pews, choir stalls and so forth. Printed from two blocks, they feature skilful combinations of Renaissance architectural elements – palaces, towers, loggias and the like – in perspective views. Tonal gradations and atmospheric effects are not permitted to impair the illusion of intarsia work. Loy also produced colour woodcuts with Renaissance decorative motifs. This 'printed wallpaper' could be cut out and arranged in strips of any desired length to form border decoration on wall and ceiling panels, doors and beds. Both the architectural and the decorative designs were generally pasted over paper printed with woodcut patterns imitating the grain of light brown ash-wood veneers. The 'grain' showed through in the blank, unprinted areas of the design. Produced for a specific practical purpose, not as collector's items, Loy's prints are extremely rare.

● Bibliography: Strauss 1975, vol. 2, pp. 617–33; Appuhn 1976.

Master NDB

This unidentified woodcutter is named after the initials on five chiaroscuro prints, two of which bear the date 1544. They reproduce compositions by Raphael (cats 93, 94), PARMIGIANINO and Rosso Fiorentino. Attributions have increased the number of Master NDB's chiaroscuro woodcuts to eleven. One of the additional works carries an inscription indicating that the artist came from Bologna. Recent investigation of the woodcuts has shown that the paper watermarks are French and also occur on prints produced by members of the school of Fontainebleau. It has therefore been suggested that Master NDB must have been active in Fontainebleau by 1544, perhaps at the behest of his fellow Bolognese artist Primaticcio, who settled in France in 1531 but visited Italy on several occasions from 1540 onwards. Stylistically, the chiaroscuros betray the influence of UGO DA CARPI.

● Bibliography: Karpinski 1976; Jenkins 2013.

Georg Matheus

Very little reliable information is available on the career of this German woodblock cutter. Born in Augsburg, he seems to have been active in his hometown, and possibly in Lyons, from *c.* 1554 to 1572. He apparently inscribed his woodcuts sometimes with his full name, for instance in a *Flight into Egypt* in Vienna (fig. 34, p. 128), and sometimes with the initial 'M', as in the example included here (cat. 92). His prints, embracing a variety of religious and mythological subjects, reproduce mainly works by Italian artists: cat. 92, for instance, shows a fresco, now destroyed, by a Raphael pupil, either Giulio Romano or Giovanni Francesco Penni, in the church of SS. Trinità dei Monti, Rome. The figures in Matheus's woodcuts, which generally exhibit clear detailing, are occasionally rather stiff. A hypothesis identifying the artist as the 'woodcutter Jörg' (a form of the name Georg used by Matheus) who signed a portrait of Martin Luther dated 1551 and was active in Wittenberg cannot be substantiated.

● Bibliography: H., vol. 23, pp. 251–5; Strauss 1973, nos 64–6.

Parmigianino

The painter, draughtsman and printmaker Girolamo Francesco Maria Mazzola, a leading exponent of the early Mannerist style, was born in Parma (hence his nickname 'il Parmigianino') in 1503. He trained and worked in his hometown before moving to Rome in 1524 and painting his principal work of this period, *The Vision of St Jerome* (National Gallery, London). After the sack of the city, in 1527, he fled to Bologna, where he remained for four years. In 1531 he returned to Parma, producing, among other major works, the 'iconic' Mannerist painting *The Madonna of the Long Neck* (fig. 4, p. 21). Imprisoned briefly for breach of contract, he was released on condition that he fulfil his obligations, but escaped to Casalmaggiore, where he died in 1540.

Parmigianino's characteristically elegant style, wedding the power of Michelangelo to the classical poise and grace of Raphael and Correggio, also informs his work as a printmaker. He was among the first Italian artists to practise etching (see cats 40–3), apparently during his Roman and Bolognese periods, and at this time he produced designs for engravings and chiaroscuro woodcuts, collaborating with UGO DA CARPI (cats 35–9), ANTONIO DA TRENTO (cats 44–55, 57–67) and other specialists. The dissemination of his work via prints made him a major force in the art of the mid-sixteenth century (he exerted a crucial influence on the school of Fontainebleau in France) and, later, among the artists active at the court of Emperor Rudolf II in Prague around 1600.

● Bibliography: Gnann 2003; Ekserdjian 2006.

Antonio da Trento

Information on the life and work of Antonio da Trento comes solely from Giorgio Vasari's *Lives of the Artists* (1550, 1568). According to Vasari, Antonio came from Trent and was employed by PARMIGIANINO in his Bologna studio to make prints of his work. All six chiaroscuro woodcuts mentioned by Vasari do indeed reproduce works by Parmigianino. The co-operation between the two artists, which may have started in Rome, before the painter's departure for Bologna in 1527, ended in 1530–31.

Antonio may have trained with UGO DA CARPI in Rome, since five of his documented chiaroscuro woodcuts employ the linear style and two-block technique characteristic of Ugo's early work. The sixth print ranks with the finest Italian examples made from more than two blocks (cat. 44). Antonio has sometimes been erroneously identified with the painter and etcher Antonio Fantuzzi, who worked at Fontainebleau from 1537 to 1550.

● Bibliography: Gnann 2002; Matile 2003, pp. 134–41.

Niccolò Vicentino

Giuseppe Niccolò Rossigliani, generally known as Niccolò Vicentino after his birthplace, Vicenza, is sometimes thought to have started his career as a woodcutter and printer around 1540, but there are strong indications that he was already active *c.* 1525 in Rome. He may have trained there with UGO DA CARPI: his work stresses flowing movement in a way comparable with the painterly approach characteristic of Ugo's mature style. Five signed chiaroscuro woodcuts by him are known. Each reproduces a work by a different artist, including PARMIGIANINO (cat. 68), Raphael and Polidoro da Caravaggio. Other items can be attributed to him on stylistic and technical grounds. His hand has been detected among a substantial number of chiaroscuro woodcuts based on designs and drawings by Parmigianino, with whom he seems to have collaborated personally. It has been suggested that these prints were produced in a workshop headed by Niccolò. The blocks were acquired and reprinted with emendations several decades later by ANDREA ANDREANI (cat. 73).

● Bibliography: Matile 2003, pp. 142–54; Gnann 2002.

Hans Wechtlin

Wechtlin, born in Strasbourg *c.* 1480–85, was active as a painter and a woodcut designer, though his work as a painter has received little attention from scholars. He is documented in Nancy in 1505 and in Wittenberg in 1506–07. In Wittenberg he will have made the acquaintance of CRANACH, while the very strong influence of DÜRER on his work suggests that he may also have spent time in the latter's workshop. He is recorded as a citizen of Strasbourg in 1514 and was still active there in 1526. It is not known when he died.

Wechtlin is best known for an extensive series of woodcuts showing episodes from the life of Christ, yet his twelve surviving chiaroscuro woodcuts are artistically finer and historically more important (he was once credited incorrectly with inventing the technique). They probably date from *c.* 1510–12, the time when BALDUNG was employing the chiaroscuro method, also in Strasbourg. Wechtlin's chiaroscuros, probably aimed at a sophisticated humanist audience, range widely in subject-matter and are among the earliest examples to reflect the influence of the Italian Renaissance in form and content.

● Bibliography: Klein 2006–07.

Hans Weiditz

Records indicate that Hans Weiditz, probably the son of the eponymous Strasbourg sculptor (1475? – 1516?), was a member of the artists' guild in Strasbourg from 1530 to 1534. He died in his native city *c.* 1536. Weiditz's only authenticated works are woodcut illustrations for Otto Brunfels's *Herbarum vivae eicones*, published in Strasbourg by Johann Schott from 1530 to 1536. Some naturalistic preparatory watercolour drawings for these, remarkable in their botanical exactitude, also survive (University of Berne). Other works are attributed to him on the basis of stylistic comparisons with the herbal woodcuts and drawings.

Seeking to match Weiditz's surviving oeuvre with the high reputation accorded him in contemporary documents, Heinrich Röttinger advanced the theory in 1904 that Weiditz was identical with the woodcut designer known as the Petrarch Master. Named after a German edition of Petrarch's *De remediis utriusque fortunae* (Augsburg, 1532), this highly original Augsburg artist produced a number of single-leaf woodcuts and a very large body of book illustrations, designed between 1514 and 1522, but mostly printed after 1530. Whether all, some or any of these works are by Weiditz remains a matter of dispute.

● Bibliography: Geisberg and Strauss 1974, vol. 4, pp. 1461–1506; Muller 2001.

Works Exhibited

1

Hans Burgkmair the Elder

St George and the Dragon

1508 and *c.* 1509–10

Chiaroscuro woodcut printed from two blocks, the tone block in beige

31.9 × 22.5 cm

Inscribed (upper left): *DIVUS·GEORGIUS / CHRISTIANORUM· / MILITUM· PRO= / PUGNATOR*; (lower left): *H· BURGKMAIR*; (lower right): *Jost de Negker.*

Watermark: Ox head with staff ending in a flower; similar to Briquet 14734

Collection of Georg Baselitz

B. VII, pp. 208–9, no. 23; H. V, 253.

Bibliography: Chmelarz 1894; Lippmann 1895, p. 142; Dodgson 1911, p. 74, no. 14; Friedländer 1925; Reichel 1926, pp. 16–18; Burkhard 1932, no. 15; Jahn 1955, p. 26; Winkelbauer 1954, p. 547; Paris and Rotterdam 1965–66, no. 9; Falk 1968, pp. 69–71; Falk 1980, p. 29; Strauss 1973, no. 11; Basle 1974, vol. 1, no. 17 (text by D. Koepplin); Hébert 1982, no. 1019a; Parshall and Landau 1994, pp. 184–97; Bartrum 1995, p. 136, no. 135; Tokyo 2005, cat. 1; Silver 2012–13, pp. 93–4; Jecmen 2012–14, pp. 76–8.

2

Hans Burgkmair the Elder

Emperor Maximilian on Horseback

1508 and 1518

Chiaroscuro woodcut printed from two blocks, the tone block in greenish beige

32.3 × 22.6 cm

Inscribed (above): *IMP·CAES·MAXIMIL·AUG*; (lower right): *1518 / H·BURGKMAIR·*

Albertina, Vienna, DG1934/65

B. VII, p. 211, no. 32; H. V, 323.

Bibliography: Loedel 1863, p. 4; Chmelarz 1894; Lippmann 1895, p. 142; Dodgson 1911, p. 76, no. VI; Friedländer 1925; Reichel 1926, pp. 16–18; Burkhard 1932, cat. 14; Winkelbauer 1954, p. 547; Falk 1968, pp. 69–73; Augsburg 1973, no. 22; Strauss 1973, no. 12; Braunschweig 1973, cat. 10; Goldfarb 1981, p. 308; Landau and Parshall 1994, pp. 184–97; Bartrum 1995, p. 135, no. 133; Baltimore und Saint Louis 2003, no. 12 (text by S. Dackerman); Braunschweig 2003–04, p. 15, cat. A., no. 3; Tokyo 2005, cat. 2; Brussels and Paris 2010–11, no. 50 (text by G. Messling); Silver 2012–13, pp. 93–5; Vienna 2012–13a, cat. 113 (text by C. Metzger); Jecmen 2012–14, pp. 76–8, fig. 21.

3

Lucas Cranach the Elder

St Christopher

1509 and second half of the sixteenth century

Chiaroscuro woodcut printed from two blocks, the tone block in yellowish brown

28 × 19.6 cm

Inscribed (upper left, on tablet): *LC*; two coats of arms also hanging from the tree

Collection of Georg Baselitz

B. VII, p. 283, no. 58; H. VI, no. 79 IIe.

Bibliography: Loedel 1863, p. 3; Seibt 1891, pp. 23–5; Lippmann 1895; Flechsig 1900, pp. 11–60; Dodgson 1911, p. 296, no. 61; Geisberg 1930, no. 594; Jahn 1955, p. 33; Paris and Rotterdam 1965–66, nos 22–3; Coburg 1972, no. 64; Strauss 1973, no. 4; Basle 1974, vol. 2, no. 402c (text by D. Koepplin); Schade 1974, pp. 34–6; Hébert 1982, no. 887; Paris 1984, no. 265, cat. 179 (text by R. Braig); Landau and Parshall 1994, pp. 190–7; Braunschweig 2003–04, p. 17, cat. A., no. 8; Tokyo 2005, cat. 3.

4

Hans Burgkmair the Elder

Lovers Surprised by Death

c. 1510

Chiaroscuro woodcut printed from three blocks, the tone blocks in blue

21.3 × 15.2 cm

Inscribed (lower left edge, top to bottom): *Jost de Negker.*; (lower left): *H·/ BURGKMAIR*

Albertina, Vienna, DG1934/75

B. VII, p. 215, no. 40; H. V, 724.

Bibliography: Loedel 1863, p. 5; Seibt 1891, pp. 28–9; Chmelarz 1894, p. 395; Dodgson 1911, p. 86, no. 46b.II; Reichel 1926, pl. 8; Geisberg 1930, no. 475; Burkhard 1932, no. 20.2; Richards 1957; Falk 1968, p. 67; Augsburg 1973, cat. 41b (text by T. Falk); Strauss 1973, no. 13; Braunschweig 1973, cat. 11; Berlin 1974, cat. 13; Basle 1974, cat. 82 (text by D. Koepplin); Falk 1980, p. 46; Goldfarb 1981, p. 308; Hébert 1982, no. 1037; Landau and Parshall 1994, pp. 198–202; Bartrum 1995, pp. 136–7, no. 136; Braunschweig 2003–04, pp. 18–21, cat. A., no. 4; Jecmen 2012–14, p. 78.

5
Lucas Cranach the Elder
The Rest on the Flight into Egypt
1509
Chiaroscuro woodcut printed from two blocks, the tone block in reddish brown
28.5 × 18.6 cm
Inscribed (lower right, on tablet): *L C* [above winged serpent] / *1509*
Albertina, Vienna, DG1929/119
B. VII, pp. 279–80, no. 3; H. VI, no. 7.

Bibliography: Seibt 1891, p. 28; Dodgson 1911, pp. 294–5, no. 58; Reichel 1926, pl. 2; Geisberg 1930, no. 540; Jahn 1955, p. 32; Coburg 1972, no. 14; Strauss 1973, no. 7; Schade 1974, p. 34; Hébert 1982, no. 832A; Landau and Parshall 1994, p. 197; Moser 2004, p. 49; Braunschweig 2003–04, p. 17, cat. A., no. 13; Brussels and Paris 2010–11, cat. 28 (text by G. Messling).

6
Hans Burgkmair the Elder
Hans Paumgartner
1512
Chiaroscuro woodcut printed from three blocks, the tone blocks in violet
29.1 × 24.1 cm
Inscribed (upper right, on tablet): *ANN·SAL·MDXII / IOANNES·PAUNGARTNER· CI* [I within C] *AUGU / STA*ᴺ [N retraced in pen and ink] *AETAT·SUAE·ANN·LVII*; (at centre left edge, top to bottom on the architecture):·*H·BURGKMAIR*
Albertina, Vienna, DG1934/69
B. VII, p. 212, no. 34; H. V, 307.

Bibliography: Herberger 1851, pp. 58–9; Loedel 1863, p. 5; Chmelarz 1894, p. 395; Lippmann 1895, p. 139; Dodgson 1911, pp. 87–8, no. 50; Reichel 1926, pp. 21–2, pl. 9; Geisberg 1930, no. 507; Burkhard 1932, no. 33; Panofsky 1942, p. 52, fig. 21; Falk 1968, pp. 57–8, fig. 31; Augsburg 1973, cat. 76 (text by T. Falk); Braunschweig 1973, cat. 13; Strauss 1973, no. 18; Falk 1980, p. 40; Landau and Parshall 1994, p. 200; Bartrum 1995, p. 137, no. 137; Braunschweig 2003–04, pp. 18–21, cat. A., no. 6; Berlin 2006, no. 104 (text by M. Roth); Vienna and Munich 2011–12, cat. 76 (text by A. Riether); Jecmen 2012–14, p. 80.

7
Hans Wechtlin
Virgin and Child
c. 1510–12
Chiaroscuro woodcut printed from two blocks, the tone block in blue-grey; blue wash added to the sky
26.5 × 17.8 cm
Inscribed (lower left, on tablet): *Io[annes] V[echtlin]* [with two crossed pilgrim's staffs]
Albertina, Vienna, DG1949/644
B. VII, p. 450, no. 2 (as J. U. Pilgrim); Le Blanc, 4, p. 196, no. 5.

Bibliography: Loedel 1863; Nagler 1858–79, vol. 4, 1871, p. 74, no. 2 (as ?Hans Ulrich Pilgrim); Seibt 1891, p. 31; Reichel 1926, pl. 21; Geisberg 1930, no. 1486; Francis 1953, p. 31; Karlsruhe 1959, no. 339; Paris and Rotterdam 1965–66, no. 33; Strauss 1973, no. 20; Geisberg and Strauss 1974, vol. 4, p. 1447; Strauss 1981, p. 28; Hébert 1982, no. 1404; Tokyo 2005, cat. 6; Klein 2006–07, vol. 1, pp. 25–7, vol. 2, fig. 46.

8
Hans Baldung Grien
Virgin and Child with Angels in a Landscape
c. 1511
Chiaroscuro woodcut printed from two blocks, the tone block in greyish brown
37.3 × 26 cm; cut down at the lower edge
Inscribed (lower right, on tablet): *HB* [monogrammed]
Albertina, Vienna, DG1931/94
P. III, p. 322, no. 66; H. II, 62.

Bibliography: Seibt 1891, p. 31; Curjel 1923, p. 57; Reichel 1926, p. 54, pl. 13; Geisberg 1930, no. 87; Karlsruhe 1959, II H, no. 19; Paris and Rotterdam 1965–66, no. 5; Strauss 1973, no. 34; Mende 1978, no. 20; Bartrum 1995, pp. 73–4, no. 60; Washington and New Haven 1981, cat. 22 (text by C. Schuler); Hébert 1982, no. 1338; Freiburg 2001–02, cat. 3 (text by S. Bock and S. Durian-Ress); Söding 2001–02, p. 22.

9
Hans Wechtlin
Christ on the Cross
c. 1510–12
Chiaroscuro woodcut printed from two blocks, the tone block in greyish blue; ornamental frame printed from four blocks
27.7 × 19.2 cm
Inscribed (lower left, on tablet): *Io[annes] V[echtlin]* [with two crossed pilgrim's staffs]
Albertina, Vienna, DG1949/643
B. VII, p. 449, no. 1 (as J. U. Pilgrim); Le Blanc, 4, p. 196, no. 4.

Bibliography: Loedel 1863; Nagler 1858–79, vol. 4, 1871, p. 74, no. 1 (as ?Hans Ulrich Pilgrim); Seibt 1891, p. 31; Reichel 1926, pl. 19; Geisberg 1930, no. 1482, Paris and Rotterdam 1965–66, no. 32; Strauss 1973, no. 19, Geisberg and Strauss 1974, vol. 4, p. 1444; Strauss 1981, p. 27; Tokyo 2005, cat. 5; Klein 2006–07, vol. 1, pp. 25–7, vol. 2, fig. 44.

10
Hans Wechtlin
Virgin and Child
c. 1510–12
Chiaroscuro woodcut printed from two blocks, the tone block in greyish green
27 × 18.5 cm
Inscribed (upper left, on foreshortened tablet resting on the cornice): *Io[annes] V[echtlin]* [with two crossed pilgrim's staffs]
Albertina, Vienna, DG1949/645
B. VII, p. 450, no. 3 (as J. U. Pilgrim); Le Blanc, 4, p. 196, no. 6.

Bibliography: Loedel 1863; Nagler 1858–79, vol. 4, 1871, p. 74, no. 3 (as ?Hans Ulrich Pilgrim); Seibt 1891, p. 31; Reichel 1926, pl. 18; Geisberg 1930, no. 1486; Winkler 1951; Karlsruhe 1959, no. 341; Geisberg and Strauss 1974, vol. 4, p. 1448; Strauss 1981, p. 29; Hébert 1982, no. 1405; Klein 2006–07, vol. 1, pp. 25–7, vol. 2, fig. 45.

11
Hans Wechtlin
Knight and Lansquenet
c. 1510–12
Chiaroscuro woodcut printed from two blocks, the tone block in blue
26.9 × 18.1 cm
Inscribed (lower left, on tablet): *Io[annes] V[echtlin]* [with a flower and two crossed pilgrim's staffs]; (upper left): *P*[?] *mariette 1665* [in pen and ink]
Albertina, Vienna, DG1949/653
B. VII, p. 452, no. 10 (as J. U. Pilgrim); Le Blanc, 4, p. 197, no. 14.

Bibliography: Loedel 1863; Nagler 1858–79, vol. 4, 1871, p. 74, no. 10 (as ?Hans Ulrich Pilgrim); Seibt 1891, p. 31; Reichel 1926, pl. 22; Geisberg 1930, no. 1497; Francis 1953, pp. 31–2; Paris and Rotterdam 1965–66, no. 36; Strauss 1973, no. 27; Geisberg and Strauss 1974, vol. 4, p. 1459; Strauss 1981, p. 36; Hébert 1982, no. 1411; Tokyo 2005, cat. 7; Klein 2006–07, vol. 1, pp. 25–7, vol. 2, fig. 50.

12
Hans Baldung Grien
Witches' Sabbath
1510
Chiaroscuro woodcut printed from two blocks, the tone block in greyish beige
37 × 25.5 cm
Inscribed (at centre right edge, on tablet hanging from a branch): *HGB* [monogrammed]; (on the tree trunk): *1510* [below a vine leaf, his journeyman's mark]; area of loss at centre left
Albertina, Vienna, DG1931/87
B. VII, pp. 319–20, no. 55; Le Blanc, 2, p. 324, no. 46; H. II, 235.

Bibliography: Seibt 1891, p. 31; Curjel 1923, pp. 46, 52; Reichel 1926, pp. 53–4, pl. 11; Geisberg 1930, no. 121; Karlsruhe 1959, II H, no. 76; Strauss 1973, no. 32; Mende 1978, no. 16; Washington and New Haven 1981, cat. 18 (text by D. Lettieri); Strauss et al. 1981, p. 59; Hébert 1982, no. 1388a; Bartrum 1995, pp. 69–70, nos 54–5; Freiburg 2001–02, cat. 34 (text by S. Bock and S. Durian-Ress); Söding 2001–02, pp. 44–5; Braunschweig 2003–04, cat. B., nos 1, 2; Hult 2005, pp. 75–85; Berlin 2006, cat. 79 (text by U. B. Ullrich); Frankfurt 2007, cat. 6–8; Vienna 2012–13b, cat. 68.

13
Hans Baldung Grien
Christ on the Cross, with the Virgin and Ss. John the Evangelist and Mary Magdalene
c. 1511–12
Chiaroscuro woodcut printed from two blocks, the tone block in orange-brown
37 × 25.8 cm
Inscribed (lower right corner, on tablet): *HGB* [monogrammed, in pen and ink]; (lower centre edge): *AD* [monogram of Albrecht Dürer, in pen and ink, not autograph]
Albertina, Vienna, DG1931/104
B. VII, p. 125, no. 57 (as Dürer); H. II, 11.

Bibliography: Thausing 1869; Seibt 1891, p. 31; Curjel 1923, p. 159; Reichel 1926, p. 54, pl. 15; Geisberg 1930, no. 59; Perseke 1941, pp. 166–7; Karlsruhe 1959, II H, no. 7; Paris and Rotterdam 1965–66, no. 3; Strauss 1973, no. 37; Mende 1978, no. 37; Strauss 1980, p. 152; Washington and New Haven 1981, cat. 24; Hébert 1982, no. 1325; Freiburg 2001–02, cat. 11 (text by S. Bock and S. Durian-Ress); Söding 2001–02, pp. 23–4.

14
Hans Baldung Grien
Adam and Eve
1511
37.5 × 25.6 cm
Chiaroscuro woodcut printed from two blocks, the tone block in greyish brown
Inscribed (upper centre, on tablet): *LAPSUS HUMA / NI GENERIS*; (lower left, on tablet): *HGB* [monogrammed, below a vine leaf, his journeyman's mark] / *1511*; outlines of the figures pricked with holes
Albertina, Vienna, DG1931/50
B. VII, pp. 306–7, no. 3; H. II, 3.

Bibliography: Seibt 1891, p. 31; Curjel 1923, p. 57; Reichel 1926, p. 54, pl. 12; Geisberg 1930, no. 59; Karlsruhe 1959, II H, no. 3; Paris and Rotterdam 1965–66, no. 2; Strauss 1973, no. 33; Mende 1978, no. 19; Washington and New Haven 1981, cat. 19; Strauss et al. 1981, p. 13; Hébert 1982, no. 1321a; Bartrum 1995, pp. 71–2, no. 58; Freiburg 2001–02, cat. 30 (text by S. Bock and S. Durian-Ress); Söding 2001–02, pp. 35–6; Tokyo 2005, cat. 4b; Frankfurt 2007, pp. 162–70, cat. 41.

15
Hans Weiditz
Man of Sorrows Seated
c. 1522
Chiaroscuro woodcut printed from two blocks, the tone block in brownish orange
28.2 × 19.8 cm
Inscribed (centre right): *ECCE HOMO*
Albertina, Vienna, DG1949/417
P. III, p. 199, no. 233 (as Upper German).

Bibliography: Röttinger 1924, p. 35 (as not by Weiditz); Geisberg 1930, no. 1501; Paris and Rotterdam 1965–66, no. 38; Strauss 1973, no. 42a; Geisberg and Strauss 1974, p. 1462.

16
Hans Weiditz
Man of Sorrows
1522
Chiaroscuro woodcut printed from two blocks, the tone block in brownish red
29.4 × 22.1 cm; cut down slightly at left and right edges
Inscribed (upper right): *1522*; (lower left): *ECCE HOMO*
Collection of Georg Baselitz
P. III, p. 322, no. 63 (as Hans Baldung Grien).

Bibliography: Seibt 1891, p. 31 (as Baldung Grien); Röttinger 1911, p. 49; Reichel 1926, pl. 27; Geisberg 1930, no. 1500; Strauss 1973, no. 42; Geisberg and Strauss 1974, p. 1462.

17
Albrecht Dürer
Ulrich Varnbühler
1522 and *c.* 1620
Chiaroscuro woodcut printed from three blocks, the tone blocks in yellowish brown and brown
Inscribed (at upper edge): *VLRICHVS VARNBULER ZC M.D.XXII.*; (in the cartouche): *Albertus Durer Noric[u]s, / hac imagine Vlrichum cognom[en]to / Varnbuler Ro[mani] Caesarei Regimin[i]s / in Imperio, a Secretis, simul[ar]chi / gramateum, vt quem amet / vnice, etiam posteritati [vul]t / cognitum reddere c[olere] que / conatur.* [restorations from Thausing 1884, vol. 2, p. 268, n. 3]
43.5 × 32.8 cm
Collection of Georg Baselitz
B. VII, pp. 163–4, no. 155; P. III, p. 173, no. 155; H. VII, 256.

Bibliography: Thausing 1884, vol. 2, pp. 268–9; Seibt 1891, pp. 31–2; Dodgson 1903b, pp. 340–1, no. 146b; Geisberg 1930, no. 730; Meder 1932, no. 256; Panofsky 1942, p. 52; Paris and Rotterdam 1965–66, no. 26; Strauss 1973, no. 31; Geisberg and Strauss 1974, vol. 2, p. 684; Bartrum 1995, p. 58, under no. 44; Schoch, Mende and Scherbaum 2002, no. 256 (text by D. Eichberger); Vienna and Munich 2011–12, no. 6 (text by A. Riether).

18
Albrecht Dürer
Rhinoceros
1515 and *c.* 1620
Chiaroscuro woodcut printed from two blocks, the tone block in green
Inscribed (upper right): *1515 / RHINOCERVS / AD* [monogrammed]
21.1 × 29.9 cm
Albertina, Vienna, DG1934/512
B. VII, pp. 147–9, no. 136; P. III, pp. 167–8, no. 136; H. VII, 273.

Bibliography: Seibt 1891, pp. 31–2; Dodgson 1903b, p. 307, no. 125c; Geisberg 1930, no. 721; Meder 1932, no. 273; Strauss 1973, no. 2; Geisberg and Strauss 1974, vol. 2, p. 684; Bartrum 1995, p. 50, under no. 35; Schoch, Mende and Scherbaum 2002, no. 241 (text by Y. Doosry); Cambridge and Evanston 2011–12, cat. 35 (text by D. Zolli).

19
Hans Sebald Beham
Head of Christ Crowned with Thorns
c. 1520–21
Chiaroscuro woodcut printed from two blocks, the tone block in brown
45.3 × 20.2 cm
Watermark: Eagle with coat of arms shield in the centre
Albertina, Vienna, DG1936/1080
B. VII, p. 182, no. 26 (as Dürer); P. III, p. 183, no. 192 (as Dürer); H. III, p. 184.

Bibliography: Seibt 1891, pp. 32–5; Pauli 1901, p. 349, no. 829b; Dodgson 1903b, pp. 457–8, no. 101; Dodgson 1903c, p. 194; Röttinger 1926, pp. 29–30 (as Peter Vischer the Elder); Geisberg 1930, no. 772 (as Master of the Celtis Illustrations); Paris and Rotterdam 1965–66, nos 6–7; Strauss 1973, no. 43; Geisberg and Strauss 1974, p. 167; Vienna 1992, p. 51 (text by C. Geissmar); Bartrum 1995, p. 101, no. 89; Nuremberg 2000, nos 70–71 (as Dürer; text by M. Mende); Schoch, Mende and Scherbaum 2002, no. A 18 (text by M. Mende); Baltimore and Saint Louis 2003, under no. 18 (text by S. Dackerman and T. Primeau).

20
Lucas Cranach the Elder
St John the Baptist Preaching
1516
Chiaroscuro woodcut printed from two blocks, the tone block in reddish brown
34 × 23.7 cm
Inscribed (lower right, on tablet): *1516* [with winged serpent]; the coat of arms of the Elector of Saxony hanging from the tree at upper right
Collection of Georg Baselitz
B. VII, p. 283, no. 60; H. VI, 85.

Bibliography: Seibt 1891, pp. 26, 28; Dodgson 1911, p. 315, no. 119; Reichel 1926, pl. 4; Geisberg 1930, no. 601; Jahn 1955, p. 50; Paris and Rotterdam 1965–66, no. 20; Coburg 1972, no. 64; Strauss 1973, no. 8; Hébert 1982, no. 893; Paris 1984, no. 284, cat. 198 (text by B. Brinkmann); Brussels and Paris 2010–11, cat. 32 (text by A. Kunz).

21
Hans Sebald Beham
The Unequal Lovers
after 1533
Chiaroscuro woodcut printed from two blocks, the tone block in olive green
24.6 × 24.9 cm
Watermark: P below a shield with the imperial orb and with an H on either side; cf. Piccard Online no. 11514
Collection of Georg Baselitz
P. III, p. 211, no. 281 (as Dürer); H. XXIII, 37.

Bibliography: Pauli 1901, p. 419, no. 1236 III; Röttinger 1921, p. 92, no. 28 (as Jakob Lucius); Geisberg 1930, no. 901 (as Jakob Lucius); Strauss 1973, no. 49; Geisberg and Strauss 1974, vol. 1, p. 231; Basle 1974, vol. 2, no. 468 (attributed to Jakob Lucius); Hébert 1983, no. 1949a.

22
After Hans Sebald Beham
Adam and Eve
c. 1530–40
Chiaroscuro woodcut printed from two blocks, the tone block in yellow ochre
35.4 × 25.7 cm
Damage at the left, right and lower edges and in the upper right corner has been made up
Collection of Georg Baselitz
H. III, p. 172.

Bibliography: Pauli 1901, pp. 12, 322, no. 687b II; Dodgson 1903b, p. 450, no. 38b; Pauli 1911, p. 63; Hébert 1983, no. 1872a; Bartrum 1995, p. 104, under no. 93.

23
Ugo da Carpi, after Titian
St Jerome
1516
Chiaroscuro woodcut printed from two blocks, the tone block in grey
Inscribed (centre): *TICIANUS*; (lower edge, centre right): *UGO*
16 × 9.9 cm
Albertina, Vienna, DG2002/324
B. 12, p. 82, no. 31; Le Blanc, 1, p. 596, no. 11.

Bibliography: Kristeller 1912, p. 49; Suida 1936, p. 288; Mauronner 1941, cat. 5; Trotter 1974, pp. 31, 55–7; Washington, Dallas and Detroit 1976–77, no. 6; Servolini 1977, p. 8, cat. 1, pl. XII; Johnson 1982, cat. 2; Karpinski 1983, p. 123; London 1983, P 18 (text by D. Landau); Wethey 1987, p. 21, cat. 15; Landau and Parshall 1994, p. 150; Joannides 2001, pp. 280–1; Rome, Weimar and Munich 2001–03, cat. 1 (text by D. Graf); Carpi 2009, no. 12 (text by S. Urbini).

24
Ugo da Carpi, after Baldassare Peruzzi
Hercules Chasing Avarice from the Temple of the Muses
c. 1516–17
Chiaroscuro woodcut printed from two blocks, the tone block in green
29.9 × 22.6 cm; damaged lower corners have been made up
Inscribed (lower left corner): *BAL·S·EN*; (lower right corner): *PER UGO*; verso inscribed: *J. Storck a Milan 1797 / In. No. 548* [in pen and ink]
Watermark: Crossbow within a circle beneath a star
Albertina, Vienna, DG2002/913

Bibliography: Vasari 1878–85, vol. 5, 1880, p. 422; Zanetti 1837, p. 10, no. 7 (as ?Ugo da Carpi); Seibt 1891, pp. 48–9 (as probably by Antonio da Trento); Reichel 1926, pl. 29; Pittaluga 1930, p. 231; Kristeller 1912, p. 49; Florence 1956, no. 1; Paris and Rotterdam 1965–66, no. 96; Vienna 1966, no. 196; Frommel 1967–68, cat. 81; Providence 1973, pp. 102–3, no. 112 (text by A. Wagner); Trotter 1974, pp. 11–29, 63–5; Servolini 1977, p. 22, cat. 5, pl. XV; Franklin 1977, p. 27; Goldfarb 1981, p. 311; Johnson 1982, cat. 5; Karpinski 1983, p. 221; Landau and Parshall 1994, pp. 153–4; Mantua and Vienna 1999, no. 52; Rome, Weimar and Munich 2001–03, cat. 2 (text by D. Graf); Sassi 2009, pp. 67–79; Carpi 2009, no. 14 (text by R. Sassi); Takahatake 2010, p. 320.

25
Ugo da Carpi, after Baldassare Peruzzi
Hercules Chasing Avarice from the Temple of the Muses
c. 1517–20
Chiaroscuro woodcut printed from two blocks, the tone block in beige
Inscribed (lower left corner): *BAL·S·EN*; (lower right corner): *PER UGO*
29.7 × 22.5 cm
Watermark: Circle enclosing an indecipherable motif
Collection of Georg Baselitz
B. XII, pp. 133–4, no. 12; Le Blanc, 1, p. 596, no. 20.

26
Ugo da Carpi, after Raphael
Hercules and Antheus
c. 1516–18
Chiaroscuro woodcut printed from two blocks, the tone block in greyish blue
Inscribed (upper left, in the frieze): *RAPHAEL / URBINAS*; (lower right): *UGO*
30.1 × 22.2 cm; small holes in the centre
Collection of Georg Baselitz
B. XII, p. 117, no. 14; P. VI, p. 28, no. 174; Le Blanc, 1, p. 596, no. 17.

Bibliography: Kristeller 1912, p. 49; Vienna 1966, no. 196; Karpinski 1971, no. 117.14; Trotter 1974, pp. 12–31, 58–9; Servolini 1977, cat. 3, pl. XIV; Johnson 1982, cat. 7; Karpinksi 1983, p. 186; Mantua and Vienna 1999, no. 49; Carpi 2009, no. 16 (text by T. Previdi).

27
Ugo da Carpi, after Raphael
Aeneas und Anchises
1518
Chiaroscuro woodcut printed from four tone blocks, in beige and grey
Inscribed (lower right, in cartouche): *RAPHAEL / URBINAS / QUISQUIS. HAS. TABELLAS / INVITO.AUTORE.INPRIMET. / EX.DIVI.LEONIS.X.AC ILL[USTRIS]. / PRI[N]CIPIS. VENETIARUM.DE / CRETIS. EXCOMINICATIO. / NIS. SENTE[N]TIA[M]. ET.ALIAS. / PENAS.INCURRET. / ROME.APUD. UGUM. DE DARPI. I[M]PRESA[M] / M.DXVIII.* ; (lower right edge): *[F?] Mariette 1728* [in pen and ink]
51 × 37.4 cm
Collection of Georg Baselitz
B. XII, pp. 104–5, no. 12; Le Blanc, 1, p. 596, no. 25.

Bibliography: Seibt 1891, pp. 44–5; Kristeller 1912, p. 49; Pittaluga 1930, p. 234; Paris and Rotterdam 1965–66, no. 87; Vienna 1966, no. 192; Karpinski 1971, no. 104.12; Oberhuber 1972, p. 108, fig. 101; Trotter 1974, pp. 70–2; Servolini 1977, pp. 8–9, cat. 7, pl. XVIII; Johnson 1982, cat. 13; Mantua and Vienna 1999, no. 2; Sassi 2009, pp. 74–5; Carpi 2009, no. 20 (text by R. Sassi).

28
Ugo da Carpi, after Raphael
The Death of Ananias
1518
Chiaroscuro woodcut printed from four blocks, the tone blocks in brown
27 × 38.1 cm; lower left corner has been made up
Inscribed (below): *RAPHAEL. URBINAS. / QUISQUIS. HAS. TABELLAS. INVITO. AUTORE. INPRIMET. EX. DIVI. LEONIS. X. / AC. ILL. PRINCIPIS. ET. SENATUS. VENETIARUM. DECRETIS. EXCOMVNICATI / ONIS. SENTENTIAM. ET. ALIAS. PENAS. INCURRET. / ROME. APUD. UGUM. DE DARPI. INMPRESSAM. M.D.XVIII.*; (lower left): *P. mariette* 1668 [in pen and ink]
Albertina, Vienna, DG2002/290
B. XII, pp. 46–7, no. 27; Le Blanc 1, p. 595, no. 9.

Bibliography: Vasari 1878–85, vol. 5, 1880, p. 421; Zanetti 1837, pp. 8–9, nos 3–4; Seibt 1891, p. 45; Kristeller 1912, p. 49; Reichel 1926, pl. 33; Pittaluga 1930, p. 234; Paris and Rotterdam 1965–66, nos 77–8; Shearman 1972, pp. 99–100; Trotter 1974, pp. 17–24, 73–5; Servolini 1977, pp. 9, 26, cat. 6, pl. XII; Johnson 1982, cat. 12; Karpinksi 1983, p. 54; Landau and Parshall 1994, p. 150, fig. 153; Mantua and Vienna 1999, no. 11; Rome, Weimar and Munich 2001–03, cat. 6 (text by D. Graf); Tokyo 2005, cat. 12a,b; Sassi 2009, pp. 73–4; Carpi 2009, no. 19 (text by M. Rossi); Takahatake 2010, pp. 320–1.

29
Ugo da Carpi, after Raphael
The Miraculous Draught of Fishes
c. 1523–27
Chiaroscuro woodcut printed from three blocks, the tone blocks in red
23.4 × 25.7 cm
Watermark: Anchor within a circle, below a star; similar to Briquet 478, 484, 485, 490, 493
Albertina, Vienna, DG2002/282
B. XII, pp. 37–8, no. 13.

Bibliography: Zanetti 1837, p. 11, no. 9; Seibt 1891, p. 45; Kristeller 1912, p. 49 (as ?Ugo da Carpi); Reichel 1926, pl. 34; Pittaluga 1930, pp. 234–5; Paris and Rotterdam 1965–66, no. 71; Vienna 1966, no. 193; Oberhuber 1972, p. 126; Trotter 1974, pp. 17–21, 101–3; Servolini 1977, cat. 19, pl. XXX; Goldfarb 1981, p. 311; Karpinski 1983, p. 38; Paris 1983–84, pp. 387–8, no. 84 (text by P. Jean-Richard); Rome, Mantua and Vienna 1999, no. 8; Weimar and Munich 2001–03, cat. 3 (text by D. Graf); Matile 2003, pp. 112–13, 119 (as ?Niccolò Vicentino); Sassi 2009 pp. 75–6; Carpi 2009, cat. 26 (text by R. Sassi).

30
Ugo da Carpi, after Raphael
Archimedes (?)
c. 1518–20
Chiaroscuro woodcut printed from five blocks, the tone blocks in beige, pale brown, brown and blackish brown
44.5 × 34.7 cm
Watermark: Sailing boat within a circle, above a star
Albertina, Vienna, DG2002/524
B. XII, pp. 97–8, no. 6; Le Blanc, 1, p. 596, no. 23.

Bibliography: Copertini 1932, vol. 2, p. 47; Vienna 1963, no. 92; Fagiolo dell'Arco 1970, p. 284, under no. 5; Popham 1971, under no. 203; Karpinski 1971, no. 97.6; Trotter 1974, pp. 46, 167–8; Servolini 1977, cat. 31, pl. XLII; Oberhuber 1972, p. 79, n. 35; Johnson 1982, cat. 14; Karpinski 1983, p. 151; London 1983, P 32 (text by D. Landau); Mantua and Vienna 1999, no. 280; Venice, Vienna and Bilbao 2004–05, no. 45; Schneede and Sitt 2007, p. 404 (text by M. Sitt); Gnann 2007, vol. 1, pp. 187–8, fig. 77; Carpi 2009, p. 166, under no. 36 (text by M. Rossi).

31
Ugo da Carpi, after Raphael
The Deposition from the Cross
c. 1520–23
Chiaroscuro woodcut printed from three blocks, the tone blocks in pale and dark green
32.9 × 26.9 cm; cut down at the sides and top
Inscribed (lower centre edge): *·RAPHAEL· URBINAS +*; (lower right corner, on the tablet): *UGO / DA / CAR / PI*; (lower right edge): *J. Mariette 1730* [in pen and ink]
Albertina, Vienna, DG 2002/287
B. XII, p. 43, no. 22; Le Blanc, 1, p. 595, no. 8.

Bibliography: Zanetti 1837, p. 9, no. 5; Seibt 1891, p. 48 (as not by Ugo da Carpi); Kristeller 1912, p. 49; Pittaluga 1930, p. 234 and fig. 170; Paris and Rotterdam 1965–66, p. 33, no. 74, pl. IX; Karpinski 1971, no. 43.22; Trotter 1974, pp. 76–7; Servolini 1977, cat. 10, pl. XXI; Shoemaker and Broun 1981, p. 160; Johnson 1982, cat. 9 (2nd state); Mantua and Vienna 1999, no. 109; Matile 2003, cat. 46; Tokyo 2005, cat. 11; Sassi 2009, p. 76; Carpi 2009, cat. 25.

32
Ugo da Carpi, after Parmigianino
Circe and the Companions of Ulysses
c. 1524–27
Chiaroscuro woodcut printed from four blocks, the tone blocks in beige, pale blue and blue
20.9 × 18.8 cm; cut down on all sides
Collection of Georg Baselitz
B. XII, p. 111, no. 7.

Bibliography: Zanetti 1837, p. 72, under no. 94; Kolloff 1878, p. 726, no. 25; Reichel 1926, pl. 26 (as by an unidentified Italian woodblock cutter); Paris and Rotterdam 1965–66, no. 102 (attributed to Ugo); Popham 1971, p. 69, under no. 85; Trotter 1974, pp. 241–3; Servolini 1977, cat. 32, pl. XLIII (as Ugo da Carpi or Niccolò Vicentino); Karpinski 1983, p. 178; Gnann 2003, pp. 89–90; Matile 2003, no. 61 (as ?Niccolò Vicentino); Tokyo 2005, cat. 31 (as Niccolò Vicentino); Gnann 2007, p. 198; Munich and Frankfurt 2007–08, cat. 56; Carpi 2009, no. 36 (text by M. Rossi).

33
Ugo da Carpi, after Parmigianino (?)
Saturn
c. 1524–27
Chiaroscuro woodcut printed from four blocks, the tone blocks in green and brown
31.6 × 43.3 cm
Inscribed (lower left): *P. Mariette 1661* [in pen and ink]
Albertina, Vienna, DG2013/13
B. XII, pp. 125–6, no. 27; Le Blanc, 1, p. 596, no. 16 I.

Bibliography: Zanetti 1837, p. 12, no. 11; Seibt 1891, p. 50; Kristeller 1912, p. 49; Hind 1930, p. 18, pl. VII; Tietze-Conrat 1939; Vienna 1963, no. 89; Paris and Rotterdam 1965–66, no. 95; Trotter 1974, pp. 36, 195–7; Servolini 1977, cat. 34, pl. XLV; Karpinski 1983, p. 201; London 1983, P 35 (text by D. Landau; as Niccolò Vicentino); Gnann 2002, pp. 290–2; Mussini 2003, p. 22; Matile 2003, cat. 69 (as Niccolò Vicentino); Gnann 2007, pp. 185–6, fig. 76; Munich and Frankfurt 2007–08, cat. 50; Carpi 2009, no. 39 (text by M. Rossi; attributed to Niccolò Vicentino); Paris, Rouen and Ajaccio 2011–12, cat. 27 (text by D. Vandecasteele).

34
Ugo da Carpi, after Parmigianino (?)
Saturn
c. 1524–27 and 1604
Chiaroscuro woodcut printed from four blocks, the tone blocks in greyish brown
32.3 × 43.4 cm
Inscribed (lower right edge): *A[ndrea] A[ndreani]* [monogrammed] *in mantoua 1604*
Collection of Georg Baselitz
B. XII, p. 126, no. 27 II; Le Blanc, 1, p. 596, no. 16 II.

Bibliography: Kolloff 1878, p. 726, no. 19 II; Lusingh Scheurkeer 1936, pl. B; New York 1986, no. 47; Rome, Weimar and Munich 2001–03, cat. 14 (as Niccolò Vicentino; text by D. Graf); Tokyo 2005, cat. 30 (attributed to Niccolò Vicentino); Munich and Frankfurt 2007–08, cat. 51.

35
Ugo da Carpi, after Parmigianino
Olympus
c. 1526–27
Chiaroscuro woodcut printed from three blocks, the tone blocks in olive green and yellow
27 × 19.2 cm
Verso inscribed: *no. 3637 / N: 325* [in pencil]
Collection of Georg Baselitz
B. XII, p. 146, no. 10, P. VI, p. 222 (as Niccolò Vicentino).

Bibliography: Baseggio 1844, pp. 18–19, no. 1 (as Niccolò Vicentino); Kolloff 1878, p. 727, no. 29 I; Vienna 1963, no. 94; Paris and Rotterdam 1965–66, nos 98–99; Trotter 1974, p. 17–18, 232–5; Servolini 1977, cat. 25, pl. XXXVI; Karpinski 1983, p. 246; Gnann 2002, p. 289; Gnann 2003, p. 88; Matile 2003, cat. 62 (as ?Niccolò Vicentino); Parma 2003, cat. 79 (text by C. Farinelli); Munich and Frankfurt 2007–08, cat. 53 (text by K. Zeitler); Gnann 2007, vol. 1, pp. 178–84; Carpi 2009, cat. 35 (text by R. Sassi).

36
Ugo da Carpi, after Parmigianino
Nymphs Bathing
c. 1526–27
Chiaroscuro woodcut printed from three blocks, the tone blocks in brownish orange and brown
30.6 × 21.1 cm (sheet)
Collection of Georg Baselitz
B. XII, p. 122, no. 22 II.

Bibliography: Zanetti 1837, p. 73, under no. 96; Kolloff 1872, p. 726, no. 22 I; Vienna 1963, no. 93; Paris and Rotterdam 1965–66, no. 89; Popham 1969, p. 51, n. 9; Trotter 1974, pp. 225–7; Karpinski 1983, p. 194; Servolini 1977, no. 23, pl. XXXIV; Parma and Vienna 2003, no. 2.4.9 (text by A. Gnann); Parma 2003, no. 85 (text by C. Farinelli); Matile 2003, p. 141, n. 330 (as Niccolò Vicentino or his workshop); Munich and Frankfurt 2007–08, cat. 52; Carpi 2009, no. 37 (text by R. Sassi); Budapest 2009–10, cat. 58.

37
Ugo da Carpi, after Parmigianino
Diogenes
c. 1527
Chiaroscuro woodcut printed from four blocks, the tone blocks in green and blue
47.8 × 34.3 cm; crease mark across the centre
Inscribed (lower left corner, on book page): *FRANCISCUS / PARMEN. / PER UGO CARP*; (lower centre edge): *P. Mariette 1679* [in pen and ink]
Albertina, Vienna, DG2003/3031

38
Ugo da Carpi, after Parmigianino
Diogenes
c. 1527
Chiaroscuro woodcut printed from four blocks, the tone blocks in green
48.5 × 35 cm; crease mark across centre
Inscribed (lower left corner, on book page): *FRANCISCUS / PARMEN. / PER UGO CARP*; (lower centre edge): *P. mariette 1690* [in pen and ink]
Collection of Georg Baselitz

39
Ugo da Carpi, after Parmigianino
Diogenes
c. 1527
Chiaroscuro woodcut printed from four blocks, the tone blocks in brown
47.6 × 34 cm
Inscribed (lower left corner, on book page): *FRANCISCUS / PARMEN· / PER UGO CARP*
Watermark: Coat of arms with two crossed axes, beneath a lily (?)
Collection of Georg Baselitz
B. XII, p. 100, no. 10; Le Blanc, 1, p. 596, no. 24.

Bibliography : Zanetti 1837, p. 9, no. 6; Seibt 1891, p. 50; Pittaluga 1930, pp. 237–8; Copertini 1932, vol. 2, p. 47; Janson 1955; Vienna 1963, no. 91; Paris and Rotterdam 1965–66, no. 86; Vienna 1966, no. 197; Popham 1969, p. 50; Fagiolo dell'Arco 1970, p. 283, C 1; Popham 1971, pp. 12–15; Trotter 1974, pp. 32–47, 162–6; Servolini 1977, cat. 12; Franklin 1977, p. 27; Johnson 1982, no. 15; Karpinski 1983, p. 155; Goldfarb 1981, p. 313; New York 1986, no. 44; Landau and Parshall 1994, p. 154; Mantua and Vienna 1999, cat. 301; Matile 2003, no. 53; Tokyo 2005, cat. 16a,b; Munich and Frankfurt 2007–08, cat. 40–2; Ekserdjian 2008, pp. 369–73; Budapest 2009–10, cat. 26–7; Takahatake 2010, p. 321; Paris, Rouen and Ajaccio 2011–12, cat. 25–6 (text by D. Vandecasteele).

40
Circle of Parmigianino
SS. Peter and John Healing the Lame Man
c. 1525–30
Etching and woodcut tone block in greyish brown
28 × 40.8 cm
Inscribed (lower left corner): *20 go* [?] [in pen and ink]; verso inscribed: *P. m.* [in pen and ink]; traces of black and red chalk at the left edge on verso
Collection of Georg Baselitz

41
Circle of Parmigianino
SS. Peter and John Healing the Lame Man
c. 1525–30
Etching
26.9 × 40.6 cm
Inscribed (lower left corner, on base of column): *I·V·R·*
Watermark: Triple mountain
Collection of Georg Baselitz

42
Circle of Parmigianino
SS. Peter and John Healing the Lame Man
c. 1525–30
Etching and two woodcut tone blocks in ochre and brown
27.9 × 40.9 cm
Inscribed (lower left corner, on base of column): *I·V·R·*
Collection of Georg Baselitz

43
Circle of Parmigianino
SS. Peter and John Healing the Lame Man
c. 1525–30
Etching and two woodcut tone blocks in reddish brown
26.9 × 40.7 cm; damaged lower corners have been made up
Inscribed (lower left corner, on base of column): *I·V·R·*
Collection of Georg Baselitz
B. XVI, p. 10, no. 7 II, and XII, pp. 78–9, no. 27; Le Blanc, 2, p. 630, no. 8.

Bibliography: Copertini 1932, vol. 2, pp. 22, 151; Vienna 1963, no. 45; Oberhuber 1963, p. 34, n. 29; Fagiolo dell'Arco 1970, p. 281; Oberhuber 1972, p. 123, n. 5, p. 131; Shearman 1972, pp. 98–101; Trotter 1974, pp. 193–4; Zerner 1979, pp. 13–14; Emison 1985, pp. 225–6; Los Angeles et al. 1988–89, no. 33; Boston 1989, no. 10 (text by R. Wallace); Landau and Parshall 1994, p. 270; Mantua and Vienna 1999, cat. 281; Matile 2003, p. 129; Ottawa and New York 2003–04, no. 26; Parma 2003, nos 1–2 (text by G. M. de Rubeis); Gnann 2003, p. 86; Mistrali 2003, no. 1; Tokyo 2005, cat. 17; Ekserdjian 2006, p. 29; Munich and Frankfurt 2007–08, cat. 30–2; Budapest 2009–10, cat. 32–4; Paris, Rouen and Ajaccio 2011–12, cat. 24 (text by D. Vandecasteele).

44
Antonio da Trento, after Parmigianino
The Martyrdom of SS. Peter and Paul
c. 1524–25
Chiaroscuro woodcut printed from three blocks, the tone blocks in reddish brown and brown
29 × 48.6 cm
Collection of Georg Baselitz
B. XII, pp. 79–80, no. 28; Le Blanc, 4, p. 218, no. 6.

Bibliography: Zanetti 1837, p. 3, no. 16; Nagler 1858–79, vol. 2, p. 153, no. 20; Kolloff 1878, pp. 153–4 no. 20; Seibt 1891, pp. 52–3; Copertini 1932, vol. 2, pp. 40–1; Pittaluga 1930, pp. 234, 242; Vienna 1963, no. 110; Paris and Rotterdam 1965–66, nos 129–31; Popham 1971, pp. 12–13; Trotter 1974, pp. 39–43, 169–72; Goldfarb 1981, p. 313; Emison 1985, pp. 247–8; Johnson 1987; Landau and Parshall 1994, pp. 154–7; Mantua and Vienna 1999, no. 257; Rome, Weimar and Munich 2001–03, cat. 19 (text by D. Graf); Gnann 2002, p. 294; Parma and Vienna 2003, cat. 2.4.13 (text by A. Gnann); Parma 2003, no. 91 (text by C. Farinelli); Matile 2003, p. 135 and no. 54; Tokyo 2005, cat. 21; Ekserdjian 2006, pp. 220–1, fig. 231; Munich and Frankfurt 2007–08, cat. 35–6; Paris, Rouen and Ajaccio 2011–12, cat. 29 (text by D. Vandecasteele).

45
Atrributed to Antonio da Trento, after Parmigianino
Sibyl Reading
c. 1524–27
Chiaroscuro woodcut printed from two blocks, the tone block in brown
27.8 × 22.1 cm; fragment inserted into the area of the sibyl's knees
Inscribed (upper right): *•R/R•V•/•*
Collection of Georg Baselitz
B. XII, pp. 89–90, no. 6 (sixteenth-century copy); Le Blanc, 1, p. 596, no. 14A (sixteenth-century copy).

Bibliography: Zanetti 1837, p. 71, no. 90; Seibt 1891, pp. 42–3; Paris and Rotterdam 1965–66, no. 85 (as Ugo da Carpi); Trotter 1974, pp. 8–10, 66–9; Franklin 1977, p. 27; Goldfarb 1981, p. 311; Johnson 1982, cat. 4 II (as Ugo da Carpi); Karpinski 1983, p. 140; Landau and Parshall 1994, p. 154; Gnann 2002, p. 294; Matile 2003, cat. 43 (as Ugo da Carpi); Tokyo 2005, cat. 10 (as Ugo da Carpi); Munich and Frankfurt 2007–08, cat. 59 (as ?Antonio da Trento); Carpi 2009, no. 18 (as Ugo da Carpi; text by T. Previdi).

46
Antonio da Trento, after Parmigianino
Virgin and Child with Saints
c. 1527–30 and *c.* 1602–10
Chiaroscuro woodcut printed from two blocks, the tone block in brown
31 × 21.4 cm
Inscribed (lower left): *A[ndrea] A[ndreani]* [monogrammed]
Collection of Georg Baselitz
B. XII, pp. 64–5, no. 24 (as anonymous); Le Blanc, 1, p. 42, no. 21.

Bibliography: Zanetti 1837, pp. 69–70, no. 87 (as anonymous); Kolloff 1872, p. 152, no. 5 II; Kolloff 1878, p. 725, no. 9 II; Copertini 1932, vol. 2, p. 40, pl. CXXVIIa (as anonymous); Zava Boccazzi 1962, p. 60, no. 13 (attributed to Antonio da Trento); Vienna 1963, no. 140; Paris and Rotterdam 1965–66, nos 136–7 (attributed to Antonio da Trento); Popham 1971, under no. 79, pl. 224; Trotter 1974, pp. 262–4; Franklin 1977, p. 31; Karpinski 1983, p. 86; Parma 2003, no. 230 (text by C. Farinelli); Matile 2003, p. 144, n. 333 (as Niccolò Vicentino); Gnann 2007, p. 222; Munich and Frankfurt 2007–08, cat. 65.

47
Antonio da Trento, after Parmigianino
Circe and the Companions of Ulysses
c. 1524–27 and *c.* 1602–10
Chiaroscuro woodcut printed from three blocks, the tone blocks in beige and brown
22.5 × 21.2 cm (sheet)
Inscribed (lower left corner): *A[ndrea] A[ndreani]* [monogrammed, in the block]; (lower left): *K·g*; [in pen and ink]; figure sketch and various inscriptions on verso
Collection of Georg Baselitz
B. XII, p. 112, no. 8.

Bibliography: Zanetti 1837, p. 72, no. 94; Kolloff 1872, p. 726, no. 25 II; Kolloff 1878, p. 154, no. 26 II; Servolini 1932, p. 60; Paris and Rotterdam 1965–66, no. 103; Trotter 1974, pp. 244–5; Karpinski 1983, p. 179; Gnann 2003, p. 90; Matile 2003, cat. 60 (as ?Niccolò Vicentino); Rome, Weimar and Munich 2001–03, cat. 22 (text by D. Graf); Gnann 2007, vol. 1, p. 198; Munich and Frankfurt 2007–08, pp. 163–5; Takahatake 2010, p. 321; Paris, Rouen and Ajaccio 2011–12, cat. 38 (attributed to Antonio da Trento; text by D. Vandecasteele).

48
Antonio da Trento, after Parmigianino
Circe and the Companions of Ulysses
c. 1524–27
Chiaroscuro woodcut printed from two blocks, the tone blocks in orange brown
24.9 × 21.6 cm; cut down at both sides
Collection of Georg Baselitz
B. XII, pp. 110–11, no. 6 (as anonymous).

Bibliography: Nagler 1835–52, vol. 4, 1837, p. 245; Kolloff 1872, p. 726, no. 24; Kolloff 1878, p. 154, no. 26; Servolini 1932, p. 60; Florence 1956, p. 18, no. 27; Zava Boccazzi 1962, p. 58, no. 5; Paris and Rotterdam 1965–66, nos 139–40 (attributed to Antonio da Trento); Popham 1971, under no. 73, pl. 122; Trotter 1974, pp. 238–40; Franklin 1977, p. 30; Karpinski 1983, pp. 176–7; Rome, Weimar and Munich 2001–03, cat. 21 (text by D. Graf); Gnann 2002, p. 295; Gnann 2003, p. 89; Matile 2003, p. 148, n. 338, under nos 60–1; Tokyo 2005, cat. 24 (attributed to Antonio da Trento); Munich and Frankfurt 2007–08, cat. 54.

49
Antonio da Trento, after Parmigianino
The Lute Player
c. 1527–30
Chiaroscuro woodcut printed from two blocks, the tone block in greyish green
11.9 × 10.9 cm
Watermark: Circle enclosing a V and an I (?)
Collection of Georg Baselitz
B. XII, p. 143, no. 3; Le Blanc, 4, p. 218, no. 11.

50
Antonio da Trento, after Parmigianino
The Lute Player
c. 1527–30
Chiaroscuro woodcut printed from two blocks, the tone block in brownish green
14 × 13.8 cm
Inscribed (on frame, below): *AT* [monogrammed]
Collection of Georg Baselitz

Bibliography: Kolloff 1878, p. 155, no. 35; Reichel 1926, pl. 35 top; Pittaluga 1930, p. 241; Servolini 1932, p. 59; Zava Boccazzi 1962, p. 58, no. 6; Vienna 1963, no. 112; Paris and Rotterdam 1965–66, no. 134; Popham 1969, p. 49; Trotter 1974, pp. 3, 45, 177–8; Franklin 1977, p. 28; Karpinksi 1983, p. 238; Matile 2003, p. 134, cat. 55; Gnann 2002, p. 294; Gnann 2007, p. 199; Ekserdjian 2006, p. 222; Munich and Frankfurt 2007–08, cat. 62; Paris, Rouen and Ajaccio 2011–12, cat. 33 (text by D. Vandecasteele).

51
Antonio da Trento, after Parmigianino
The Madonna of the Roses
c. 1524–27
Chiaroscuro woodcut printed from two blocks, the tone block in green
20.4 × 24.8 cm; damaged lower left corner has been made up
Inscribed (lower centre border): *669·* [in pen and ink]
Watermark: Circle enclosing an indecipherable motif
Collection of Georg Baselitz
B. XII, pp. 56–57, no. 12 (as anonymous after Parmigianino).

Bibliography: Zanetti 1837, p. 21; Kolloff 1878, p. 152, no. 3; Pittaluga 1930, p. 241; Alten 1943, p. 12; Zava Boccazzi 1962, p. 59, no. 8; Vienna 1963, no. 114; Paris and Rotterdam 1965–66, no. 125; Popham 1969, p. 49; Trotter 1974, pp. 46, 184–6; Karpinski 1983, p. 129; Matile 2003, no. 57; Tokyo 2005, cat. 20; Gnann 2007, pp. 87, 198; Munich and Frankfurt 2007–08, cat. 58 (text by K. Zeitler); Budapest 2009–10, cat. 53; Paris, Rouen and Ajaccio 2011–12, cat. 34 (attributed to Antonio da Trento; text by D. Vandecasteele).

52
Antonio da Trento, after Parmigianino
St John the Baptist in the Wilderness
c. 1527–30
Chiaroscuro woodcut printed from two blocks, the tone block in green
13.9 × 13.9 cm
Inscribed (lower section of frame): *AT* [monogrammed]
Albertina, Vienna, DG2002/464
B. XII, p. 73, no. 17; Le Blanc, 4, p. 218, no. 5

Bibliography: Zanetti 1837, p. 3, no. 18; Kolloff 1878, p. 152, no. 6; Servolini 1932, p. 59; Zava Boccazzi 1962, p. 58, no. 1; Vienna 1963, no. 113; Paris and Rotterdam 1965–66, nos 126–7; Popham 1969, p. 49; Trotter 1974, pp. 38–47, 173–6; Franklin 1977, p. 28; Karpinski 1983, p. 107; Matile 2003, p. 134, cat. 56; Tokyo 2005, cat. 18b; Gnann 2007, pp. 198–9; Munich and Frankfurt 2007–08, cat. 61 (text by K. Zeitler); Budapest 2009–10, cat. 44; Paris, Rouen and Ajaccio 2011–12, cat. 32 (text by D. Vandecasteele).

53
Antonio da Trento, after Parmigianino
Narcissus
c. 1527–30/1
Chiaroscuro woodcut printed from two blocks, the tone block in green
28.5 × 18.1 cm
Collection of Georg Baselitz

54
Antonio da Trento, after Parmigianino
Narcissus
c. 1527–30/1
Chiaroscuro woodcut printed from two blocks, the tone block in brown
28.9 × 18 cm
Collection of Georg Baselitz

55
Antonio da Trento, after Parmigianino
Narcissus
c. 1527–30/1
Chiaroscuro woodcut printed from two blocks, the tone block in reddish brown
29 × 18.3 cm; crease mark across the centre
Several inscriptions on verso, including (lower left edge): *E[...] Mark* [perhaps a previous owner, in pencil]
Collection of Georg Baselitz
B. XII, p. 148, no. 13; Le Blanc, 4, p. 218, no. 10.

Bibliography: Zanetti 1837, pp. 18–19, no. 21; Nagler 1835–52, vol. 4, 1837, p. 244; Kolloff 1878, p. 155, no. 36; Artioli 1901, p. 125; Servolini 1932, p. 60; Copertini 1932, vol. 2, p. 39, pl. CXXIII; Weimar 1957, p. 16, no. 31; Zava Boccazzi 1962, p. 58, no. 7; Vienna 1963, no. 116; Paris and Rotterdam 1965–66, no. 135; Popham 1969, p. 49; Trotter 1974, pp. 45–7, 187–9; Franklin 1977, p. 27; Karpinski 1983, p. 249; New York 1986, no. 46; Rome, Weimar and Munich 2001–03, cat. 23 (text by D. Graf); Gnann 2002, pp. 294–5; Parma 2003, no. 82 (text by C. Farinelli); Tokyo 2005, cat. 19a,b; Ottawa and New York 2003–04, no. 61; Ekserdjian 2006, p. 222; Gnann 2007, pp. 199–200; Munich and Frankfurt 2007–08, cat. 63–4; Budapest 2009–10, cat. 42; Paris, Rouen and Ajaccio 2011–12, cat. 35–6 (text by D. Vandecasteele).

56
Niccolò Vicentino, after Parmigianino
Augustus and the Tiburtine Sibyl
c. 1529–30
Chiaroscuro woodcut printed from four blocks, the tone blocks in blue and greenish blue
34.2 × 25.6 cm; traces of emendations in pen and brown ink; damaged upper right corner has been made up
Inscribed (lower left): *P. mariette 1670* [in pen and ink]
Collection of Georg Baselitz
B. XII, pp. 90–1, no. 8; Le Blanc, 4, p. 116, no. 5.

Bibliography: Nagler 1835–52, vol. 20, 1850, p. 208, no. 5; Zanetti 1837, p. 28, no. 33 (attributed to Niccolò Vicentino); Kolloff 1878, p. 154, under no. 22; Reichel 1926, p. 34; Paris and Rotterdam 1965–66, no. 145; Popham 1969, p. 49; Popham 1971, p. 13; Trotter 1974, pp. 45, 182–3; Goldfarb 1981, p. 317; Los Angeles et al. 1988–89, no. 52; Gnann 2002, pp. 292–5; Parma and Vienna 2003, under no. 2.4.12 (text by A. Gnann); Parma 2003, under no. 93 (text by C. Farinelli); Gnann 2007, p. 189; Munich and Frankfurt 2007–08, cat. 68; Budapest 2009–10, cat. 47.

57
Antonio da Trento, after Parmigianino
Augustus and the Tiburtine Sibyl
c. 1529–30
Chiaroscuro woodcut printed from two blocks, the tone block in brown
34.9 × 26.6 cm (sheet);
34 × 26 cm (block)
Collection of Georg Baselitz

58
Antonio da Trento, after Parmigianino
Augustus and the Tiburtine Sibyl
c. 1529–30
Chiaroscuro woodcut printed from two blocks, the tone block in reddish brown
36.6 × 28.2 cm
Collection of Georg Baselitz
B. XII, p. 90, no. 7; Le Blanc, 4, p. 218, no. 7.

Bibliography: Nagler 1835–52, vol. 4, 1837, p. 244; Zanetti 1837, p. 18, no. 19; Seibt 1891, p. 52; Kolloff 1878, p. 154, no. 22; Artioli 1901, p. 124; Reichel 1926, p. 34; Pittaluga 1930, p. 241; Copertini 1932, vol. 2, p. 39, pl. CXXIV; Florence 1956, p. 18, no. 24; Zava Boccazzi 1962, p. 58, no. 4; Vienna 1963, no. 111; Paris and Rotterdam 1965–66, no. 133; Popham 1969, p. 49, fig. 1; Popham 1971, p. 13, fig. 24; Trotter 1974, pp. 179–81; Franklin 1977, p. 28; Goldfarb 1981, pp. 315–17; Karpinski 1983, p. 141; New York 1986, no. 45; Los Angeles et al. 1988–89, no. 49; Gnann 2002, p. 294; Parma and Vienna 2003, no. 2.4.12 (text by A. Gnann); Parma 2003, no. 93 (text by C. Farinelli); Ottawa and New York 2003–04, no. 62; Tokyo 2005, cat. 22; Ekserdjian 2006, p. 221, fig. 238; Gnann 2007, p. 189; Munich and Frankfurt 2007–08, cat. 66–7; Budapest 2009–10, cat. 46.

59
Antonio da Trento, after Parmigianino
St Matthew
c. 1524–27
Chiaroscuro woodcut printed from three blocks, the tone block in brown
15.5 × 10.6 cm
Albertina, Vienna, DG2002/443

60
Antonio da Trento, after Parmigianino
St Thomas
c. 1524–27
Chiaroscuro woodcut printed from three blocks, the tone block in brown
15.1 × 10.5 cm
Albertina, Vienna, DG2002/449

61
Antonio da Trento, after Parmigianino
St Simon
c. 1524–27
Chiaroscuro woodcut printed from three blocks, the tone blocks in brown
15.5 × 10.6 cm
Albertina, Vienna, DG2002/445

62
Antonio da Trento, after Parmigianino
St Paul
c. 1524–27
Chiaroscuro woodcut printed from three blocks, the tone blocks in brown
15.1 × 10.8 cm
Albertina, Vienna, DG2002/447

63
Antonio da Trento, after Parmigianino
St John the Evangelist
c. 1524–27
Chiaroscuro woodcut printed from three blocks, the tone blocks in beige and brown
13.1 × 8.6 cm
Collection of Georg Baselitz
B. XII, pp. 69–71, nos 1–12.

64
Antonio da Trento, after Parmigianino
St Peter
c. 1524–27
Chiaroscuro woodcut printed from three blocks, the tone blocks in ochre
15.3 × 10.5 cm
Albertina, Vienna, DG2002/441

65
Antonio da Trento, after Parmigianino
St Jude
c. 1524–27
Chiaroscuro woodcut printed from three blocks, the tone blocks in brown
12.4 × 7.4 cm
Albertina, Vienna, DG2002/444

66
Antonio da Trento, after Parmigianino
St Andrew
c. 1524–27
Chiaroscuro woodcut printed from three blocks, the tone blocks in green and brown
14.5 × 9.9 cm
Albertina, Vienna, DG2002/439

67
Antonio da Trento, after Parmigianino
St Philip
c. 1524–27
Chiaroscuro woodcut printed from three blocks, the tone blocks in red
12.4 × 7 cm
Albertina, Vienna, DG2002/460

Bibliography: Nagler 1835–52, vol. 4, 1837, pp. 243–4; Mariette 1854–56, p. 304 (as Ugo da Carpi); Zanetti 1837, p. 19, no. 23 (attributed to Antonio da Trento); Kolloff 1878, pp. 152–3, nos 7–19 (as Ugo da Carpi [?]); Copertini 1932, vol. 2, pp. 40, 47 (as Ugo da Carpi and his school); Servolini 1932, p. 60; Quintavalle 1948, p. 116; Zava Boccazzi 1962, p. 59, no. 1 (attributed to Antonio da Trento); Vienna 1963, nos 121–9; Popham 1971, vol. 1, p. 16 (as Antonio da Trento [?]); Trotter 1974, pp. 293–5; Karpinski 1983, pp. 93–102; Gnann 2002, p. 294; Gnann 2007, pp. 174, 195–6.

68
Niccolò Vicentino, after Parmigianino
Christ Healing the Lepers
c. 1527–29
Chiaroscuro woodcut printed from three blocks, the tone blocks in violet
29.1 × 40.7 cm; small area of loss at lower right edge
Inscribed (lower right, barely legible): *IOSEPH• NICOLAUS VICENTINI*
Collection of Georg Baselitz
B. XII, p. 39, no. 15; Le Blanc, 4, p. 116, no. 3; P. VI, pp. 220–1.

Bibliography: Nagler 1835–52, vol. 20, 1850, p. 208, no. 3; Zanetti 1837, p. 26, no. 28; Kolloff 1872, p. 725, no. 5; Pittaluga 1930, p. 245; Servolini 1932, p. 66; Copertini 1932, vol. 2, p. 41; Florence 1956, p. 16, no. 16; Weimar 1957, p. 12, no. 15; Vienna 1963, no. 101; Paris and Rotterdam 1965–66, no. 144; Vienna 1966, no. 201; Popham 1969, p. 51; Popham 1971, p. 13, fig. 27; Trotter 1974, pp. 39, 251–3; Goldfarb 1981, p. 317; Karpinski 1983, p. 41; Los Angeles et al. 1988–89, pp. 140–1, no. 51; Landau and Parshall 1994, pp. 159; Mantua and Vienna 1999, no. 283; Rome and Weimar 2001, cat. 13 (text by D. Graf); Gnann 2002, pp. 289–92; Parma and Vienna 2003, no. 2.4.10 (text by A. Gnann); Matile 2003, pp. 58, 143, 223; Parma 2003, no. 100 (text by C. Farinelli); Ottawa and New York 2003–04, p. 217, under no. 63; Ekserdjian 2006, p. 223, fig. 53; Munich and Frankfurt 2007–08, cat. 69; Paris, Rouen and Ajaccio 2011–12, cat. 30 (text by D. Vandecasteele).

69
Niccolò Vicentino, after Polidoro da Caravaggio
The Death of Ajax
c. 1525–27
Chiaroscuro woodcut printed from three blocks, the tone blocks in green
31.4 × 41.6 cm
Inscribed (lower right corner): *PULIDORO · CAR / IOs · NIC· VICEN*; (lower left): *T Mariette 1725* [in pen and ink]
Albertina, Vienna, DG2002/342

Bibliography: Zanetti 1837, p. 27, no. 31; Kolloff 1872, p. 726, no. 23; Seibt 1891, p. 54; Servolini 1932, p. 66; Paris and Rotterdam 1965–66, nos 147–8; Kultzen 1973, p. 638; Trotter 1974, p. 28; Karpinski 1983, p. 154; Gnann 1997, p. 96; Mantua and Vienna 1999, cat. 220; Matile 2003, cat. 47a, b.

70
Niccolò Vicentino, after Polidoro da Caravaggio
The Death of Ajax
c. 1525–27 and 1608
Chiaroscuro woodcut printed from three blocks, the tone blocks in beige and grey
31.7 × 42.1 cm
Inscribed (lower right corner): *POLIDORO DA CARAVAGIO / INVENT[OR] A[ndrea] A[ndreani] in mantoua 1608*
Collection of Georg Baselitz
B. XII, pp. 99–100, no. 9; Le Blanc, 4, pp. 116–17, no. 7; Weigel 1865, p. 509, no. 6072.

71
Niccolò Vicentino, after Raphael (?)
Hercules and the Nemean Lion
c. 1525–27 and 1602–10
Chiaroscuro woodcut printed from two blocks, the tone block in ochre
25.3 × 19.7 cm
Inscribed (lower left corner): *RAPH[AEL] • UR[BINAS] / A[ndrea] A[ndreani]*
Collection of Georg Baselitz
B. XII, p. 119, no. 17; Le Blanc, 4, p. 117, no. 9; P. VI, pp. 221–2.

Bibliography: Zanetti 1837, pp. 27–8, no. 32; Kolloff 1872, p. 726, no. 20; Seibt 1891, p. 49; Reichel 1926, p. 58, under pl. 37; Pittaluga 1930, p. 245; Servolini 1932, p. 66; Vienna 1966, p. 129, under no. 195; Trotter 1974, pp. 92–5; Rome, Weimar and Munich 2001–03, cat. 10 (text by D. Graf); Matile 2003, pp. 50–1, cat. 50; Tokyo 2005, no. 25.

72
Niccolò Vicentino, after Parmigianino
The Adoration of the Magi
c. 1527–29
Chiaroscuro woodcut printed from three blocks, the tone blocks in beige
29.2 × 23.9 cm; cut down at the upper, lower and right edge
Inscribed (lower right corner): *F•[P]*; verso inscribed: *Mariette* [in pen and ink]
Collection of Georg Baselitz
B. XII, p. 30, no. 3; Le Blanc, 4, p. 116, no. 2.

Bibliography: Nagler 1835–52, vol. 20, 1850, p. 208, no. 2; Pittaluga 1930, pp. 248–9; Copertini 1932, vol. 2, p. 42; Servolini 1932, p. 71; Vienna 1963, no. 100; Popham 1969, p. 51, n. 9; Popham 1971, p. 13, under no. 137; Trotter 1974, pp. 258–9; Frankfurt 1980, under no. 25; Karpinski 1983, p. 87; Gnann 2002, p. 292; Parma and Vienna 2003, cat. 2.4.11 (text by A. Gnann); Ottawa and New York 2003–04, no. 63; Tokyo 2005, cat. 28; Munich and Frankfurt 2007–08, cat. 70; Paris, Rouen and Ajaccio 2011–12, cat. 31 (text by D. Vandecasteele).

73
Niccolò Vicentino, after Parmigianino
Virgin and Child with St Sebastian and a Bishop
c. 1527–29 and 1605
Chiaroscuro woodcut printed from four blocks, the tone blocks in beige
39.8 × 30 cm
Inscribed (lower right corner): *A[ndrea] A[ndreani]* [monogrammed] *in mantoua 1605•*
Collection of Georg Baselitz
B. XII, p. 66, no. 26 (as Ugo da Carpi); Le Blanc, 1, p. 595, no. 6 (as Ugo da Carpi).

Bibliography: Kolloff 1878, p. 725, no. 11 (as Ugo da Carpi); Seibt 1891, p. 50 (as not by Ugo da Carpi); Servolini 1932, p. 52 (as anonymous); Vienna 1963, no. 90 (as Ugo da Carpi); Paris and Rotterdam 1965–66, no. 79 (as Ugo da Carpi); Popham 1971, under no. 464; Trotter 1974, pp. 37, 247–50; Servolini 1977, cat. 30 (as Ugo da Carpi); Karpinski 1983, p. 88; Paris 2001, p. 110, under no. 32 (text by D. Cordellier); Gnann 2002, p. 293; Matile 2003, cat. 65 (as ?Niccolò Vicentino); Gnann 2007, pp. 189, 210–11, fig. 79.

74
Niccolò Vicentino, after Perino del Vaga (?)
Faith
c. 1539–45
Chiaroscuro woodcut printed from three blocks, the tone blocks in grey and greyish blue
14.1 × 9.4 cm
Collection of Georg Baselitz

75
Niccolò Vicentino, after Perino del Vaga (?)
Hope
c. 1539–45
Chiaroscuro woodcut printed from three blocks, the tone blocks in brown
14.5 × 9.7 cm
Albertina, Vienna, DG2002/480

76
Niccolò Vicentino, after Perino del Vaga (?)
Charity
c. 1539–45
Chiaroscuro woodcut printed from three blocks, the tone blocks in brown
14.5 × 10.1 cm
Collection of Georg Baselitz

77
Niccolò Vicentino, after Perino del Vaga (?)
Fortitude
c. 1539–45
Chiaroscuro woodcut printed from three blocks, the tone blocks in brown
14.5 × 9.8 cm
Collection of Georg Baselitz

78
Niccolò Vicentino, after Perino del Vaga (?)
Temperance
c. 1539–45
Chiaroscuro woodcut printed from three blocks, the tone blocks in brown
14.4 × 9.8 cm
Verso inscribed: *P. Mariette 1689* [in pen and ink]
Albertina, Vienna, DG2002/482

79
Niccolò Vicentino, after Perino del Vaga (?)
Prudence
c. 1539–45
Chiaroscuro woodcut printed from three blocks, the tone blocks in yellow and blue-green
14.2 × 9.8 cm
Collection of Georg Baselitz
B. XII, pp. 128–9, nos 1–6 (as anonymous).

Bibliography: Zanetti 1837, pp. 73–4, nos 97–99 (as Ugo da Carpi and Antonio da Trento); Kolloff 1872, p. 726, nos 13–18 (as possibly Ugo da Carpi); Pittaluga 1930, pp. 239, 327, n. 31 (as Ugo da Carpi); Copertini 1932, vol. 2, a. 36 (as in the style of Ugo da Carpi); Servolini 1932, p. 60 (attributed to Antonio da Trento); Florence 1956, nos 21–23 (as in the manner of Niccolò Vicentino); Weimar 1957, nos 20–26 (as in the manner of Niccolò Vicentino); Zava Boccazzi 1962, p. 60, nos 14–19 (attributed to Antonio da Trento); Vienna 1963, nos 105–10 (as Niccolò Vicentino [?]); Paris and Rotterdam 1965–66, nos 152–6 (attributed to Niccolò Vicentino); Trotter 1974, pp. 290–2; Karpinski 1983, pp. 207–12; Rome, Weimar and Munich 2001–03, cat. 15–18 (attributed to Niccolò Vicentino; text by D. Graf); Parma 2003, cat. 101–3 (*Prudence* as by Ugo da Carpi, otherwise as anonymous; text by C. Farinelli).

80
Domenico Beccafumi
An Apostle
c. 1540–45
Chiaroscuro woodcut printed from three blocks, the tone blocks in grey and grey-blue
28.9 × 17.7 cm
Inscribed (lower right edge): *Du Beccafumi.* [in pen and ink]; verso inscribed: *Mariette* [in pen and ink]
Collection of Georg Baselitz
B. XII, p. 147, no. 12 (as anonymous); P. VI, p. 151, no. 9.

Bibliography: Florence 1956, cat. 39–40; Sanminiatelli 1956, p. 59; Sanminiatelli 1967, p. 134, no. 7; Karpinski 1983, p. 248; Siena 1990, cat. 163 (text by A. De Marchi); Landau 1991, p. 451; Landau and Parshall 1994, p. 274; Lincoln 2000, pp. 52–8.

81
Domenico Beccafumi
St Philip
c. 1540–45
Chiaroscuro woodcut printed from three blocks, the tone blocks in brown
28.5 × 17.3 cm
Albertina, Vienna, DG2002/391
B. XII, p. 76, no. 23 (as anonymous).

Bibliography: Heinecken 1778–90, vol. 2, 1788, p. 300; Seidlitz 1885, p. 258, no. 14 (as after Beccafumi); Vienna 1966, no. 203; Sanminiatelli 1967, p. 134, no. 7; Karpinski 1983, p. 113; Siena 1990, cat. 164–5 (text by A. De Marchi); Landau and Parshall 1994, p. 281; Lincoln 2000, pp. 52–8; Tokyo 2005, cat. 37.

82
Domenico Beccafumi
St Philip
c. 1544–47
Chiaroscuro woodcut printed from three blocks, the tone blocks in reddish brown
41 × 21.2 cm
Inscribed (lower right): *P. mariette 1689* [in pen and ink]
Albertina, Vienna, DG2013/17
B. XII, p. 71, no. 13 (as anonymous after Beccafumi); Le Blanc, 1, p. 226, no. 5; P. VI, p. 151, Nr. 6.

83
Domenico Beccafumi
St Philip
c. 1544–47
Chiaroscuro woodcut printed from three blocks, the tone blocks in grey and blue
39.6 × 20.9 cm
Inscribed (lower right): *P. mariette 1678* [in pen and ink]
Albertina, Vienna, DG2002/385
B. XII, p. 71, no. 13 (as anonymous after Beccafumi); Le Blanc, 1, p. 226, no. 5; P. VI, p. 151, no. 6.

Bibliography: Heinecken 1778–90, vol. 2, 1788, p. 300; Seidlitz 1885, p. 258, no. 13 (as after Beccafumi); Pittaluga 1930, pp. 250–1; Servolini 1932, p. 77; Vienna 1966, no. 203; Florence 1956, cat. 39–42; Sanminiatelli 1967, p. 134, no. 9; Karpinski 1983, p. 103; Siena 1990, cat. 165–7 (text by A. De Marchi); Lincoln 2000, pp. 52–8, 107–9.

84
Domenico Beccafumi
St Peter
c. 1544–47
Chiaroscuro woodcut printed from four blocks, the tone blocks in green and grey
41 × 21.1 cm
Inscribed (lower left corner): *P. mariette 1662* [in pen and ink]
Albertina, Vienna, DG2013/18
B. XII, pp. 71–2, no. 14 (as anonymous after Beccafumi); Le Blanc, 1, p. 226, no. 6; P. VI, p. 150, no. 5.

Bibliography: Heinecken 1778–90, vol. 2, 1788, p. 300; Seidlitz 1885, p. 258, no. 12 (as after Beccafumi); Reichel 1926, p. 39, pl. 59 (as after Beccafumi); Paris and Rotterdam 1965–66, no. 44 (as anonymous); Pittaluga 1930, p. 250; Servolini 1932, p. 77; Florence 1956, cat. 46–7; Vienna 1966, cat. 202, fig. 32; Sanminiatelli 1967, p. 135, no. 10; Karpinski 1983, p. 104; Siena 1990, cat. 165–8 (text by A. De Marchi); Landau and Parshall 1994, p. 274; Lincoln 2000, pp. 52–8.

85
Domenico Beccafumi
An Apostle
c. 1544–47
Chiaroscuro woodcut printed from three blocks, the tone blocks in brown
39.7 × 19 cm
Albertina, Vienna, DG2002/387
B. XII, p. 72, no. 15 (as anonymous after Beccafumi); P. VI, p. 151, no. 7.

Bibliography: Seidlitz 1885, p. 258, no. 15 (as after Beccafumi); Pittaluga 1930, pp. 250–1; Servolini 1932, p. 77; Florence 1956, cat. 48–9; Sanminiatelli 1956, p. 59; Sanminiatelli 1967, p. 135, no. 11; Karpinski 1983, p. 105; Siena 1990, cat. 169 (text by A. De Marchi); Lincoln 2000, pp. 52–8; Tokyo 2005, cat. 38.

86
Domenico Beccafumi
Two Apostles
c. 1544–47
Engraving with woodcut tone block in ochre
41.3 × 20.9 cm; traces of red paint on the right
Albertina, Vienna, DG2002/388
B. XII, p. 151, no. 18; Le Blanc, 1, p. 227, no. 9 (as anonymous).

Bibliography: Mariette 1854–1856, vol. 1, p. 97; Heinecken 1778–90, vol. 2, 1788, pp. 300–1; Seidlitz 1885, p. 257, no. 3, p. 258, no. 17; Troche 1933, pp. 28–9; Florence 1956, cat. 52; Sanminiatelli 1956, p. 59; Vienna 1966, no. 204, Sanminiatelli 1967, p. 134, no. 8; Karpinski 1983, p. 254; Siena 1990, cat. 154 (text by A. De Marchi); Landau and Parshall 1994, p. 274; Lincoln 2000, pp. 52–8; Tokyo 2005, p. 55, cat. 38.

87
Domenico Beccafumi
Group of Men and Women
c. 1545–47
Engraving with two woodcut tone blocks, in pale blue and blue
14.3 × 22.2 cm; area of loss in the back of the rear-view figure
Albertina, Vienna, DG2002/395

Bibliography: Heinecken 1778–90, vol. 2, 1788, p. 298 (as anonymous); Reichel 1926, pl. 60 below (as anonymous); Vienna 1966, no. 206; Sanminiatelli 1967, p. 136, no. 1 (as not by Beccafumi); De Marchi 1990, p. 420; Siena 1990, cat. 161 (text by A. De Marchi); Hartley 1991, p. 424; Landau and Parshall 1994, p. 274; Tokyo 2005, cat. 35.

88
Antonio Campi, after Parmigianino
The Holy Family with St Catherine of Alexandria
1547
Chiaroscuro woodcut printed from two blocks, the tone block in reddish brown
19 × 12.8 cm (sheet), 18 × 12.2 cm (image)
Inscribed (upper left): *ANTONIUS / CREMONENSIS / 1547*
Collection of Georg Baselitz

Bibliography: Nagler 1858–79, vol. 1, 1858, no. 1068, 6; Pittaluga 1930, p. 329, n. 44; Servolini 1932, p. 78; Cremona 1985, pp. 320–3, no. 3.2 (text by F. Buonincontri); Geneva 2002, cat. 62 (text by N. Strasser).

89
Alessandro Gandini, after Girolamo da Treviso
Virgin and Child with Saints
c. 1540–50 and 1610
Chiaroscuro woodcut printed from three blocks, the tone blocks in ochre and brown
35.9 × 24.2 cm
Inscribed (on the step of the throne): *Taglio d'Alex'. ghandinj* [in the darker tone block]; (lower centre): *A[ndrea] A[ndreani]* [monogrammed] */ IN MANTOVA / MDCX*; [in the line block]; verso inscribed: *Fraca*[?] [in pen and ink]
Collection of Georg Baselitz
B. XII, pp. 65–6, no. 25.

Bibliography: Nagler 1835–52, vol. 5, 1837, p. 126; Zanetti 1837, p. 40, no. 42; Nagler 1858–79, vol. 1, 1858, no. 614; Kolloff 1872, p. 725, no. 10 II; Kristeller 1920, p. 148; Reichel 1926, p. 34; Servolini 1932, p. 97; Vienna 1963, no. 142; Paris and Rotterdam 1965–66, no. 122; Trotter 1974, pp. 33–6, 209–11; Gould 1975, p. 114; Karpinski 1976, p. 24; Karpinski 1983, p. 87; Rome, Weimar and Munich 2001–03, cat. 20 (text by D. Graf); Johnson 2013, pp. 5–9.

90
Alessandro Gandini, after Parmigianino
Feast in the House of Simon the Pharisee
c. 1540–50
Chiaroscuro woodcut printed from three blocks, the tone blocks in grey and black
24.6 × 37.5 cm
Inscribed (lower right, on the base of the seat): *Taglio d'Alex.ro Ghandinj*
Albertina, Vienna, DG2002/285
B. XII, p. 41, no. 18.

Bibliography: Zanetti 1837, pp. 12, 39–40; Nagler 1858–79, vol. 1, 1858, no. 614; Reichel 1926, p. 34; Servolini 1932, pp. 92–3; Trotter 1974, pp. 22–34, 120–4; Karpinski 1983, p. 44; Johnson 2013, pp. 5–8, fig. 2.

91
Alessandro Gandini, after Parmigianino
Feast in the House of Simon the Pharisee
c. 1540–50 and 1609
Chiaroscuro woodcut printed from four blocks, the tone blocks in grey
28.5 × 40.3 cm (sheet), 25.3 × 37 cm (image)
Inscribed (lower right corner): *RAPH[A]EL VRB[INAS] / IN VEN[IT] / A[ndrea] A[ndreani]* [monogrammed] */ In mantoua / 1609*; verso inscribed: *Lisa & Leonard / L [pomegranate] L Baskin / 1965* [in pen and ink]
Collection of Georg Baselitz
B. XII, pp. 40–1, no. 17 (as Ugo da Carpi); Le Blanc, 1, p. 595, no. 7 (as Ugo da Carpi).

Bibliography: Zanetti 1837, pp. 12, 39–40 (as Ugo da Carpi); Nagler 1858–79, vol. 1, 1858, no. 614 (Ugo da Carpi); Kolloff 1872, p. 725, no. 6 (as Ugo da Carpi); Kristeller 1920, p. 148; Paris and Rotterdam 1965–66, no. 73 (as Ugo da Carpi); Trotter 1974, pp. 22–34, 120–4; Servolini 1977, no. 29, pl. XL (as Ugo da Carpi); Rome, Weimar and Munich 2001–03, cat. 4 (as Ugo da Carpi; text by D. Graf); Gnann 2002, p. 290 (as Ugo da Carpi); Gnann 2007, pp. 184–5, 433 (as Ugo da Carpi); Carpi 2009, cat. 27 (text by T. Previdi); Johnson 2013, pp. 5–8, fig. 4.

92
Georg Matheus
Martha Leading Mary Magdalene to Christ
c. 1540–60
Chiaroscuro woodcut printed from two blocks, the tone block in brown
24.5 × 35 cm
Inscribed (lower centre): *·M·* [in the tone block]; verso inscribed: *F[?]a[?]co Mazzuoli* [in pen and ink]
Collection of Georg Baselitz
B. XI, p. 37, no. 12; Le Blanc, 2, p. 623, no. 2; P. IV, p. 312, no. 2; H. XXIII, 7.

Bibliography: Nagler 1835–52, vol. 8, 1839, p. 433, no. 2; Nagler 1858–79, vol. 1, 1858, p. 719, no. 1614, vol. 4, 1871, p. 454, no. 1449; Paris and Rotterdam 1965–66, no. 27; Strauss 1973, no. 65; Trotter 1974, pp. 10, 117–19; Franklin 1977, p. 28; Karpinski 1983, p. 37; Paris 1983–84, cat. 91 (text by P. Jean-Richard); Mantua and Vienna 1999, p. 181, cat. 118.

93
Master NDB, after Raphael (?)
The Massacre of the Innocents
c. 1540–50
Chiaroscuro woodcut printed from three blocks, the tone blocks in pale brown and brown
29.3 × 50.7 cm; area of loss at upper right corner
Inscribed (lower edge, centre): *RAPH[AEL]. URB[INAS]. INVEN[IT].*; (lower right corner, on the block of stone): *NDB / 1544*
Collection of Georg Baselitz

94
Master NDB, after Raphael (?)
The Massacre of the Innocents
c. 1540–50
Woodcut; small areas of loss at right edge and upper right corner
31.1 × 52 cm
Collection of Georg Baselitz
B. XII, pp. 33–4, no. 7.

Bibliography: Zanetti 1837, p. 37, no. 40, p. 38, no. 41; Passavant 1860, vol. 2, p. 217; Nagler 1858–79, vol. 4, 1871, pp. 743–4, no. 1; Seibt 1891, p. 63; Pouncey and Gere 1962, vol. 1, p. 81, n. 1; Paris and Rotterdam 1965–66, no. 123; Trotter 1974, pp. 131–5; Karpinski 1976, cat. 1; Karpinski 1983, p. 32; Mantua and Vienna 1999, p. 291, cat. 206–7; Matile 2003, p. 155; Jenkins 2013, pp. 138–9.

95
Erasmus Loy
Courtyard with Renaissance Architecture
c. 1550
Chiaroscuro woodcut printed from two blocks, the tone block in reddish brown
44.2 × 36.1 cm (sheet), 42.4 × 35.6 cm (image)
Inscribed (lower centre edge): *Mit Kö: Kaÿ: und Khü Maÿ / freÿhait: nit Nachzudruckhen*
Watermark: R above two crossed keys (watermark of the city of Regensburg), similar to Briquet 1139
Collection of Georg Baselitz
H. XXIII, 12.

Bibliography: Strauss 1973, no. 63a; Strauss 1975, vol. 2, p. 621.

96
Erasmus Loy
View of Architecture with a Figure in the Background
c. 1550
Chiaroscuro woodcut printed from two blocks, the tone block in reddish brown
39.2 × 30.2 cm (sheet), 34.7 × 28.8 cm (image)
Inscribed (lower centre edge): *Mit Kö: Kaÿ: und Khü Maÿ / freÿhait: nit Nachzudruckhen*
Watermark: R above two crossed keys (watermark of the city of Regensburg), similar to Briquet 1139
Albertina, Vienna, DG1984/102
H. XXIII, 14.

Bibliography: Strauss 1975, vol. 2, p. 625.

97
Frans Floris
David Playing the Harp before Saul
1555
Chiaroscuro woodcut printed from four blocks, the tone blocks in pale red and reddish brown, on brownish paper
33.4 × 48.1 cm; various tears, small areas have been made up
Inscribed (on the base of the throne): *SAVL· ·I· REG·CA·XVI*; (on the step): *FRĀ[N] CISCVS·FLORIS INVĒ[N]TOR · IVDOCE DE CVRIA· EXCVDEBAT: 1555.*
Collection of Georg Baselitz
Le Blanc, 2, p. 241, no. 1; H. VI, p. 251.

Bibliography: Winkler 1916, p. 125; Paris and Rotterdam 1965–66, nos 191–2; Vienna 1966–67, no. 117; Strauss 1973, no. 101; Van de Velde 1975, pp. 395–6, cat. 15; Berlin 1979, no. 59; Amsterdam and Cleveland 1992–93, no. 3; Braunschweig 2003–04, p. 36; Wouk 2009, pp. 56–7; Paris 2010, cat. 5 (text by E. Hinterding); Wouk 2011, vol. 1, pp. LIV–LVI, no. 1.

98
Frans Floris
Ceres
c. 1560–70
Chiaroscuro woodcut printed from three tone blocks, in pink and red
43 × 29.5 cm
Verso inscribed: *Mariette 1752* [in pen and ink]
Albertina, Vienna, DG85339

Bibliography: Judson 1970, p. 93, n. 4; Amsterdam and Cleveland 1992–93, no. 4; Wouk 2011, vol. 1, no. 7.

99
Adriaen Thomasz. Key
Joab Killing Absalom
c. 1570–80
Chiaroscuro woodcut printed from three blocks, the tone blocks in green
30.1 × 47.6 cm
Inscribed (lower right, on a stone): *ATK* [monogrammed]
Watermark: Coat of arms shield with linked letters, the first a P, above the inscription *P PRICARD*; cf. Briquet 9613
Albertina, Vienna, DG2013/23
B. IX, p. 407 (as anonymous); H. IX, p. 241, no. 1.

Bibliography: Bruillot 1832, p. 41, no. 298; Nagler 1858–79, vol. 1, 1858, p. 247, no. 1; Wurzbach 1904, p. 264; Reichel 1926, p. 26, fig. 6; Winkler 1927, p. 228; Delen 1935, p. 86; Judson 1970, p. 93, n. 4; Strauss 1973, no. 115; Amsterdam and Cleveland 1992–93, no. 8b; Braunschweig 2003–04, p. 37; Jonckheere 2007, cat. A. 123; Wouk 2011, vol. 1, p. LV.

100
Adriaen Thomasz. Key
Nebuchadnezzar Casting Daniel's Companions into the Fiery Furnace
c. 1570–80
Chiaroscuro woodcut printed from three blocks, the tone blocks in pale green and blue-green, on cloth
24.4 × 31.5 cm; browning lower left
Inscribed (upper right, on tablet hanging on wall): *ATK* [monogrammed]; verso inscribed (upper left): *Of / König Vienna 1849 / rare 30*[?] [in pen and ink]
Collection of Georg Baselitz
H. IX, p. 241, no. 2.

Bibliography: Bruillot 1832, p. 41, no. 298; Nagler 1858–79, vol. 1, 1858, p. 247, no. 2; Wurzbach 1904, p. 264; Reichel 1926, p. 26, fig. 6; Winkler 1927, p. 228; Delen 1935, p. 86; Judson 1970, p. 93, n. 4; Paris and Rotterdam 1965–66, no. 256; Vienna 1966–67, no. 118; Judson 1970, p. 93, n. 4; Strauss 1973, no. 116; Amsterdam and Cleveland 1992–93, no. 8b; Braunschweig 2003–04, p. 37; Jonckheere 2007, cat. A. 122; Wouk 2011, vol. 1, p. LV.

101
Crispin van den Broeck (?)
Feast in the House of Simon the Pharisee
c. 1570
Etching with tone woodcut block in greyish blue
23.2 × 23.5 cm
Albertina, Vienna, DG2013/22
H. III, p. 225, no. 43.

Bibliography: Wurzbach 1904, vol. 1, p. 187, no. 7; Delen 1935, vol. II 2, p. 102 (as ?Crispin van den Broeck); Rotterdam 1965, no. 92; Wescher 1974, p. 177; Vienna 1967–68, p. 91; Van de Velde 1975, p. 400, cat. 27 (as ?Crispijn van den Broeck); Strauss 1973, no. 109; Amsterdam and Cleveland 1992–93, no. 18 (as school of Frans Floris); Braunschweig 2003–04, p. 37; Wouk 2011, vol. 1, p. LVII, no. 2 (as anonymous).

102
Hendrick Goltzius
Hercules Killing Cacus
1588
Woodcut
41.2 × 32.9 cm
Indecipherable watermark
Collection of Georg Baselitz
B. III, p. 72, no. 231; H. VIII, p. 122 I.

Bibliography: Seibt 1891, p. 67; Hirschmann 1921, no. 373 I; Paris and Rotterdam 1965–66, no. 217; Strauss 1973, no. 134 I; Strauss 1982, p. 256 S4; Amsterdam and Cleveland 1992–93, no. 25 IV; Amsterdam, New York and Toledo 2003–04, no. 34 (text by N. M. Orenstein); Tokyo 2005, no. 44a; Leesberg 2012, vol. 1, p. LVI, vol. 2, no. 304 II.

103
Hendrick Goltzius
Hercules Killing Cacus
1588
Chiaroscuro woodcut printed from three blocks, the tone blocks in yellow and green
41.1 × 33.3 cm
Inscribed (left centre, top to bottom on a rock): *A° .88 / H Goltzius inve:*
Collection of Georg Baselitz
B. III, p. 72, no. 231; H. VIII, p. 122 III.

Bibliography: Hirschmann 1921, no. 373 III; Ames 1949, pp. 426–36; Paris and Rotterdam 1965–66, nos 219–20; Vienna 1967–68, no. 317; Strauss 1973, no. 134 IV; Strauss 1982, p. 256 S2; Amsterdam and Cleveland 1992–93, no. 25 II; Amsterdam, New York and Toledo 2003–04, no. 34 (text by N. M. Orenstein); Tokyo 2005, no. 44c; Leesberg 2012, vol. 1, p. LVI, vol. 2, no. 304 Ih.

104
Hendrick Goltzius
Allegory of Time, Nature and Eternity (The Demiurge)
c. 1588
Chiaroscuro woodcut printed from three blocks, the tone blocks in beige and grey
36.8 × 27 cm (sheet), 34.8 × 26.3 cm (image); crease mark across centre
Inscribed (lower centre): *HG* [monogrammed]. *f* [both in tone block]
Collection of Georg Baselitz
B. III, pp. 73–4, no. 238; H. VIII, p. 123.

Bibliography: Seibt 1891, p. 67; Hirschmann 1921, no. 374 I 3; Ames 1949, pp. 432–6; Vienna 1967–68, no. 318; Strauss 1973, no. 135; Amsterdam and Cleveland 1992–93, no. 26a; Amsterdam, New York and Toledo 2003–04, no. 35.2 (text by N. M. Orenstein); Leesberg 2012, vol. 2, no. 294a.

105
Hendrick Goltzius
Allegory of Time, Nature and Eternity (The Demiurge)
c. 1588
Chiaroscuro woodcut printed from three blocks, the tone blocks in ochre and blue-green
35.3 × 26.1 cm (sheet), 35 × 26.4 cm (image)
Inscribed (lower centre): *HG* [monogrammed]. *f* [both in tone block]
Collection of Georg Baselitz
B. III, pp. 73–4, no. 238; H. VIII, p. 123.

Bibliography: Seibt 1891, p. 67; Hirschmann 1921, no. 374 I 1; Ames 1949, pp. 432–6; Paris and Rotterdam 1965–66, no. 222; Vienna 1967–68, no. 318; Strauss 1973, no. 135; Berlin 1979, no. 81; Strauss 1982, pp. 264–5 S2; Amsterdam and Cleveland 1992–93, no. 26b; Amsterdam, New York and Toledo 2003–04, no. 35.1 (text by N. M. Orenstein); Tokyo 2005, no. 45; Paris 2010, no. 6a (text by E. Hinterding); Leesberg 2012, vol. 2, no. 294b.

106
Hendrick Goltzius
Oceanus
c. 1589–90
Chiaroscuro woodcut printed from three blocks, the tone blocks in beige and green
35 × 26.5 cm
Inscribed (lower centre edge): *HG* [monogrammed]. *F*
Collection of Georg Baselitz
B. III, p. 73, no. 1; H. VIII, p. 121.

Bibliography: Seibt 1891, p. 67; Hirschmann 1921, no. 367; Reichel 1926, p. 44; Ames 1949, pp. 432–6; Paris and Rotterdam 1965–66, nos 203–4; Strauss 1973, no. 136; Strauss 1982, p. 259; Amsterdam and Cleveland 1992–93, no. 27c; Leesberg 2012, vol. 2, no. 295b.

107
Hendrick Goltzius
Thetis
c. 1589–90
Chiaroscuro woodcut printed from three blocks, the tone blocks in beige and green
38.3 × 29.5 cm (sheet), 35 × 26.5 cm (image)
Inscribed (lower centre edge):
HG [monogrammed]. *fe*
Collection of Georg Baselitz
B. III, p. 73, no. 4; H. VIII, p. 121.

Bibliography: Seibt 1891, p. 67; Hirschmann 1921, no. 368; Reichel 1926, pp. 44, 66; Ames 1949, pp. 432–6; Paris and Rotterdam 1965–66, nos 205–7; Strauss 1973, no. 137; Strauss 1982, pp. 260–1; Amsterdam and Cleveland 1992–93, no. 28 IIIa; Leesberg 2012, vol. 2, no. 300 IIIa.

108
Hendrick Goltzius
Pluto
c. 1589–90
Chiaroscuro woodcut printed from three blocks, the tone blocks in beige and green
34.5 × 25.9 cm (image); area of loss at lower edge has been made up
Inscribed (lower centre):
HG [monogrammed]. *fe*
Collection of Georg Baselitz
B. III, p. 73, no. 2; H. VIII, p. 121.

Bibliography: Seibt 1891, p. 67; Hirschmann 1921, no. 369; Reichel 1926, p. 44; Ames 1949, pp. 433–6; Paris and Rotterdam 1965–66, nos 208–9; Strauss 1973, no. 138; Strauss 1982, p. 259; Amsterdam and Cleveland 1992–93, no. 29b; Amsterdam, New York and Toledo 2003–04, no. 35.7 (text by N. M. Orenstein); Leesberg 2012, vol. 2, no. 297 IIa.

109
Hendrick Goltzius
Proserpina
c. 1589–90
Chiaroscuro woodcut printed from three blocks, the tone blocks in brown
34.4 × 25.8 cm (image); crease marks across centre
Inscribed (centre left edge, at the foot of the tree): *HG* [monogrammed, in the lighter tone block]
Collection of Georg Baselitz
B. III, p. 73, no. 5; H. VIII, p. 121.

Bibliography: Seibt 1891, p. 67; Hirschmann 1921, no. 370; Reichel 1926, p. 44; Ames 1949, p. 434; Paris and Rotterdam 1965–66, nos 210–12; Vienna 1967–68, no. 319; Strauss 1973, no. 139; Berlin 1979, no. 82; Strauss 1982, pp. 262–3; Amsterdam and Cleveland 1992–93, no. 30d; Amsterdam, New York and Toledo 2003–04, no. 35.5 (text by N. M. Orenstein); Leesberg 2012, vol. 2, no. 298d.

110
Hendrick Goltzius
Day (Helios)
c. 1589–90
Chiaroscuro woodcut printed from three blocks, the tone blocks in beige and green
38.3 × 29.5 cm (sheet), 27 × 35 cm (image)
Inscribed (lower centre):
HG [monogrammed]. *fe.*
Indecipherable watermark
Collection of Georg Baselitz
B. III, p. 73, no. 3; H. VIII, p. 121.

Bibliography: Seibt 1891, p. 67; Hirschmann 1921, no. 371; Reichel 1926, p. 44; Ames 1949, pp. 434–6; Paris and Rotterdam 1965–66, nos 213–14; Strauss 1973, no. 140; Strauss 1982, p. 260; Amsterdam and Cleveland 1992–93, no. 31b; Paris 2010, p. 55 (text by E. Hinterding); Leesberg 2012, vol. 2, no. 299b.

111
Hendrick Goltzius
Night (Nyx)
c. 1589–90
Chiaroscuro woodcut printed from three blocks, the tone blocks in beige and green
34.8 × 26.2 cm
Inscribed (lower centre):
HG [monogrammed] *fe.*
Collection of Georg Baselitz
B. III, p. 73, no. 6; H. VIII, p. 121.

Bibliography: Seibt 1891, p. 67; Hirschmann 1921, no. 372 II; Reichel 1926, p. 44; Ames 1949, pp. 434–6; Paris and Rotterdam 1965–66, nos 215–16; Strauss 1973, no. 141; Strauss 1982, p. 263 S2; Amsterdam and Cleveland 1992–93, no. 32b; Paris 2010, no. 6–I (text by E. Hinterding); Leesberg 2012, vol. 2, no. 300b.

112
Hendrick Goltzius
Landscape with Watermill
c. 1593–98
Chiaroscuro woodcut printed from three blocks, the tone blocks in light green and green
13.8 × 17.4 cm (sheet), 11.6 × 15.1 cm (image)
Inscribed (lower left): *HG.* [monogrammed]
Collection of Georg Baselitz
B. III, p. 75, no. 1; H. VIII, p. 127 II.

Bibliography: Seibt 1891, p. 67; Hirschmann 1921, no. 378 II; Reichel 1926, pp. 44–5, 66; Ames 1949, pp. 429–30; Paris and Rotterdam 1965–66, nos 235–7; Strauss 1973, no. 128; Strauss 1982, no. 242 S2; Amsterdam and Cleveland 1992–93, no. 49 Ia; Geneva 2002, no. 109a (text by N. Strasser); Amsterdam, New York and Toledo 2003–04, no. 70.2 (text by M. Plomp); Tokyo 2005, no. 53b; Leesberg 2012, vol. 2, no. 307 IIa.

113
Hendrick Goltzius
Landscape with Trees and a Shepherd Couple
c. 1593–98
Chiaroscuro woodcut printed from three blocks, the tone blocks in pale green and green
14 × 17.6 cm (sheet), 11.7 × 15.3 cm (image)
Inscribed (lower centre edge): *HG* [monogrammed]
Collection of Georg Baselitz
B. III, p. 75, no. 2; H. VIII, p. 127 II.

Bibliography: Seibt 1891, p. 67; Hirschmann 1921, no. 379 II; Reichel 1926, pp. 44–5; Strauss 1973, no. 129; Ames 1949, pp. 429–30; Paris and Rotterdam 1965–66, nos 239–40; Vienna 1967–68, pp. 216–17; Strauss 1982, no. 243 S2; Amsterdam and Cleveland 1992–93, no. 50 II; Geneva 2002, no. 109b (text by N. Strasser); Amsterdam, New York and Toledo 2003–04, no. 70.2 (text by M. Plomp); Tokyo 2005, pp. 65–6; Leesberg 2012, vol. 2, no. 308 II.

114
Hendrick Goltzius
Landscape with Farm
c. 1593–98
Chiaroscuro woodcut printed from three blocks, the tone blocks in pale green and green
17.6 × 14.2 cm (sheet), 11.5 × 14.8 cm (image)
Inscribed (lower centre): *HG* [monogrammed]
Collection of Georg Baselitz
B. III, p. 75, no. 3; H. VIII, p. 127 II.

Bibliography: Seibt 1891, p. 67; Hirschmann 1921, no. 380; Reichel 1926, pp. 44–5, 66; Ames 1949, pp. 429–30; Paris and Rotterdam 1965–66, no. 242; Strauss 1973, no. 130; Strauss 1982, no. 244 S2; Amsterdam and Cleveland 1992–93, no. 51 II; Geneva 2002, no. 109c (text by N. Strasser); Amsterdam, New York and Toledo 2003–04, no. 70.5 (text by M. Plomp); Leesberg 2012, vol. 2, no. 309 II.

115
Hendrick Goltzius
Coastal Scene with a Large Rock
c. 1593–98
Chiaroscuro woodcut printed from three blocks, the tone blocks in pale green and green
11.5 × 14.7 cm
Inscribed (lower centre, on a rock): *HG* [monogrammed]
Collection of Georg Baselitz
B. III, p. 75, no. 4; H. VIII, p. 127 II.

Bibliography: Seibt 1891, p. 67; Hirschmann 1921, no. 381 II; Reichel 1926, pp. 44–5; Ames 1949, pp. 429–30; Paris and Rotterdam 1965–66, nos 244–5; Strauss 1973, no. 131; Strauss 1982, no. 245 S3; Amsterdam and Cleveland 1992–93, no. 52 II; Geneva 2002, no. 109d (text by N. Strasser); Amsterdam, New York and Toledo 2003–04, no. 70.6 (text by M. Plomp); Leesberg 2012, vol. 2, no. 310 II.

116
Hendrick Goltzius
Gillis van Breen
c. 1588
Chiaroscuro woodcut printed from three blocks, the tone blocks in ochre and brown
20.5 × 14.1 cm
Inscribed (upper right corner): *HG* [monogrammed] *fe*
Collection of Georg Baselitz
B. III, p. 74, no. 239; H. VIII, p. 124 III.

Bibliography: Seibt 1891, p. 67; Hirschmann 1921, no. 375 II, II; Reichel 1926, pp. 44, 65; Ames 1949, pp. 426–36; Paris and Rotterdam 1965–66, nos 224–5; Strauss 1973, no. 121a; Strauss 1982, p. 265 S2; Amsterdam and Cleveland 1992–93, no. 23 IIb; Amsterdam, New York and Toledo 2003–04, no. 47 (text by M. Schapelhouman); Leesberg 2012, vol. 1, p. LVI, vol. 2, no. 305 IIb.

117
Hendrick Goltzius
Mars
c. 1589–90
Chiaroscuro woodcut printed from three blocks, the tone blocks in orange-brown and brown
24.4 × 14.7 cm
Inscribed (upper left): *HG* [monogrammed]
Collection of Georg Baselitz
B. III, p. 72, no. 229; H. VIII, p. 118 II.

Bibliography: Hirschmann 1921, no. 365 II; Ames 1949, pp. 428–36; Paris and Rotterdam 1965–66, no. 199; Strauss 1973, no. 125 II; Strauss 1982, p. 251, S2; Amsterdam and Cleveland 1992–93, no. 34; Leesberg 2012, vol. 2, no. 302 IIc.

118
Hendrick Goltzius
Bacchus
c. 1589–90
Chiaroscuro woodcut printed from two blocks, the tone block in light brown
23.8 × 14.3 cm
Inscribed (lower right): *H Goltzius* [?] [in pen and ink, in an early hand]
Collection of Georg Baselitz
B. III, p. 72, no. 228; H. VIII, p. 118 I.

Bibliography: Hirschmann 1921, no. 364 I; Ames 1949, pp. 428–36; Paris and Rotterdam 1965–66, no. 197; Strauss 1973, no. 126 I; Strauss 1982, p. 251 S1; Amsterdam and Cleveland 1992–93, no. 33 I; Tokyo 2005, no. 52; Leesberg 2012, vol. 2, no. 301 I.

119
Unknown woodcutter (Domenico Campagnola?), after Titian
Tree with two Goats
c. 1530–40
Chiaroscuro woodcut printed from two blocks, the tone block in grey
49.2 × 21.7 cm
Inscribed (lower right edge): *T[iziano]* [in pen and ink]; buckling mark across centre, border line retraced in pen and ink at upper left corner
Albertina, Vienna, DG2002/329
B. XII, pp. 151–2, no. 20; P. VI, p. 222, no. 20.

Bibliography: Tietze and Tietze-Conrat 1938, pp. 475–7; Mauroner 1941, cat. 25 (as Domenico delle Greche), Florence 1956, no. 80 (as after ?Domenico Campagnola); Weimar 1957, no. 43; Vienna 1966, no. 168; Berlin 1971, cat. 7 (as Ugo da Carpi); Dreyer 1972, pp. 298–9 (as Ugo da Carpi); Washington, Dallas and Detroit 1976–77, no. 25 (as ?Domenico Campagnola); Karpinski 1983, p. 256; London 1983, cat. P 38 (text by D. Landau); Rome, Weimar and Munich 2001–03, cat. 24 (attributed to Niccolò Boldrini; text by D. Graf).

120
Attributed to Niccolò Boldrini, after Raphael
St John the Baptist
Second third of the sixteenth century
Chiaroscuro woodcut printed from two blocks, the tone block in brown
38.8 × 27.6 cm
Inscribed (lower left edge): *RAPHA[EL]·UR[BINAS]·IN[VENTOR]*
Watermark: Coat of arms shield bearing a plant (?)
Collection of Georg Baselitz
B. XII, pp. 73–4, no. 18 (as Ugo da Carpi); Le Blanc, 1, pp. 595–6 (as Ugo da Carpi), no. 10; P. VI, p. 221, no. 18 (as Ugo da Carpi).

Bibliography: Zanetti 1837, p. 34, no. 38 (attributed to Niccolò Boldrini); Passavant 1860, p. 288 (as Ugo da Carpi); Seibt 1891, p. 49 (as not by Ugo da Carpi); Reichel 1926, p. 30 (as Ugo da Carpi); Servolini 1932, p. 51 (as Ugo da Carpi); Florence 1956, no. 3 (as Ugo da Carpi); Trotter 1974, pp. 112–13 (as ?Ugo da Carpi); Servolini 1977, p. 8, cat. 16, pl. XXVII (as Ugo da Carpi); Karpinski 1983, p. 108; Edinburgh 1994, p. 108 (text by A. Weston-Lewis); Carpi 2009, no. 17 (as Ugo da Carpi; text by R. Sassi).

121
Niccolò Boldrini, after Pordenone
Marcus Curtius on Horseback
second third of the sixteenth century
Chiaroscuro woodcut printed from three blocks, the tone blocks in ochre and brown
39.5 × 25.9 cm; cut down at the left, right and lower edges
Albertina, Vienna, DG2002/353
B. XII, p. 151, no. 19 (as anonymous); Le Blanc I, p. 429, no. 22.

Bibliography: Reichel 1926, pp. 38–9, 61 (as unknown sixteenth-century Italian woodcutter); Vienna 1966, no. 212 (as anonymous sixteenth-century master); Washington, Dallas and Detroit 1976–77, no. 74; Karpinski 1983, p. 255.

122
Unknown woodcutter, after Federico Barocci
The Holy Family Resting on the Return from Egypt
Last third third of the sixteenth century
Chiaroscuro woodcut printed from two blocks, the tone block in brown
35.6 × 28.7 cm
Inscribed (lower left edge): *•F[edericus]•B[arotius]•V[rbinas]•I[nvenit]*
Collection of Georg Baselitz
B. XII, pp. 36–7, no. 11.

Bibliography: Reichel 1926, pp. 61–2; Servolini 1932, p. 98; Olsen 1962, p. 154; Paris and Rotterdam 1965–66, no. 41; Vienna 1966, no. 215; Cleveland and Yale 1978, no. 80 (text by L. S. Richards); Rome, Weimar and Munich 2001–03, cat. 31 (text by D. Graf); Saint Louis and London 2012–13, p. 109 (text by J. S. Mann).

123
Giovanni Gallo, after Marco Pino
Cain and Abel
c. 1570–80
Chiaroscuro woodcut printed from four blocks, the tone blocks in beige and blue
40 × 26.1 cm
Inscribed (lower edge): *Marcus Senensis invē / Ioanes Gallus incid.* [cropped]
Albertina, Vienna, DG2002/583

Bibliography: Weimar 1957, no. 40; Vienna 1966, no. 214, fig. 30; Rome, Weimar and Munich 2001–03, cat. 31 (text by D. Graf); Zezza 2003, D. 9.

124
Giovanni Gallo, after Marco Pino
Perseus with the Head of Medusa
c. 1570–80
Chiaroscuro woodcut printed from four blocks, the tone blocks in orange and reddish brown
35.9 × 22.7 cm
Inscribed (lower right, in the border): *Marcus Senensis invē[nit] / Ioãnes Gallus incid[it].*; verso inscribed: *Mariette 1728 / Desneux* [in pen and ink]
Albertina, Vienna, DG2002/587
B. XII, p. 124, no. 25; Le Blanc II, p. 266, no. 4.

Bibliography: Nagler 1835–52, vol. 5, 1837, p. 3; Servolini 1932, p. 92; Paris and Rotterdam 1965–66, no. 119; Siena 1980, no. 84 (text by F. Bellini); Karpinski 1983, p. 198; Zezza 2003, V. 48, cat. D 10, pl. 49.

125
Giovanni Gallo, after Marco Pino
The Lamentation of Christ
c. 1570–80
Chiaroscuro woodcut printed from four blocks, the tone blocks in green
44 × 28.4 cm
Inscribed (lower right, in the border): *Marcus Senensis invē[nit] / Ioanes Gallus incid[it].*; verso inscribed: *P. mariette 1668 / Desneux* [in pen and ink]
Albertina, Vienna, DG2002/586
B. XII, pp. 43–4, no. 23; Le Blanc II, p. 266, no. 2.

Bibliography: Nagler 1835–52, vol. 5, 1837, pp. 2–3; Servolini 1932, p. 92; Vienna 1966, no. 213; Siena 1980, p. 222 (text by F. Bellini); Karpinski 1983, p. 50; Zezza 2003, cat. D.12.

126
Andrea Andreani, after Jacopo Ligozzi
Virtue Assailed by Love, Error, Ignorance and Opinion
1585
Chiaroscuro woodcut printed from four blocks, in brown
46.2 × 32.1 cm; area of loss at lower right corner has been made up
Inscribed (lower left corner): *FRANCISCO / MEDICI / Sereniss:º Magno / Ethrurie Duci. / Andreas Andreanus / incisit ac dicavit Iacobus Ligotius Veronens̄ / invenit / ac / Pinxit;* (lower right corner): *In / Firenze / 1585 / Lettere Vocale / figurate ·A·Amore ·E·Errore / I· Ignora:^{za} O·Opinio^{e} / ·V· Virtu*
Collection of Georg Baselitz
B. XII, p. 130, no. 9.

Bibliography: Kolloff 1872, p. 720, no. 25 II; Seib 1891, p. 57; Servolini 1932, p. 104; Paris and Rotterdam 1965–66, nos 61–2; Stechow 1967; Van Gastel 2007, p. 26; Franklin 1977, p. 30; Karpinski 1983, p. 215; Poppi 1992, p. 23; Rome, Weimar and Munich 2001–03, cat. 38 (text by D. Graf); Matile 2003, p. 166; Hirschboek 2010, pp. 6–13.

127
Andrea Andreani, after Giambologna
Rape of a Sabine Woman
1584
Chiaroscuro woodcut printed from two blocks, the tone block in greyish green
45.3 × 20.2 cm
Inscribed (lower right): *Hoc opus exculpsit / Io:Bologna Andreas / Andreani incisit atq' / dicavit. Ad Illustriss. / & Eccel: Ioannē Medicē*
Watermark: Eagle (?) within a circle
Albertina, Vienna, DG2002/572
B. XII, p. 94, no. 3.

Bibliography: Baglione 1649, p. 395; Kolloff 1872, p. 722, no. 30; Reichel 1926, p. 35; Pittaluga 1930, p. 253; Servolini 1932, p. 104; Paris and Rotterdam 1965–66, no. 56; Vienna 1966, no. 221; Franklin 1977, p. 29; Edinburgh, London and Vienna 1978–79b, no. 209c (text by M. Leithe-Jasper); Goldfarb 1981, p. 319; Karpinski 1983, p. 148; Rome, Weimar and Munich 2001–03, cat. 35; Braunschweig 2003–04, cat. A 25; Tokyo 2005, no. 64; Van Gastel 2007, fig. 3; Boorsch 2008–09, p. 48.

128
Andrea Andreani, after Giambologna
Rape of a Sabine Woman
1584
Chiaroscuro woodcut printed from four blocks, the tone blocks in brown
44.7 × 20.9 cm; areas of loss at upper left, upper right and lower right corners have been made up
Inscribed (lower left corner): *Raptā Sabinā à Ioa: / Bolog: marm: exculptā / Andreas Andrean' Mant. Īci: / atqu' Equiti Nicc: Gaddio / dicavit M.D.LXXXIIII. Flor.*
Collection of Georg Baselitz
B. XII, p. 93, no. 1.

Bibliography: Baglione 1649, p. 395; Kolloff 1872, p. 722, no. 28; Seibt 1891, p. 56; Reichel 1926, p. 35; Pittaluga 1930, p. 253; Servolini 1932, p. 104; Vienna 1966, no. 219; Edinburgh, London and Vienna 1978–79b, no. 209a (text by M. Leithe-Jasper); Goldfarb 1981, p. 319; Karpinski 1983, p. 147 (left); Matile 2003, no. 73; Braunschweig 2003–04, p. 31; Van Gastel 2007, fig. 2.

129

Andrea Andreani, after Giambologna

Rape of a Sabine Woman

1584

Chiaroscuro woodcut printed from four blocks, the tone blocks in ochre and brown

44.4 × 20.5 cm

Inscribed (lower right): *Raptā Sabinam, à / Io: Bolog·marm:excul·/ Andreas Andrean' Māt: / incisit, atq. Bernard / Vechiett dicavit año / M·D·LXXXIIII*; *P. mariette 1652 [?]* and *P. mariette 1674 [?]* [both in pen and ink]

Albertina, Vienna, DG2002/570

B. XII, pp. 93–4, no. 2

Bibliography: Baglione 1649, p. 395; Kolloff 1872, p. 722, no. 29; Seibt 1891, p. 56; Reichel 1926, p. 35; Pittaluga 1930, p. 253; Servolini 1932, p. 104; Paris and Rotterdam 1965–66, no. 54; Vienna 1966, Nr. 220; Edinburgh, London and Vienna 1978–79b, no. 209b (text by M. Leithe-Jasper); Goldfarb 1981, p. 319; Karpinski 1983, p. 147 (right); Rome, Weimar and Munich 2001–03, cat. 34; Van Gastel 2007, fig. 1; Boorsch 2008–09, p. 48.

130

Andrea Andreani, after Giambologna

Rape of the Sabine Women

1585

Chiaroscuro woodcut printed from three sets of four blocks, the tone blocks in ochre and brown, on six sheets of paper

75.2 × 94.5 cm

Verso inscribed: *F. Rechberger 1800*; (lower left): *Andreas Andrean' Mantuan' / eam incisit, impressit· / Anno Domini· / M·D $\overline{\text{LXXXV}}$ / Florentiae; Hec est hystoria[um] Sabinar[um] in are scupltar[um] per Doūm / Io: Bolognam Sereniss: Magni Etre Ducis scupltorē celeberr̄*

Albertina, Vienna, DG2002/574

B. XII, pp. 94–6, no. 4.

Bibliography: Baglione 1649, p. 395; Kolloff 1872, p. 722, no. 31 I.; Reichel 1926, p. 35; Servolini 1932, p. 104; Florence 1956, no. 55; Weimar 1957, no. 47; Paris and Rotterdam 1965–66, no. 56; Vienna 1966, no. 222; Edinburgh, London and Vienna 1978–79b, no. 210 (text by M. Leithe-Jasper); Goldfarb 1981, pp. 307, 317–25; Karpinski 1983, p. 149; Rome, Weimar and Munich 2001–03, cat. 36; Matile 2003, p. 166; Van Gastel 2007, pp. 19–20, fig. 9; Boorsch 2008–09, p. 48.

131

Andrea Andreani, after Giambologna

Christ before Pilate

1585

Chiaroscuro woodcut printed from two sets of four blocks, the tone blocks in brownish red, on two sheets of paper

44.8 × 65.1 cm

Inscribed (on the throne plinth): *MD L XXXV*; (on the shield of the soldier on the right): *Gianbologna 'scolpi·/ Andrea Andriano= / Io'ntagliatore, / A.Giovambatista. Deti gen= / til'huomo Fiorentino*

Collection of Georg Baselitz

B. XII, pp. 41–2, no. 19.

Bibliography: Baglione 1649, p. 395; Kolloff 1872, p. 718, no. 11; Seibt 1891, pp. 56–7; Servolini 1932, p. 104; Florence 1956, no. 56; Paris and Rotterdam 1965–66, no. 47; Edinburgh, London and Vienna 1978–79a, nos 208–9 (text by M. Leithe-Jasper); Karpinski 1983, p. 45; Matile 2003, p. 166; Tokyo 2005, no. 65b; Van Gastel 2007, pp. 23–4, fig. 11; Paris 2010, no. 9-II (text by G. Luijten).

132

Andrea Andreani, after Jacopo Ligozzi

Virgin and Child with the Infant John the Baptist and SS. Catherine of Siena and Francis

1585

Chiaroscuro woodcut printed from three blocks, the tone blocks in ochre and brown

46.2 × 37.4 cm

Inscribed (upper left corner): *Iacopo Ligozia Veronese Pictor'del / Sereniss: Gran Duca. d. Tosc. Inven[tor]· / Andrea Andriano / Mant.^{o} Intagliator^{e} / All Ill^{o} Signor / Nicolo Gaddi / in Fiorenza / ·1585·*

Collection of Georg Baselitz

B. XII, p. 67, no. 27.

Bibliography: Kolloff 1872, p. 720, no. 24; Seibt 1891, p. 57; Servolini 1932, p. 104; Weimar 1957, no. 49; Paris and Rotterdam 1965–66, no. 52; Goldfarb 1981, p. 325; Poppi 1992, p. 23; Rome, Weimar and Munich 2001–03, cat. 37 (text by D. Graf); Tokyo 2005, no. 67; Van Gastel 2007, p. 26.

133

Andrea Andreani, after Raffaellino da Reggio

The Entombment of Christ

1585

Chiaroscuro woodcut printed from four blocks, the tone blocks in orange-red and reddish brown

Inscribed (lower left): *Raff. da Reggio Inuent: Andrea Andriano / Mant^{o}: Intagliatore / All Illmo et l'ec:^{mo} sig.^{r} Don Giovañ Medici / 1585*

41.8 × 32.7 cm

Collection of Georg Baselitz

B. XII, p. 44, no. 24.

Bibliography: Kolloff 1872, pp. 718–19, no. 16; Pittaluga 1930, p. 253; Servolini 1932, pp. 104–5; Vienna 1966, no. 218; Paris and Rotterdam 1965–66, nos 49–50; Florence 1966, p. 52, under no. 80; Franklin 1977, p. 30; Goldfarb 1981, p. 325; Karpinski 1983, p. 51; Jaffé 1994, p. 203, under no. 336; Van Gastel 2007, p. 29.

134

Andrea Andreani, after Alessandro Casolani

Christ Carrying the Cross

1591

Chiaroscuro woodcut printed from three blocks, the tone blocks in reddish brown and brown

36.9 × 26.4 cm; foxing at upper left edge

Inscribed (lower margin): *CALI* [monogrammed] / *A^{l} Sig.^{r} Fabio Buonsignori Nobile senese / Andrea Andreani Intagliatore in Siena 1591.*

Collection of Georg Baselitz

B. XII, pp. 42–3, no. 21.

Bibliography: Kolloff 1872, p. 718, no. 12; Seibt 1891, p. 58; Servolini 1932, p. 107; Paris and Rotterdam 1965–66, no. 48; Karpinski 1983, p. 48; Siena 1980, no. 90 (text by N. Fargnoli); Ciampolini 2010, vol. 1, pp. 124–5.

135

Andrea Andreani, after Beccafumi

The Sacrifice of Isaac

1586

Chiaroscuro woodcut printed from five sets of four blocks, the tone blocks in grey, on ten sheets of paper

73.5 × 169.5 cm

Inscribed (lower left): *Al Ser.m^{o} S.^{re} il Sr Franc.^{o} M.^{a} della Rovere / Duca d'Vrb.^{o} etc. / Fra le nobiliss.^{e} pitture di chiaroscuro ch'adornano il marmo/ reo Pavim.^{to} del Duomo di Siena, v'ha quella del figlio d'Abra.^{o} / offerto in sacrificio: inventione di D.nico Beccafumi pittore / Sanese: la qle Andrea Andriani da Mantoua ha ridotto / in q.a breve forma: riponendo intorno ad essa tutte le forze del suo / ingegno: cosi come con tutto l'affetto del cuore la dona, e dedi / ca al chiariss.^{o} nome di V.A. che per l'egregie sue virtù viverà / glorioso, mentre havrà vita il mondo. In Siena a di xij di / Novembre. M.D.Lxxxvj.*

Albertina, Vienna, DG24089–90

B. XII, pp. 22–4, no. 4.

Bibliography: Baglione 1649, p. 395; Kolloff 1872, pp. 716–17, no. 3; Seibt 1891, pp. 57–8; Pittaluga 1930, p. 254; Servolini 1932, p. 107; Siena 1980, no. 86 (text by N. Fargnoli); Goldfarb 1981, pp. 325–6; Karpinski 1983, pp. 14–15; Lincoln 2000, p. 50; Bury 2001, no. 161; Matile 2003, pp. 166–7; Boorsch 2008–09, p. 48, cat. 13.

136

Andrea Andreani, after Alessandro Casolani

Woman Contemplating a Skull

c. 1591

Chiaroscuro woodcut printed from four blocks, the tone blocks in reddish brown and brown

28.4 × 21.2 cm

Inscribed (lower left corner): *P. Vischer* [in pen and ink]

Collection of Georg Baselitz

B. XII, pp. 148–9, no. 14.

Bibliography: Kolloff 1872, pp. 723–4, no. 35; Seibt 1891, p. 59; Reichel 1926, p. 59; Pittaluga 1930, p. 254; Servolini 1932, p. 108; Weimar 1957, no. 50; Paris and Rotterdam 1965–66, nos 64–5; Vienna 1966, no. 223; Siena 1980, no. 89; Goldfarb 1981, p. 327; Karpinski 1983, p. 250; Bury 2001, no. 160; Rome, Weimar and Munich 2001–03, cat. 40 (text by D. Graf); Fischer 2001, p. 262, under cat. 181; Tokyo 2005, no. 68; Ciampolini 2010, vol. 1, p. 124, pl. 83.

137
Andrea Andreani, after Alessandro Casolani
The Lamentation of Christ
1593
Chiaroscuro woodcut printed from four sets of four blocks, the tone blocks in brown, on thirteen sheets of paper
174.8 × 119.8 cm
Inscribed (lower left corner): *Vincentio Gonzagae Mantuae, et / Montisferrati duci Sereniẞimo etc / Ab Alexandro Casulano Senensi lineis co / loribusq. Ductum opus, domi Octavij Prenati / Canonici ab Andrea vero Andriano / Mantuano varijs novisq. Ligneis formis in= / cisum ac intimo cordis affectu dicatum. / Senis M·D·XCIII·; labels on verso inscribed: F. Gawet 1822* [in pen and ink] Vienna, Albertina, DG24096–97

Bibliography: Baglione 1649, p. 395; Kolloff 1872, p. 718, no. 15; Siena 1980, no. 91; Karpinski 2001, p. 40; Bury 2001, p. 213; Boorsch 2008–09, p. 48, fig. 10; Ciampolini 2010, vol. 1, p. 124.

Andrea Andreani, after Mantegna
The Triumphs of Caesar
1599

138.0
Title page with a portrait of Mantegna and dedication
Chiaroscuro woodcut printed from four blocks, the tone blocks in yellow ochre and brown
39.4 × 37.2 cm
Inscribed: *SER.mo PRINCIPI VINCĒTIO GŌ ZAGÆ.D.G / MANTVÆ AC MONTIS FERRATI OPTIMO DVCI / TABVLÆ TRVNPHI CÆSARIS. OLIM NVTV ECCELSI FRANCISCI GONZAGÆ INCLITÆ / VRBIS MANTVÆ TVNC MARCHIONIS. IIIJ. PROPE D.SEBASTIANI ÆDES, IN MAIORI EIVS / AVLA, AB ANDREA MANTINEA MANTVANO EA.DILIGENTIA PICTÆ, VT IAM PER ANNOS / SVPRA CENTVM, NON SOLVM INCOLARVM, VERVMETIĀ EX VARIIS ORBIS PARTIBVS, / ADVENARVM OCVLOS TANQUĀM MIRABILE QVODDAM AD SVI INSPECTIONEM ATTRA- / HANT, QVEMADMODVM NON SOLVM OPVS IPSŪ ADHVC OSTENDIT, VERŪETIAM GEOR- / GII VASARII HISTORICI IN VITIS PICTORVM TESTIMONIO COMPROBATVR. / ANDREAS ANDRIANVS PARITER MANTVANVS, QVO ABSENTIVM VOLVNTATI, MELIO- / RI QVA POSSET RATIONE SATISFACERET, ET MVNICIPIS TANTI VIRI FAMA LATVIS PER / ORA VIRVM ET COMMODIVS VOLITARET. IDCIRCO HIS TYPIS LIGNEIS NOVA SVAR / FORMAR ADŪBRATIŌE INCISIT, TVÆQ CELSITVDINIS INVICTO NOMINI OMNIVM VIR- / TVTIS AMATORVM AVGVSTO MECÆNATI, QVOD IPSVM A SENARVM ETIAM SI CARA / SIBI VRBE, AD PATRIĀ BENIGNE REVOCAVERIS, QVOD ET AD OPVS PERFICIENDVM ET AD / VICTVM NECESSARIA, SPONTE, ATQ ABVNDANTISSIME SVPPEDITAVERIS MAXIMA / HVMILITATE DICAVIT. / VTINĀ NOVVS HAC ÆTATE VIRIBVS, ET ANIMO CÆSAR, SICVTI PAR EST, / IMPERIO NOVO, NOVISQ POTIARE TRIVMPHIS. / BERNAR. MALPITIVS PICT. MANT. F. MANTVAE. M.DXCVIIII.*
Collection of Georg Baselitz
B. XII, pp. 103–4.

Bibliography: Kolloff 1872, p. 722, no. 32; Reichel 1926, p. 36; Paris and Rotterdam 1965–66, no. 59; Vienna 1966, p. 142; Martindale 1979, p. 187, Doc. 33; Goldfarb 1981, p. 327; Karpinski 1983, p. 156; Lincoln 2000, p. 45; Rome, Weimar and Munich 2001–03, cat. 41; Matile 2003, p. 167; Tokyo 2005, no. 69a; Boorsch 2008–09, p. 48, cat. 12.

138.1
Andrea Andreani, after Mantegna
Trumpeters, bearers of standards and banners ('The Trumpeters')
Chiaroscuro woodcut printed from four blocks, the tone blocks in yellowish brown and brown
39.8 × 38.7 cm
Collection of Georg Baselitz
B. XII, p. 101, no. 11, 1.

138.2
Andrea Andreani, after Mantegna
Captured statues and siege equipment, a representation of a captured city and inscriptions ('The Triumphal Carts')
Chiaroscuro woodcut printed from four blocks, the tone blocks in yellowish brown and brown
38.7 × 39.9 cm
Collection of Georg Baselitz
B. XII, p. 101, no. 11, 2.

138.3
Andrea Andreani, after Mantegna
Trophies and bearers of coins and vases ('The Trophy Bearers')
Chiaroscuro woodcut printed from four blocks, the tone blocks in yellowish brown and brown
39.5 × 38.5 cm
Collection of Georg Baselitz
B. XII, pp. 101–2, no. 11, 3.

138.4
Andrea Andreani, after Mantegna
Bearers of coins and vases, youths leading oxen, trumpeters ('The Vase Bearers')
Chiaroscuro woodcut printed from four blocks, the tone blocks in yellowish brown and brown
38.9 × 38.3 cm
Collection of Georg Baselitz
B. XII, p. 102, no. 11, 4.

138.5
Andrea Andreani, after Mantegna
Trumpeters, youths leading oxen, elephants with attendants ('The Elephants')
Chiaroscuro woodcut printed from four blocks, the tone blocks in yellowish brown and brown
39.3 × 38.3 cm
Collection of Georg Baselitz
B. XII, p. 102, no. 11, 5.

138.6
Andrea Andreani, after Mantegna
Bearers of coins and plate, trophies of royal armour ('The Corselet Bearers')
Chiaroscuro woodcut printed from four blocks, the tone blocks in yellowish brown and brown
39.6 × 38.5 cm
Collection of Georg Baselitz
B. XII, p. 102, no. 11, 6.

138.7
Andrea Andreani, after Mantegna
Captives, musicians ('The Captives')
Chiaroscuro woodcut printed from four blocks, the tone blocks in yellowish brown and brown
39.2 × 38.5 cm; same image on verso, printed from the line block and one tone block
Collection of Georg Baselitz
B. XII, p. 102, no. 11, 7.

138.8
Andrea Andreani, after Mantegna
Musicians and standard bearers ('The Musicians')
Chiaroscuro woodcut printed from four blocks, the tone blocks in yellowish brown and brown
39.2 × 38.3 cm
Collection of Georg Baselitz
B. XII, p. 102, no. 11, 8.

138.9
Andrea Andreani, after Mantegna
Julius Caesar on his Chariot
Chiaroscuro woodcut printed from four blocks, the tone blocks in yellowish brown and brown
39 × 38.3 cm
Collection of Georg Baselitz
B. XII, pp. 102–3, no. 11, 9.

Bibliography: Baglione 1649, p. 395; Portheim 1886, pp. 278–80; Seibt 1891, pp. 59–60; Kolloff 1872, pp. 722–3, no. 32; Kristeller 1902, p. 293, n. 1, p. 462; Reichel 1926, pp. 36–7; Pittaluga 1930, p. 254; Servolini 1932, pp. 108–14; Paris and Rotterdam 1965–66, no. 60; Vienna 1966, nos 226–8; Stanford 1978, no. 173 (text by M. S. Sopher); Martindale 1979, passim; Goldfarb 1981, pp. 327–8; London 1981–82, no. 71 (text by R. Signorini); Karpinski 1983, pp. 157–65; Lincoln 2000, pp. 45–6; Karpinski 2001; Rome, Weimar and Munich 2001–03, cat. 42–50 (text by D. Graf); Tokyo 2005, no. 69,b,k; Arlt 2005, pp. 66–7; Boorsch 2008–09, p. 48, cat. 12; Paris 2010, no. 11 (text by P. Fuhring); Innsbruck 2011, under cat. 2.1 (text by V. Sandbichler).

138.10
Andrea Andreani, after Mantegna
Seven cut-out pilasters for *The Triumphs of Caesar*
1598
Chiaroscuro woodcut printed from two blocks, the tone block in brown (five central pilasters), and from three blocks, the tone blocks in yellow and brown (two outer pilasters); Andreani's view of Mantua, 1607, on versos of the two outer pilasters each approx.
37.5 × 80 cm
Collection of Georg Baselitz
B. XII, p. 104.

Bibliography: Kolloff 1872, p. 723; Kristeller 1902, p. 293, n. 1; Reichel 1926, p. 36; Karpinski 1983, p. 166; Karpinski 2001.

Endnotes

The Chiaroscuro Woodcut: An Introduction

Achim Gnann

1 In rare cases an engraving or etching can take the place of the line block (cats 41–3, 86, 87).
2 Vasari 1878–85, vol. 1, pp. 212–13.
3 Vasari 1878–85, vol. 5, p. 357; Borghini 1584, p. 109; Armenini 1587, ch. 7, p. 54.
4 Loedel 1863, pp. 5–6; Landau and Parshall 1994, pp. 179–87.
5 Seibt 1891, pp. 17–18; Jecmen 2012–14, p. 68.
6 Schottenloher 1922, comp. fig. VI; Gräff 1910, p. 336; Stijnman 2011, p. 9.
7 Schottenloher 1922, fig. p. 1.
8 Schottenloher 1922, fig. p. 2.
9 Schottenloher 1922, fig. p. 14.
10 Falk 1968, pp. 13–21; Augsburg 1973, nos 1, 3, 5.
11 Reichel 1926, p. 10.
12 Reichel 1926, pp. 39–40.

Georg Baselitz and the Collecting of Prints

David Ekserdjian

1 See Krautheimer and Krautheimer-Hess 1970, vol. 1, p. 305, for Ghiberti's collection, with further references.
2 Vasari 1986, p. 258, and Vasari 1878–85, vol. 2, pp. 245–6.
3 Bober and Rubinstein 1986, p. 127, no. 94, and Kruft 1983, pp. 605–7.
4 Bober and Rubinstein 1986, p. 127, no. 94, where it is listed as 'owner unknown (formerly J. Hewitt)'.
5 See Krautheimer and Krautheimer-Hess 1970, vol. 2, pp. 337–52, Appendix A, for a 'Handlist of Antiques' from which Ghiberti drew inspiration.
6 Ragghianti Collobi 1974.
7 Gregory 2012, esp. ch. 3, 'Vasari's use of prints as aides-mémoires', pp. 133–60.
8 Müller-Hofstede 1989.
9 Wood 2010–11.
10 See respectively Penny 2008, pp. 206–35, esp. p. 222, and Ingamells 1985, pp. 348–60, esp. p. 357.
11 Lugt (1921), pp. 387–9.
12 See Newman 1986, pp. 344–54, and Ekserdjian 1998, pp. 28–9, for an exception.
13 Hilaire 2003 and Paris 1960. Degas, for whom see New York 1997–98, was an exception.
14 Bernadec 1991 and http://www.nationalgallery.org.uk/lucian-freud-says-thank-you-to-the-nation-with-a-corot-painting, 4 February 2013.
15 Goethe 1981, p. 145.
16 Hocke 1957.
17 In Germany it used to be customary to list the cumulative number of copies of a book in an edition: my copy of *Die Welt as Labyrinth*, which was published in June 1963, belongs in the 41,000–45,000 bracket.
18 Shearman 1967. Hocke's study is listed there on p. 208, in the bibliography.
19 Ekserdjian 2006, pp. 190–211, esp. p. 193, fig. 201.
20 Franklin 1994, p. 61, fig. 43, and Berti 1973, plate LV.
21 Zerner 1969 remains the fundamental work on the subject and is a great favourite of Baselitz's.
22 Geneva 2002, p. 323.
23 Munich and Frankfurt 2007–08.
24 Munich and Frankfurt 2007–08, pp. 30–2, no. 1.
25 London 1985.
26 Boerner and Stogdon 2012, no. 12.
27 Luijten 1994 and Geneva 2002, esp. Nathalie Strasser, 'Paramètres maniéristes: Facettes d'une collection', pp. 308–23, for Baselitz as a collector.
28 'Author's Foreword', in Auden 2007, p. xxx.
29 Monbeig Goguel 1988 and Pestilli 2013, p. 159, for Bernardo De Dominici's account of Paolo De Matteis (1662–1728) touching up drawings by Correggio.
30 Washington, Mexico City and San Francisco 1997–98, pp. 42–3, figs 26 and 27.
31 Luijten 1994, pp. 267–79, nos 98–103, which represent five of Possenti's seven known prints.
32 '[Q]uasi un uomo salvatico'; Vasari 1878–85, vol. 5, p. 233.
33 Vasari 1878–85, vol. 5, p. 173.
34 See Ekserdjian 2006, p. 222 and fig. 239, for a suggestion that it does not represent Narcissus, nor indeed any specific subject.

I Beginnings: Lucas Cranach in Wittenberg and Hans Burgkmair in Augsburg

1 Buff 1892, no. 8560. For Peutinger, see Herberger 1851; Chmelarz 1894, p. 393; Pfeiffer 1955; and Falk 1968, pp. 45–7, 81.
2 Reichel 1926, p. 15. Cranach probably undertook his experiments with printing in gold and silver at Peutinger's instigation. In a letter to Duke Georg of Saxony Peutinger mentions having sent the ducal court a copy of his book *Romanae vetustatis fragmenta*, printed by Ratdolt in Augsburg in 1505 and containing a collection of inscriptions from the city printed in gold. Buff 1892, no. 8561.
3 Landau and Parshall 1994, fig. 197.
4 Landau and Parshall 1994, fig. 198.
5 Winkelbauer 1954.
6 For de Negker, see Herberger 1851, pp. 58–9; Seibt 1891, p. 29; Chmelarz 1894, p. 394; Dodgson 1898, p. 378; Friedländer 1925, p. 2; Reichel 1926, pp. 18–22; Berlin 1974, pp. 38–9 (text by Renate Kroll); Falk 1973; Landau and Parshall 1994, pp. 200–1 and 211, n. 55.
7 Landau and Parshall 1994, figs 203, 205.
8 Flechsig 1900, pp. 23–43.
9 Landau and Parshall, 1994, p. 192, point out that, although this form of the coat of arms was added later to some woodcuts by Cranach dated 1506, no evidence of an alteration of this kind has been found in copies of St Christopher and Venus and Cupid.
10 Washington and Boston 1983, cat. 133.
11 Falk 1968, p. 61. It will be remembered that Erhard Ratdolt, whom Burgkmair provided with some designs for liturgical woodcuts, had begun using colour printing in books in Venice twenty-two years earlier.
12 Buff 1892, no. 8594.
13 However, mention should be made of a portrait of Emperor Maximilian executed after a design of 1518 by Dürer. This exists in four versions. The first state of the second version, attributed to de Negker, includes printing in gold from a tone block. See Schoch, Mende and Scherbaum 2002, p. 456 (text by D. Eichberger). The tone block has survived in the Albertina (HO2006/668), where it was discovered by Christof Metzger.

II Strasbourg: Hans Wechtlin and Hans Baldung Grien

1 Bartrum 1995, pp. 66–7; Klein 2006–07, vol. 1, pp. 87–8.
2 Buff 1892, no. 8575.
3 Gustav Radbruch has shown that belief in witches was widespread in the city's humanist circles and among its high-ranking clergy. *Hexenhammer* (Witch Hammer), which described witch trials that had taken place in various towns in Alsace, was published for the first time in Strasbourg, in 1487. In addition, the sermons attacking witchcraft collected in *Die Emeis* (The Ant), which appeared there in 1516, were probably the work of the popular local preacher Johannes Geiler von Kaisersberg, for whom Baldung created a number of woodcuts. The subject was clearly much discussed in the city. Thus the ground was well prepared for Baldung's woodcut. Radbruch 1950.

III The Chiaroscuro Woodcut Elsewhere in the German-speaking World

1 A further work should be mentioned in this context: a chiaroscuro woodcut of *Christ on the Mount of Olives* by Hans Schäufelein, possibly produced *c.* 1510 in Augsburg and known in only a single impression (British Museum, London, 1917-7-14-8). Bartrum 1995, no. 152.
2 Quoted in Panofsky 1955, p. 44.
3 Pauli 1901, no. 687.
4 Goetze 1893, pp. 112–13, no. 34.

IV Beginnings in Italy: Ugo da Carpi

1 '[H]avendo io trovato modo di stampare chiaro et scuro, cosa nova, et mai più non fatta'. Quoted in Carpi 2009, p. 182, no. 37.
2 Strauss 1973, p. XII, and, most recently, Roeck 2013, pp. 42–52.

V Ugo da Carpi's Pupils and Followers

1 Kolloff 1878. The oeuvre proposed by Kolloff has lost next to none of its validity.
2 Vasari 1878–85, vol. 5, p. 421.
3 Gnann 2007, nos 203–12, 411–12, 414.
4 Gnann 2007, nos 715–17. The woodcut's immediate model has not survived.
5 Vasari 1878–85, vol. 5, p. 227.
6 Vasari 1878–85, vol. 5, pp. 422–3.
7 For a different opinion, see Johnson 1982, p. 4, and Matile 2003, p. 132, n. 303.
8 Karpinski 1983, fig. p. 144.

VI Domenico Beccafumi

1 Vienna 1966, p. 132.
2 Siena 1990, figs pp. 196–7, 670.

VII Cremona and Bologna

1 Cremona 1985, nos 3.2–4, 3.6–7.
2 Cremona 1985, no. 3.8.
3 Johnson 2013.
4 With one exception, the print exists only in copies of a second edition, issued by Andreani in 1610. The Rijksprentenkabinet in Amsterdam possesses an early impression taken from the darker tone block (Johnson 2013, fig. 5).
5 Popham 1971, p. 266. The inventory is of the collection of Cavaliere Francesco Baiardo, a friend of Parmigianino, who owned 495 drawings and various paintings by the artist.
6 Gnann 2007, no. 522.
7 Trotter 1974, pp. 120–4, and Johnson 2013.
8 Karpinski 1976.
9 Jenkins 2013.
10 Paris 2012–13, pp. 101–2, fig. 28.
11 Washington 1987–88, no. 114.
12 Zerner 1969, J.M. 39.
13 Mantua and Vienna 1999, no. 116.

VIII Germany and the Netherlands in the Second Half of the Sixteenth Century

1 Appuhn 1976, fig. 65; Maierbacher-Legl 1997, figs 77, 78a.
2 Geisberg 1930, nos 838, 1307, 1331. For Lorenz Stoer, see Wood 2003.
3 An artist from the German-speaking world not represented here who must be mentioned is Tobias Stimmer, who produced a pair of chiaroscuro woodcuts showing Ecclesia and Synagoga after the Gothic sculptures at the south portal of Strasbourg Minster. Stimmer's designs, dating from *c.* 1571–74, were carried out by Bernhard Jobin, a local woodcutter, printer and publisher. Basle 1984, nos 147–8 (text by P. Tanner).
4 Strauss 1973, no. 100. The existence of an impression in the Albertina, mentioned by Strauss, could not be confirmed.
5 Konrad Oberhuber, in Vienna 1967–68, p. 101.
6 Amsterdam and Cleveland 1992–93, p. 38.
7 Amsterdam and Cleveland 1992–93, no. 2.
8 Vienna 1967–68, pp. 90–1.
9 Reichel 1926, p. 44.
10 Ames 1949, pp. 429–30.
11 Amsterdam and Cleveland 1992–93, no. 23 Ia.

IX Developments in Italy

1 Matile 2003, p. 60.
2 Most recently discussed in Madrid 2012, no. 12.
3 Zezza 2003, p. 255, n. 48.
4 Stechow 1967, Hirschboek 2010, pp. 22–8.

Bibliography

Alten 1943
Wilken von Alten, 'Unbekannte Meisterzeichnungen in der Bremer Kunsthalle', *Die Wittheit zu Bremen*, no. 5, 1943, pp. 12–19.

Ames 1949
Winslow Ames, 'Some Woodcuts by Hendrick Goltzius and their Program', *Gazette des Beaux-Arts*, vol. 91, 1949, pp. 425–36.

Amsterdam and Cleveland 1992–93
Chiaroscuro Woodcuts: Hendrick Goltzius (1558–1617) and His Time, Nancy Bialler, exh. cat., Rijksprentenkabinet, Rijksmuseum, Amsterdam, and The Cleveland Museum of Art, Cleveland, OH, 1992–93.

Amsterdam, New York and Toledo 2003–04
Hendrick Goltzius (1558–1617): Drawings, Prints and Paintings, Huigen Leeflang and Ger Luijten, exh. cat., Rijksmuseum, Amsterdam; The Metropolitan Museum of Art, New York; and The Toldeo Museum of Art, Toledo, 2003–04.

Appuhn 1976
Horst Appuhn, 'V. Papiertapeten, Riesenholzschnitte und ihre Verwendung im 16. Jahrhundert', in idem and Christian von Heusinger, *Riesenholzschnitte und Papiertapeten der Renaissance*, Unterschneidheim, 1976, pp. 87–103.

Arlt 2005
Thomas Arlt, *Andrea Mantegnas Triumph Caesars: Ein Meisterwerk der Renaissance in neuem Licht*, Vienna, Cologne and Weimar, 2005.

Armenini 1587
Giovanni Battista Armenini, *De' veri precetti della pittura*, Ravenna, 1587.

Artioli 1901
Romeolo Artioli, 'Arte Retrospettiva: Sesta Esposizione del Gabinetto delle Stampe a Romea', *Emporium*, vol. 13, 1901, pp. 117–30.

Auden 2007
W. H. Auden, *Collected Poems*, Edward Mendelson (ed.), London, 2007.

Augsburg 1973
Hans Burgkmair 1473–1973: Das graphische Werk, Tilman Falk et al., exh. cat., Städtische Kunstsammlungen, Augsburg, 1973.

B.
Adam von Bartsch, *Le Peintre-graveur*, 23 vols, Leipzig, 1843–76.

Baglione 1649
Giovanni Baglione, *Le Vite De' Pittori Scultori et Architetti dal Pontificato di Gregorio XIII fino a tutto quello d'Urbano VIII*, Rome, 1649, facsimile with commentary and index, Costanza Gradara Pesci (ed.), Velletri, 1924.

Baltimore and Saint Louis 2003
Painted Prints: The Revelation of Color in Northern Renaissance & Baroque Engravings, Etchings & Woodcuts, Susan Dackerman with Thomas Primeau and Deborah Carton, exh. cat., The Baltimore Museum of Art and Saint Louis Museum of Art, 2013.

Bartrum 1995
Giulia Bartrum, *German Renaissance Prints 1490–1550*, London, 1995.

Baseggio 1844
Giambattista Baseggio, *Intorno Tre Celebri Intagliatori in Legno Vicentini*, 2nd edn, Bassano, 1844.

Basle 1974
Lukas Cranach: Gemälde, Zeichnungen, Druckgraphik, Dieter Koepplin and Tilman Falk, exh. cat., 2 vols, Kunstmuseum, Basle, 1974.

Basle 1984
Tobias Stimmer 1539–1584, Dieter Koepplin and Paul Tanner (eds), exh. cat., Kunstmuseum, Basle, 1984.

Berlin 1971
Tizian und sein Kreis: 50 venezianische Holzschnitte aus dem Berliner Kupferstichkabinett Staatliche Museen Preussischer Kulturbesitz, Peter Dreyer, exh. cat., Kupferstichkabinett, Staatliche Museen Preussischer Kulturbesitz, Berlin, n.d. [1971].

Berlin 1974
Hans Burgkmair, 1473–1531: Holzschnitte, Zeichnungen, Holzstöcke, Renate Kroll and Werner Schade, exh. cat., Altes Museum, Berlin, 1974.

Berlin 1979
Manierismus in Holland um 1600: Kupferstiche, Holzschnitte und Zeichnungen aus dem Berliner Kupferstichkabinett, Hans Mielke, exh. cat., Kupferstichkabinett, Museen Preussischer Kulturbesitz, Berlin, 1979.

Berlin 2006
Dürers Mutter: Schönheit, Alter und Tod im Bild der Renaissance, Michael Roth with Uta Barbara Ullrich, exh. cat., Kupferstichkabinett, Staatliche Museen zu Berlin, 2006.

Bernadec 1991
Marie-Laure Bernadac, *Musée Picasso: Les Chefs-d'oeuvre*, Paris, 1991.

Berti 1973
Luciano Berti, *L'opera completa del Pontormo*, Milan, 1973.

Bober and Rubinstein 1986
Phyllis P. Bober and Ruth Rubinstein, *Renaissance Artists and Antique Sculpture: A Handbook of Sources*, London, 1986.

Boerner and Stogdon 2012
C. G. Boerner with N. G. Stogdon, *The Breinin Collection: From Schongauer to Picasso*, Düsseldorf and New York, 2012.

Boorsch 2008–09
Suzanne Boorsch, 'The Oversize Print in Italy', in *Grand Scale: Monumental Prints in the Age of Dürer and Titian*, Larry Silver, Suzanne Boorsch, Stephen Goddard and Alison Stewart, exh. cat., Davis Museum and Cultural Center, Wellesley College; Yale University Art Gallery, New Haven, CT; and Philadelphia Museum of Art, 2008–09, pp. 35–51.

Borghini 1584
Raffaello Borghini, *Il Riposo*, Florence, 1584.

Boston 1989
Italian Etchers of the Renaissance & Baroque, Sue Welsh Reed, Richard Wallace et al., exh. cat., Museum of Fine Arts, Boston, 1989.

Braunschweig 1973
Burgkmair und die graphische Kunst der deutschen Renaissance: Ausstellung aus Anlass des 500. Geburtstages Hans Burgkmairs, Christian von Heusinger, exh. cat., Kupferstichkabinett, Herzog Anton Ulrich-Museum, Braunschweig, 1973.

Braunschweig 2003–04
Von Cranach bis Baselitz: Meisterwerke des Clairobscur-Holzschnitts, Claus Kemmer and Jochen Köhn, exh. cat., Herzog Anton Ulrich-Museum, Braunschweig, 2003–04.

Bruillot 1832
François Brulliot, *Dictionaire des Monogrammes, Marques figurées, Lettres Initiales, Noms Abrégés etc.*, vol. 1, Munich, 1832.

Brussels and Paris 2010–11
Die Welt des Lucas Cranach: Ein Künstler im Zeitalter von Dürer, Tizian und Metsys, exh. cat., Guido Messling, Palais des Beaux-Art, Brussels, and Musée du Luxembourg, Musée du Sénat de la République française, Paris, 2010–11.

Budapest 2009–10
The Alchemy of Beauty: Parmigianino – Drawings and Prints, Zoltán Kárpáti with Eszter Seres, exh. cat., Museum of Fine Arts, Budapest, 2009–10.

Buff 1892
Adolf Buff (ed.), 'Rechnungsauszüge, Urkunden und Urkundenregesten aus dem Augsburger Stadtarchive: Erster Theil (von 1442–1519)', *Jahrbuch der Kunsthistorischen Sammlungen des Allerhöchsten Kaiserhauses*, vol. 13, 1892, pp. XIIII–LLXXIV.

Burkhard 1932
Arthur Burkhard, *Hans Burgkmair d. Ä.*, Meister der Graphik, vol. 15, Hermann Voss (ed.), Berlin, 1932.

Bury 2001
Michael Bury, *The Print in Italy 1550–1620*, London, 2001.

Cambridge and Evanston 2011–12
Prints and the Pursuit of Knowledge in Early Modern Europe, Susan Dackerman (ed.), exh. cat., The Harvard Art Museum, Cambridge, MA, and The Mary and Leigh Block Museum of Art, Northwestern University, Evanston, IL, 2011–12.

Carpi 2009
Ugo da Carpi: l'opera incisa – xilografie e chiaroscuri da Tiziano, Raffaello e Parmigianino, M. Rossi, exh. cat., Loggia di primo ordine di Palazzo dei Pio, Carpi, 2009.

Chmelarz 1894
August Chmelarz, 'Jost de Negker's Helldunkelblätter Kaiser Max und St. Georg', *Jahrbuch der Kunsthistorischen Sammlungen des Allerhöchsten Kaiserhauses*, vol. 15, 1894, pp. 392–7.

Ciampolini 2010
Marco Ciampolini, *Pittori senesi del Seicento*, 3 vols, Siena, 2010.

Cleveland and Yale 1978
The Graphic Art of Federico Barocci: Selected Drawings and Prints, Edmund S. Pillsbury and Louise S. Richards, exh. cat., The Cleveland Museum of Art, OH, and Yale University Art Gallery, New Haven, CT, 1978.

Coburg 1972
Lucas Cranach d. Ä 1472–1553: Graphik, Heino Maedebach, exh. cat., Kupferstichkabinett, Kunstsammlungen Veste Coburg, 1972.

Copertini 1932
Giovanni Copertini, *Il Parmigianino*, 2 vols, Parma, 1932.

Cremona 1985
I Campi e la cultura artistica cremonese del Cinquecento, exh. cat., Santa Maria della Pietà, Vecchio Ospedale, Museo Civico and Sala Manfredini, Cremona, 1985.

Curjel 1923
Hans Curjel, *Hans Baldung Grien*, Munich, 1923.

De Klerck 1999
Bram De Klerck, *The Brothers Campi: Images and Devotion – Religious Painting in Sixteenth-century Lombardy*, Amsterdam, 1999.

De Marchi 1990
Andrea De Marchi, 'Beccafumi e la sua "maniera": difficoltà del disegno senese', in Siena 1990, pp. 412–25.

Delen 1935
Adrien Jean Joseph Delen, *Histoire de la gravure dans les anciens Pays-Bas & dans les Provinces Belges des origines jusqu 'à la fin du XVIIIe siècle*, Paris, 1935.

Dodgson 1898
Campbell Dodgson, 'Zu Jost de Negker', *Repertorium für Kunstwissenschaft*, vol. 21, 1898, pp. 377–81.

Dodgson 1903a
Campbell Dodgson, 'Fünf unbeschriebene Holzschnitte Lucas Cranachs', *Jahrbuch der Königlich Preussischen Kunstsammlungen*, vol. 24, 1903, pp. 284–90.

Dodgson 1903b
Campbell Dodgson, *Early German and Flemish Woodcuts Preserved in the Department of Prints and Drawings in the British Museum*, vol. 1, London, 1903.

Dodgson 1903c
Campbell Dodgson, 'Hans Sebald Beham and a New Catalogue of his Works', *The Burlington Magazine*, vol. 1, no. 2, April 1903, pp. 189–201.

Dodgson 1911
Campbell Dodgson, *Catalogue of Early German and Flemish Woodcuts Preserved in the Department of Prints and Drawings in the British Museum*, vol. 2, London, 1911.

Dreyer 1972
Peter Dreyer, 'Ugo da Carpis venezianische Zeit im Lichte neuer Zuschreibungen', *Zeitschrift für Kunstgeschichte*, vol. 35, 1972, pp. 282–301.

Edinburgh 1994
Raphael: The Pursuit of Perfection, Aidan Weston-Lewis with Timothy Clifford and John Dick, exh. cat., National Gallery of Scotland, Edinburgh, 1994.

Edinburgh, London and Vienna 1978–79a
Giambologna 1524–1608: Sculptor to the Medici, Charles Avery, Anthony Radcliffe and Manfred Leithe-Jasper (eds), exh. cat., Royal Scottish Museum, Edinburgh; Victoria and Albert Museum, London; and Kunsthistorisches Museum, Vienna, 1978–79.

Edinburgh, London and Vienna 1978–79b
Giambologna 1524–1608: Ein Wendepunkt der europäischen Plastik, Charles Avery, Anthony Radcliffe and Manfred Leithe-Jasper (eds), exh. cat., Royal Scottish Museum, Edinburgh; Victoria and Albert Museum, London; and Kunsthistorisches Museum, Vienna, 1978–79.

Ekserdjian 1998
David Ekserdjian, 'A Portrait by Lely and a Drawing after Correggio: An Artist's Use of His Collection of Drawings', *Apollo*, vol. 142, no. 435, May 1998, pp. 28–9.

Ekserdjian 2006
David Ekserdjian, *Parmigianino*, New Haven, CT, and London, 2006.

Ekserdjian 2008
David Ekserdjian, 'Two Drawings by Parmigianino for Prints', *Master Drawings*, vol. 46, no. 3, autumn 2008, pp. 367–73.

Emison 1985
Patricia Anne Emison, 'Invention and the Italian Renaissance Print, Mantegna to Parmigianino', Ph.D. thesis, Columbia University, New York, 1985.

Fagiolo dell' Arco 1970
Maurizio Fagiolo dell' Arco, *Il Parmigianino, un saggio sull'ermetismo nel Cinquecento*, Rome, 1970.

Falk 1968
Tilman Falk, *Hans Burgkmair: Studien zu Leben und Werk des Augsburger Malers*, Munich, 1968.

Falk 1973
Tilman Falk, 'Hans Burgkmair und seine Graphik', in Augsburg 1973, n.p.

Falk 1980
Tilman Falk, *Sixteenth Century Artists: Hans Burgkmair the Elder, Hans Schäufelein, Lucas Cranach the Elder*, The Illustrated Bartsch, vol. 11 (formerly vol. 7, part 2), New York, 1980.

Fischer 2001
Chris Fischer, *Italian Drawings in the Department of Prints and Drawings, Statens Museum for Kunst: Central Italian Drawings – Schools of Florence, Siena, the Marches and Umbria*, Copenhagen, 2001.

Flechsig 1900
Eduard Flechsig, *Cranachstudien, erster Teil*, Leipzig, 1900.

Florence 1956
Mostra di chiaroscuri italiani dei secoli XVI, XVII, XVIII, Maria Fossi, exh. cat., Gabinetto Disegni e Stampe degli Uffizi, Florence, 1956.

Florence 1966
Mostra di Disegni degli Zuccari: Taddeo e Federico Zuccari, e Raffaellino da Reggio, John A. Gere, exh. cat., Gabinetti Disegni e Stampe degli Uffizi, Florence, 1966.

Francis 1953
Henry Sayles Francis, 'Woodcuts by Hans Wechtlin', *The Bulletin of the Cleveland Museum of Art*, vol. 40, no. 2, pt 1, February 1953, pp. 30–2.

Frankfurt 1980
Städel: Italienische Zeichnungen des 15. und 16. Jahrhunderts aus eigenen Beständen, Lutz S. Malke, exh. cat., Städelsches Kunstinstitut und Städtische Galerie, Frankfurt am Main, 1980.

Frankfurt 2007
Hexenlust und Sündenfall: Die seltsamen Phantasien des Hans Baldung Grien, Bodo Brinkmann with Bertholde Hinz, exh. cat., Städel Museum, Frankfurt am Main, 2007.

Franklin 1977
Colin and Charlotte Franklin, *A Catalogue of Early Colour Printing from Chiaroscuro to Aquatint*, Oxford, 1977.

Franklin 1994
David Franklin, *Rosso in Italy: The Italian Career of Rosso Fiorentino*, New Haven, CT, and London, 1994.

Freiburg 2001–02
Hans Baldung Grien in Freiburg, Saskia Durian-Ress (ed.), exh. cat., Augustinermuseum, Freiburg im Breisgau, 2001–02.

Friedländer 1925
Max J. Friedländer, 'Burgkmairs Hl. Georg von 1508: Bemerkungen zu den Anfängen des Deutschen Tonschnitts', *Jahrbuch der Preussischen Kunstsammlungen*, vol. 46, 1925, pp. 1–2.

Frommel 1967–68
Christoph L. Frommel, 'Baldassare Peruzzi als Maler und Zeichner', *Römisches Jahrbuch für Kunstgeschichte*, vol. 11, 1967–68, suppl.

Geisberg 1930
Max Geisberg, *Der deutsche Einblatt-Holzschnitt in der ersten Hälfte des 16. Jahrhunderts: Die Gesamtverzeichnisse*, Munich, 1930.

Geisberg and Strauss 1974
Max Geisberg, *The German Single-leaf Woodcut 1500–1550*, rev. ed., Walter L. Strauss (ed.), 4 vols, New York, 1974.

Geneva 2002
Le Beau Style 1520–1620: Gravures Maniéristes de la Collection Georg Baselitz, Nathalie Strasser, Rainer Michael Mason and Georg Baselitz, exh. cat., Musée d'art et d'histoire, Geneva, 2002.

Gnann 2002
Achim Gnann, 'La collaborazione del Parmigianino con Ugo da Carpi, Niccolò Vicentino e Antonio da Trento', in *Parmigianino e il manierismo europeo: Atti del Convegno internazionale di studi*, Lucia Fornari Schianchi (ed.), Cinisello Balsamo, 2002, pp. 288–97.

Gnann 2003
'Parmigianino e la grafica', in Parma and Vienna 2003, pp. 83–91.

Gnann 2007
Achim Gnann, *Parmigianino: Die Zeichnungen*, 2 vols, Studien zur internationalen Architektur- und Kunstgeschichte, vol. 58, Petersberg, 2007.

Goethe 1981
Johann Wolfgang von Goethe, *Werke: Hamburger Ausgabe*, vol. 7, Munich, 1981.

Goetze 1893
Edmund Goetze, *Sämtliche Fabeln und Schwänke von Hans Sachs*, vol. 1, Halle, 1893.

Goldfarb 1981
Hilliard T. Goldfarb, 'Chiaroscuro Woodcut Technique and Andrea Andreani', *The Bulletin of the Cleveland Museum of Art*, vol. 67, no. 9, November 1981, pp. 307–30.

Gould 1975
Cecil Gould, *The Sixteenth-century Italian Schools*, National Gallery Catalogues, London, 1975.

Gräff 1910
Walter Gräff, 'Älteste deutsche Farbenholzschnitte', *Zeitschrift für Bücherfreunde*, n.s., vol. 1, no. 2, 1910, pp. 336–40.

Gregory 2012
Sharon Gregory, *Vasari and the Renaissance Print*, Aldershot, 2012.

H.
[Friedrich W. H. Hollstein,] *Hollstein's German Engravings, Etchings and Woodcuts, ca. 1400–1700*, 78 vols, Amsterdam, Rosendaal and Rotterdam, 1954–2010.

Hartley 1991
Craig Hartley, 'Beccafumi "glum & gloomy"', *Print Quarterly*, vol. 8, no. 4, 1991, pp. 418–25.

Hébert 1982
Michèle Hébert, *Bibliothèque nationale, Département des Estampes: Inventaire des gravures des Ecoles du Nord*, 1440–1550, vol. 1, Paris, 1982.

Heinecken 1778–90
Karl Heinrich von Heinecken, *Dictionnaire des artistes dont nous avons des estampes, avec une notice detaillée de leurs ouvrages gravés*, 4 vols, Leipzig, 1778–90.

Herberger 1851
Theodor Herberger, 'Conrad Peutinger in seinem Verhältnisse zum Kaiser Maximilian I.', *Combinierter Jahres-Bericht des historischen Kreis-Vereins für den Regierungsbezirk von Schwaben und Neuburg*, Augsburg, 1851, pp. 31–72.

Hilaire 2003
Michel Hilaire, 'The Story of a Collection', in *French Paintings from the Musée Fabre, Montpellier*, Michel Hilaire, Jörg Zutter and Olivier Zeder, exh. cat., National Gallery of Australia, Canberra, 2003, pp. 11–41.

Hind 1930
Arthur M. Hind, *Early Italian Engraving: Annual Lecture on Aspects of Art of the British Academy*, London, 1930.

Hirschboek 2010
Martin Hirschboeck, *Jacopo Ligozzi: An Allegory of Virtue*, London, 2010.

Hirschmann 1921
Otto Hirschmann, *Verzeichnis des Graphischen Werks von Hendrick Goltzius 1558–1617*, Leipzig, 1921.

Hocke 1957
Gustav René Hocke, *Die Welt as Labyrinth: Manier und Manie in der europäischen Kunst*, Hamburg, 1957.

Hult 2005
Linda C. Hult, *The Witch as Muse: Gender and Power in Early Modern Europe*, Philadelphia, 2005.

Ingamells 1985
John Ingamells, *The Wallace Collection: Catalogue of Pictures*, vol. 1: *British, German, Italian, Spanish*, London, 1985.

Innsbruck 2011
All'antica: Götter & Helden auf Schloss Ambras, Sabine Haag (ed.), exh. cat., Schloss Ambras, Innsbruck, 2011.

Jaffé 1994
Michael Jaffé, *The Devonshire Collection of Italian Drawings: Roman and Neapolitan Schools*, 4 vols, London, 1994.

Jahn 1955
Johannes Jahn, *Lucas Cranach als Graphiker*, Leipzig, 1955.

Janson 1955
Horst W. Janson, 'The Case of the Naked Chicken', *College Art Journal*, vol. 15, no. 2, winter 1955, pp. 124–7.

Jecmen 2012–14
Gregory Jecmen, 'Color Printing and Tonal Etching: Innovative Techniques in the Imperial City, 1487–1536', in *Imperial Augsburg: Renaissance Prints and Drawings 1475–1540*, Gregory Jecmen and Freyda Spira, exh. cat., National Gallery of Art, Washington; Jack S. Blanton Museum of Art, University of Texas at Austin; Frances Lehman Loeb Art Center at Vassar College, Poughkeepsie, NY, 2012–14, pp. 67–101.

Jenkins 2013
Catherine Jenkins, 'The Chiaroscuro Woodcuts of the Master ND at Fontainebleau', *Print Quarterly*, vol. 30, no. 2, 2013, pp. 131–43.

Joannides 2001
Paul Joannides, *Titian to 1518: The Assumption of Genius*, New Haven, CT, and London, 2001.

Johnson 1982
Jan Johnson, 'I chiaroscuri di Ugo da Carpi / Ugo da Carpi's Chiaroscuro Woodcuts', *Il conoscitore di stampe / Print Collector*, vols 57–8, nos 3–4, 1982, pp. 2–87.

Johnson 1987
Jan Johnson, 'States and Versions of a Chiaroscuro Woodcut', *Print Quarterly*, vol. 4, no. 2, 1987, pp. 154–8.

Johnson 2013
Jan Johnson, 'Alessandro Gandini: Uncovering the Identity of a Chiaroscuro Woodcutter', *Print Quarterly*, vol. 30, no. 1, 2013, pp. 3–13.

Jonckheere 2007
Koenraad Jonckheere, *Adriaen Thomasz. Key*, Turnhout, 2007.

Judson 1970
J. Richards Judson, *Dirck Barendsz.*, Amsterdam, 1970.

Karlsruhe 1959
Hans Baldung Grien, Jan Lauts, exh. cat., Staatliche Kunsthalle, Karlsruhe, 1959.

Karpinski 1971
Caroline Karpinski, *Le Peintre Graveur Illustré*, vol. 1: *Italian Chiaroscuro Woodcuts*, London, 1971.

Karpinksi 1976
Caroline Karpinski, 'Le Maitre ND de Bologne', *Nouvelles de l'estampe*, vol. 26, 1976, pp. 23–7.

Karpinksi 1983
Caroline Karpinski, *Italian Chiaroscuro Woodcuts*, The Illustrated Bartsch, vol. 48 (formerly vol. 12), New York, 1983.

Karpinski 2001
Caroline Karpinksi, 'Mantegna's *Triumphs* in Andreani's Form', *Apollo*, vol. 153, no. 472, June 2001, pp. 39–64.

Klein 2006–07
Alice Klein, 'Hans Wechtlin, Peintre et Graveur à Strasbourg à la veille de la Réforme', Ph.D. thesis, 2 vols, Marc Bloch Faculté d´Histoire de l'Art, Université de Strasbourg, 2006–07.

Kolloff 1872
Eduard Kolloff, 'Andrea Andreani', in *Meyer's Allgemeines Künstler-Lexikon*, vol. 1, Leipzig, 1872, pp. 715–27.

Kolloff 1878
Eduard Kolloff, 'Antonio da Trento', in *Meyer's Allgemeines Künstler-Lexikon*, vol. 2, Leipzig, 1878, pp. 149–55.

Krautheimer and Krautheimer-Hess 1970
Richard Krautheimer and Trude Krautheimer-Hess, *Lorenzo Ghiberti*, 2 vols, Princeton, 1970.

Kristeller 1902
Paul Kristeller, *Andrea Mantegna*, Berlin and Leipzig, 1902.

Kristeller 1912
Paul Kristeller, 'Carpi, Ugo da', in Ulrich Thieme and Felix Becker, *Allgemeines Lexikon der bildenden Künstler von der Antike bis zur Gegenwart*, vol. 6, Leipzig, 1912, pp. 47–9.

Kristeller 1920
Paul Kristeller, 'Gandini, Alessandro', in Ulrich Thieme and Felix Becker, *Allgemeines Lexikon der bildenden Künstler von der Antike bis zur Gegenwart*, vol. 13, Leipzig, 1920, p. 148.

Kruft 1983
Hanno-Walter Kruft, 'An Antique Model for David's "Death of Marat"', *The Burlington Magazine*, vol. 125, no. 967, October 1983, pp. 605–7.

Kultzen 1973
Rolf Kultzen, [Review of Alessandro Marabottini, *Polidoro da Caravaggio*, Rome, 1969], *The Art Bulletin*, vol. 55, no. 4, December 1973, pp. 637–9.

Landau 1991
David Landau, [Review of Siena 1990], *Print Quarterly*, vol. 8, no. 4, 1991, pp. 450–1.

Landau and Parshall 1994
David Landau and Peter Parshall, *The Renaissance Print 1470–1550*, New Haven, CT, and London, 1994.

Le Blanc
Charles Le Blanc, *Manuel de l'amateur d'estampes [...]*, 4 vols, Paris, 1854–90.

Leesberg 2012
Marjolein Leesberg, *Hendrick Goltzius*, The New Hollstein: Dutch and Flemish Etchings, Engravings and Woddcuts 1450–1700, Ger Luijten (ed.), 4 vols, Ouderkerk aan den Ijssel, 2012.

Lincoln 2000
Evelyn Lincoln, *The Invention of the Italian Renaissance Printmaker*, New Haven, CT, and London, 2000.

Lippmann 1895
Friedrich Lippmann, 'Farbenholzschnitte von Lucas Cranach', *Jahrbuch der Königlich Preussischen Kunstsammlungen*, vol. 16, 1895, pp. 138–42.

Loedel 1863
Heinrich Loedel, *Des Strassburger Malers und Formschneiders Johann Wechtlin genannt Pilgrim Holzschnitte in Clairobscur in Holz nachgeschnitten von Heinrich Loedel nebst Bemerkungen über die Erfindung des Clairobscur und die ältere Technik des Formschnitts von demselben und einem Briefe des Herrn Geh. Oberfinanzraths Sotzmann*, Leipzig, 1863.

London 1981–82
Splendours of the Gonzaga, David Chambers and Jane Martineau (eds), exh. cat., Victoria and Albert Museum, London, 1981–82.

London 1983
The Genius of Venice, 1500–1600, Jane Martineau and Charles Hope (eds), exh. cat., Royal Academy of Arts, London, 1983.

London 1985
Old Master Prints from Chatsworth, auction cat., Christie's, London, 5 December 1985.

Los Angeles et al. 1988–89
Mannerist Prints: International Style in the Sixteenth Century, Bruce Davis, exh. cat., Los Angeles County Museum of Art; The Toledo Museum of Art; John and Mable Ringling Museum of Art, Sarasota; Arthur M. Huntington Art Gallery, University of Texas at Austin; and The Baltimore Museum of Art, 1988–89.

Lugt
Frits Lugt, *Les Marques de collections de dessins et d'estampes*, Amsterdam, 1921; suppl., The Hague, 1956.

Luijten 1994
Ger Luijten (ed.), *La Bella Maniera: Druckgraphik des Manierismus aus der Sammlung Georg Baselitz*, Berne and Berlin, 1994.

Lusingh Scheurkeer 1936
Th. H. Lusingh Scheurkeer, 'Parmigianino and Boulle', *The Burlington Magazine*, vol. 68, no. 399, June 1936, pp. 287–8.

Madrid 2012
El Último Rafael, Tom Henry and Paul Joannides, exh. cat., Prado, Madrid, 2012.

Maierbacher-Legl 1997
Gerdi Maierbacher-Legl, *Truhe und Schrank: Graphisch dekorierte Möbel der süddeutschen Spätrenaissance*, Berlin, 1997.

Mantua and Vienna 1999
Romea e lo stile classico di Raffaello, Konrad Oberhuber (ed.) and Achim Gnann, exh. cat., Palazzo del Te, Mantua, and Albertina, Vienna, 1999.

Mariette 1854–56
Pierre-Jean Mariette, *Abecedario et autres notes inédites de cet amateur sur les arts et les artistes*, vol. 3, Paris, 1854–56.

Martindale 1979
Andrew Martindale, *The Triumphs of Caesar by Andrea Mantegna in the Collection of Her Majesty The Queen at Hampton Court*, London, 1979.

Matile 2003
Michael Matile, *Italienische Holzschnitte der Renaissance und des Barock: Bestandskatalog der Graphischen Sammlung der ETH Zürich*, coll. cat., Eidgenössische Technische Hochschule, Zurich; Basle, 2003.

Mauroner 1941
Fabio Mauroner, *Le Incisioni di Tiziano*, Venice, 1941.

Meder 1932
Joseph Meder, *Dürer-Katalog: Ein Handbuch über Albrecht Dürers Stiche, Radierungen, Holzschnitte, deren Zustände, Ausgaben und Wasserzeichen*, Vienna, 1932.

Mende 1978
Matthais Mende, *Hans Baldung Grien: Das Graphische Werk – Vollständiger Bildkatalog der Einzelholzschnitte, Buchillustrationen und Kupferstiche*, Unterschneidheim, 1978.

Mielke 2011
Ursula Mielke, *Crispijn van den Broeck*, The New Hollstein: Dutch and Flemish Etchings, Engravings and Woodcuts 1450–1700, Ger Luijten (ed.), 2 vols, Ouderkerk aan den Ijssel, 2011.

Mistrali 2003
Emilio Mistrali, *Parmigianino incisore: Catalogo completo delle incisioni*, Parma, 2003.

Monbeig Goguel 1988
Catherine Monbeig Goguel, 'Taste and Trade: The Retouched Drawings in the Everard Jabach Collection at the Louvre', *The Burlington Magazine*, vol. 130, no. 1028, November 1988, pp. 821–35.

Moser 2004
Peter Moser, *Lucas Cranach: Sein Leben, seine Welt und seine Bilder*, Bamberg, 2004.

Muller 1989
Jeffrey M. Muller, *Rubens: The Artist as Collector*, Princeton, 1989.

Muller 2001
Frank Muller, *Artistes dissidents dans l'Allemagne du seizième siècle: Lautensack, Vogtherr, Weiditz*, Baden-Baden, 2001.

Müller-Hofstede 1989
Justus Müller-Hofstede, *Rubens: The Artist as Collector*, Princeton, 1989.

Munich and Frankfurt 2007–08
Parmigianino und sein Kreis: Druckgraphik aus der Sammlung Baselitz, Achim Gnann with Kurt Zeitler, exh. cat., Staatliche Graphische Sammlung, Alte Pinakothek, Munich, 2007–08, and Städel Museum, Frankfurt am Main, 2008.

Mussini 2003
Massimi Mussini, 'Parmigianino e l'incisione', in Parma 2003, pp. 15–41.

Nagler 1835–52
Georg Kaspar Nagler, *Neues allgemeines Künstlerlexikon*, 22 vols, Munich, 1835–52.

Nagler 1858–79
Georg Kaspar Nagler, *Die Monogrammisten und diejenigen bekannten und unbekannten Künstler aller Schulen welche sich zur Bezeichnung ihrer Werke eines figürlichen Zeichens, der Initialen des Namens, der Abbreviatur desselben etc. bedient haben*, 5 vols, Munich, 1858–79.

New York 1986
From Michelangelo to Rosso: Engravings and Chiaroscuro Woodcuts of the Sixteenth Century Illustrating Mannerism in Italy and the School of Fontainebleau – Loan Exhibition from a Private Collection, Frederick G. Schab, exh. cat., William H. Schab Gallery, New York, 1986.

New York 1987
Drawings by Raphael and his Circle from British and North American Collections, John A. Gere, exh. cat., The Pierpont Morgan Library, New York, 1987.

New York 1997–98
The Private Collection of Edgar Degas, Ann Dumas, Colta Ives, Susan Alyson Stein and Gary Tinterow, exh. cat., The Metropolitan Museum of Art, New York, 1997–98.

Newman 1986
John Newman, 'Reynolds and Hone: "The Conjuror" Unmasked', in *Reynolds*, Nicholas Penny (ed.), exh. cat., Royal Academy of Arts, London, 1986, pp. 344–54.

Nuremberg 2000
Albrecht Dürer: Ein Künstler in seiner Stadt, Matthias Mende with Rudolf Endres, Franz Machilek and Karl Schlemmer, exh. cat., Stadtmuseum Fembohaus, Nuremberg, 2000.

Nuremberg 2011
Die gottlosen Maler von Nürnberg: Konvention und Subversion der Beham-Brüder, Jürgen Müller and Thomas Schauerte, exh. cat., Albrecht-Dürer-Haus, Nuremberg, 2011.

Oberhuber 1963
Konrad Oberhuber, 'Parmigianino als Radierer', *Alte und Moderne Kunst*, vol. 8, no. 68, May–June 1963, pp. 33–6.

Oberhuber 1972
Konrad Oberhuber, *Raphaels Zeichnungen, Abteilung IX: Entwürfe zu Werken Raphaels und seiner Schule im Vatikan 1511/12 bis 1520*, Berlin, 1972.

Olsen 1962
Harald Olsen, *Federico Barocci*, Copenhagen, 1962.

Von der Osten 1983
Gert von der Osten, *Hans Baldung Grien: Gemälde und Dokumente*, Berlin, 1983.

Ottawa and New York 2003–04
The Art of Parmigianino, David Franklin, exh. cat., National Gallery of Canada, Ottawa, and The Frick Collection, New York, 2003–04.

P.
Johann David Passavant, *Le Peintre-graveur*, 6 vols, Leipzig, 1860–64.

Panofsky 1942
Erwin Panofsky, 'Conrad Celtes and Kunz van der Rosen: Two Problems in Portrait Identification', *The Art Bulletin*, vol. 24, no. 1, March 1942, pp. 39–54.

Panofsky 1955
Erwin Panofsky, *The Life and Art of Albrecht Dürer*, 4th ed., Princeton, 1955.

Paris 1960
Les Dessins Italiens de la Collection Bonnat, Jacob Bean, exh. cat., Louvre, Paris, 1960.

Paris 1983–84
Hommage à Raphael: Raphael dans les collections françaises, exh. cat., Musée du Louvre, Paris, 1983–84.

Paris 1984
Altdorfer et le Renaissance fantastique dans l'art allemand, exh. cat., Centre Culturel du Marais, Paris, 1984.

Paris 2001
Un siècle de dessin à Bologne, 1480–1580: De la Renaissance à la réforme tridentine, Marzia Faietti and Dominique Cordellier, exh. cat., Musée du Louvre, Paris, 2001.

Paris 2010
Un cabinet particulier: Les Estampes de la Collection Frits Lugt, Fondation Custodia, exh. cat., Institut Néerlandais, Paris, 2010.

Paris 2012–13
Luca Penni: Un disciple de Raphaël à Fontainebleau, Domonique Cordellier, exh. cat., Louvre, Paris, 2012–13.

Paris and Rotterdam 1965–66
Clair-obscurs: Gravure sur bois imprimées en couleurs de 1500 à 1800 provenant de collections hollandaises, exh. cat., Institut Néerlandais, Paris, and Musée Boymans-van Beuningen, Rotterdam 1965–66.

Paris, Rouen and Ajaccio 2011–12
Parmesan: Dessins et gravures en clair-obscur, Carnets d´études, vol. 19, Emanuelle Brugerolles (ed.), exh. cat., Ecole nationale supérieure des Beaux-Arts, Paris; Musée des Beaux-Arts, Rouen; and Musée Fesch, Ajaccio, 2011–12.

Parma 2003
Parmigianino tradotto: La fortuna di Francesco Mazzola nelle stampe di riproduzione fra il Cinquecento e l'Ottocento, Massimo Mussini and Grazia Maria De Rubeis, exh. cat., Biblioteca Palatina, Parma, 2003.

Parma and Vienna 2003
Parmigianino e il manierismo europeo, Lucia Fornari Schianchi and Sylvia Ferino-Pagden (eds), exh. cat., Galleria Nazionale, Parma, and Kunsthistorisches Museum, Vienna, 2003.

Passavant 1860
Johann David Passavant, *Raphael d'Urbin et son père Giovanni Santi*, vol. 2, Paris, 1860.

Pauli 1901
Gustav Pauli, *Hans Sebald Beham: Ein kritisches Verzeichnis seiner Kupferstiche, Radierungen und Holzschnitte*, Strasbourg, 1901.

Pauli 1911
Gustav Pauli, *Hans Sebald Beham: Nachträge zu dem kritischen Verzeichnis seiner Kupferstiche, Radierungen und Holzschnitte*, Strasbourg, 1911.

Penny 2008
Nicholas Penny, *The Sixteenth-century Italian Paintings*, vol. 2: *Venice 1540–1600*, National Gallery Catalogues, New Haven, CT, and London, 2008.

Perseke 1941
Helmut Perseke, *Hans Baldungs Schaffen in Freiburg*, Freiburg im Breisgau, 1941.

Pestilli 2013
Livio Pestilli, *Paolo de Matteis: Neapolitan Painting and Cultural History in Baroque Europe*, Aldershot, 2013.

Pfeiffer 1955
Rudolf Pfeiffer, 'Conrad Peutinger und die Humanistische Welt', in *Augusta 955–1955: Forschungen und Studien zur Kultur-und Wirtschaftsgeschichte Augsburgs*, Augsburg, 1955, pp. 179–86.

Pittaluga 1930
Mary Pittaluga, *L'incisione italiana nel Cinquecento*, Milan, [1930].

Popham 1969
Arthur E. Popham, 'Observations on Parmigianino's Designs for Chiaroscuro Woodcuts', in *Miscellanea I. Q. van Regteren Altena*, Amsterdam, 1969, pp. 48–51.

Popham 1971
Arthur E. Popham, *Catalogue of the Drawings of Parmigianino*, 3 vols, New Haven, CT, and London, 1971.

Poppi 1992
Jacopo Ligozzi: Le Vedute del Sacro Monte della Verna, I Dipinti di Poppi e Bibbiena, Lucilla Conigliello, exh. cat., Castello dei Conti Guidi, Poppi, 1992.

Portheim 1886
Friedrich Portheim, 'Andrea Mantegna's Triumph Caesar's', *Repertorium für Kunstwissenschaft*, vol. 9, 1886, pp. 266–80.

Pouncey and Gere 1962
Philip Pouncey and John A. Gere, *Italian Drawings in the Department of Prints and Drawings in the British Museum: Raphael and his Circle*, 2 vols, London, 1962.

Providence 1973
Drawings and Prints of the First Maniera, 1515–1535, exh. cat., Department of Art, Brown University at the Museum of Art, Rhode Island School of Design, Providence, 1973.

Quintavalle 1948
Armando Ottavio Quintavalle, *Il Parmigianino*, Milan, 1948.

Radbruch 1950
Gustav Radbruch, *Elegentiae Juris Criminalis*, 2nd rev. and expanded ed., Basle, 1950.

Ragghianti Collobi 1974
Licia Ragghianti Collobi, *Il Libro de' Disegni del Vasari*, 2 vols, Florence, 1974.

Reichel 1926
Anton Reichel, *Die Clair-Obscur-Schnitte des XVI., XVII. und XVIII. Jahrhunderts*, Zurich, Leipzig and Vienna, 1926.

Richards 1957
Louise S. Richards, 'Two Woodcuts', *The Bulletin of the Cleveland Museum of Art*, vol. 44, no. 4, April 1957, pp. 63–7.

Roeck 2013
Bernd Roeck, 'Artisti, artigiani, mercanti: Tedeschi a Venezia nella prima età moderna', in *La chiesa di San Bartolomeo e la comunità tedesca a Venezia*, Natalino Bonazza, Isabella Lenardo and Gianmario Guidarelli (eds), Venice, 2013, pp. 29–53.

Rome, Weimar and Munich 2001–03
Chiaroscuro: Italienische Farbholzschnitte der Renaissance und des Barock, Dieter Graf and Hermann, exh. cat., Casa di Goethe, Rome; Kunstsammlungen, Weimar; and Haus der Kunst, Munich, 2001–03.

Rotterdam 1965
Zuid-Nederlandse grafiek uit de zestiende eeuw, exh. cat., Prentenkabinet Museum Boymans-van Beuningen, Rotterdam, 1965.

Röttinger 1911
Heinrich Röttinger, 'Neues zum Werke Hans Weiditz', *Mitteilungen der Gesellschaft für vervielfältigende Kunst*, no. 3, 1911, pp. 46–52.

Röttinger 1921
Heinrich Röttinger, *Beiträge zur Geschichte des sächsischen Holzschnittes (Cranach, Brosamer, der Meister MS, Jakob Lucius aus Kronstadt)*, Strasbourg, 1921.

Röttinger 1924
Heinrich Röttinger, 'Augsburger Einzelblätter um 1530 (Weiditz, Beck, Amberger)', *Mitteilungen der Gesellschaft für vervielfältigende Kunst*, nos 2–3, 1924, pp. 34–40.

Röttinger 1926
Heinrich Röttinger, *Dürers Doppelgänger*, Studien zur deutschen Kunstgeschichte, vol. 235, Strasbourg, 1926.

Saint Louis and London 2012–13
Federico Barocci: Renaissance Master of Color and Line, Judith W. Mann and Babette Bohn with Carol Piazzotta, exh. cat., Saint Louis Art Museum und The National Gallery, London, 2012–13.

Sanminiatelli 1956
Donato Sanminiatelli, 'L'esposizione di chiaroscuri agli Uffizi' (review of Florence 1956), *Paragone Arte*, vol. 7, no. 73, January 1956, pp. 53–60.

Sanminiatelli 1967
Donato Sanminiatelli, *Domenico Beccafumi*, Milan, 1967.

Sassi 2009
Raimondo Sassi, 'Ugo incisiore di chiaroscuri da Peruzzi, Raffaello e Parmigianino', in Carpi 2009, pp. 61–80.

Schade 1974
Werner Schade, *Die Malerfamilie Cranach*, Dresden, 1974.

Schneede and Sitt 2007
Uwe M. Schneede and Martina Sitt (eds), *Die Sammlungen der Hamburger Kunsthalle*, vol. 1: *Die deutschen, englischen, französischen, italienischen und spanischen Gemälde 1350–1800*, coll. cat., Kunsthalle, Hamburg, 2007.

Schoch 2001
Rainer Schoch, 'Albertvs Dvrer noricvs faciebat: Bemerkungen zur Rolle der Druckgraphik im Werk Albrecht Dürers', in Rainer Schoch, Matthias Mende and Anna Scherbaum, *Albrecht Dürer: Das druckgraphische Werk*, vol. 1: *Kupferstiche, Eisenradierungen und Kaltnadelblätter*, Munich, Berlin, London and New York, 2001, pp. 9–23.

Schoch, Mende and Scherbaum 2002
Rainer Schoch, Matthias Mende and Anna Scherbaum, *Albrecht Dürer: Das druckgraphische Werk*, vol. 2: *Holzschnitte und Holzschnittfolgen*, Munich, Berlin, London and New York, 2002.

Schottenloher 1922
Karl Schottenloher, *Die liturgischen Druckwerke Erhard Ratdolts aus Augsburg, 1485–1522*, Mainz, 1922.

Seibt 1891
Wilhelm Seibt, *Helldunkel, Chiaroscuro, Camaïeu: Holzschnitte in Helldunkel*, Frankfurt am Main, 1891.

Seidlitz 1885
Woldemar von Seidlitz, 'Katalog der Druckgraphik von und nach Beccafumi', in *Meyer's Allgemeines Künstler-Lexikon*, vol. 3, Leipzig, 1885, pp. 256–8.

Servolini 1932
Luigi Servolini, *La xilografia a chiaroscuro italiana nei secoli XVI, XVII e XVIII*, Lecco, 1932.

Servolini 1977
Luigi Servolini, *Ugo da Carpi: I chiaroscuri e le altre opere*, Florence, 1977.

Shearman 1967
John Shearman, *Mannerism*, Harmondsworth, 1967.

Shearman 1972
John Shearman, *Raphael's Cartoons in the Collection of Her Majesty the Queen and the Tapestries for the Sistine Chapel*, London, 1972.

Shoemaker and Broun 1981
Innis H. Shoemaker and Elizabeth Broun, *The Engravings of Marcantonio Raimondi*, exh. cat., Spencer Museum of Art, University of Kansas, Lawrence, and Ackland Art Museum, University of North Carolina at Chapel Hill, 1981.

Siena 1980
L'Arte a Siena sotto i Medici 1555–1609, Fiorella Sricchia Santoro (ed.), exh. cat., Palazzo Pubblico, Siena, 1980.

Siena 1990
Domenico Beccafumi e il suo tempo, exh. cat., Chiesa di Sant' Agostino, Oratorio di San Bernardino, Spedale di Santa Maria della Scala, Palazzo Pubblico, Palazzo Bindi Sergardi, Duomo and Pinacoteca, Siena, 1990.

Silver 2012–13
Larry Silver, 'Der Papier-Kaiser: Burgkmair, Augsburg und das Bild des Kaisers', in *Kaiser Maximilian I. und die Kunst der Dürerzeit*, Eva Michel and Marie Luise Sternath (eds), exh. cat., Albertina, Vienna, 2012–13, pp. 91–9.

Söding 2001–02
Ulrich Söding, 'Hans Baldung Grien in Freiburg: Themenwahl und Stilentwicklung', in Freiburg 2001–02, pp. 13–59.

Stanford 1978
Seventeenth-century Italian Prints, Marcus S. Sopher with Claudia Lazzaro-Bruno, exh. cat., Stanford Art Gallery, Stanford University, Stanford, CA, 1978.

Stechow 1967
Wolfgang Stechow, 'On Büssinck, Ligozzi and an Ambigouos Allegory', in *Essays in the History of Art Presented to Rudolf Wittkower*, London, 1967, pp. 193–6.

Stijnman 2011
Ad Stijnman, 'Zur Geschichte des Farbdrucks vom Mittelalter bis um 1800', in *Lichtspiel und Farbenpracht: Entwicklungen des Farbdrucks 1500–1800 – Aus den Beständen der Herzog August Bibliothek*, Melanie Grimm, Claudia Klein-Tebbe and Ad Stijnman, exh. cat., Herzog August Bibliothek, Wolfenbüttel, 2011, pp. 9–28.

Strauss 1973
Walter L. Strauss, *Clair-Obscur: Der Farbholzschnitt in Deutschland und den Niederlanden im 16. und 17. Jahrhundert*, Nuremberg, 1973.

Strauss 1975
Walter L. Strauss, *The German Single-leaf Woodcut 1550–1600*, 3 vols, New York, 1975.

Strauss 1980
Walter L. Strauss, *Sixteenth-century German Artists: Albrecht Dürer*, The Illustrated Bartsch, vol. 10 (formerly vol. 7, part 1), New York, 1980.

Strauss 1981
Walter L. Strauss, *Sixteenth-century German Artists: Monogrammists, Pilgrim, Graf, Deutsch, Erlinger, Resch, Schoen, Meldemann, Huber, Woensam, Duvet, Krug*, The Illustrated Bartsch, vol. 13 (formerly vol. 7, part 4), New York, 1981.

Strauss 1982
Walter L. Strauss, *Hendik Goltzius*, The Illustrated Bartsch, vol. 3 (commentary), New York, 1982.

Strauss et al. 1981
Walter L. Strauss, Ellen S. Jacobowitz, James H. Marrow and Stephanie LStepanek, *Sixteenth-century German Artists: Baldung Grien, Springinklee, van Leyden*, The Illustrated Bartsch, vol. 12 (formerly vol. 7, part 3), New York, 1981

Suida 1936
Wilhelm Suida, 'Tizian, die beiden Campagnola und Ugo da Carpi', *Critica d'arte*, vol. 1, no. 6, December 1936, pp. 285–8.

Takahatake 2010
Naoko Takahatake, [Review of Carpi 2009], *Print Quarterly*, vol. 27, no. 3, 2010, pp. 317–21.

Thausing 1869
Moritz von Thausing, 'Hans Baldung Grien und nicht Dürer', *Jahrbücher für Kunstwissenschaft*, vol. 2, 1869, pp. 211–18.

Thausing 1884
Moritz Thausing, *Dürer: Geschichte seines Lebens und seiner Kunst*, 2 vols, Leipzig, 1884.

Tietze and Tietze-Conrat 1938
Hans Tietze and Erika Tietze-Conrat, 'Titian's Woodcuts', *Print Collector's Quarterly*, vol. 25, 1938, pp. 333–477.

Tietze-Conrat 1939
Erika Tietze-Conrat, 'Pordenone and not Parmiggianino', *The Burlington Magazine*, vol. 74, no. 431, February 1939, p. 91.

Tokyo 2005
Chiarsocuro Woodcuts from the Frits Lugt Collection in Paris, Akira Kofuku and Shinsuke Watanabe with Erik Hinterding, exh. cat., The National Museum of Western Art, Tokyo, 2005.

Troche 1933
Ernst Günter Troche, 'Zeichnungen von Domenico Beccafumi im Kupferstichkabinett', *Berliner Museen: Berichte aus den Preussischen Kunstsammlungen*, vol. 54, 1933, pp. 25–30.

Trotter 1974
William Henry Trotter, 'Chiaroscuro Woodcuts of the Circles of Raphael and Parmigianino: A Study in Reproductive Graphics', Ph.D. thesis, The University of North Carolina at Chapel Hill, 1974 (facsimile 1976).

Van de Velde 1975
Carl van de Velde, *Frans Floris (1519/20–1570): Leven en Werken*, 2 vols, Brussels, 1975.

Van Gastel 2007
Joris van Gastel, 'Hoc opus exculpsit Io. Bologna. Andreas Andreanus Incisit: Andrea Andreani's *Chiaroscuro* Houtsneden naar Giambologna', *Bulletin van het Rijksmuseum*, vol. 55, no. 1, 2007, pp. 15–39.

Vasari 1878–85
Giorgio Vasari, *Le vite de' più eccellenti pittori, scultori ed architettori [...], con nuove annotazioni e commenti di Gaetano Milanesi*, 9 vols, Florence, 1878–85.

Vasari 1986
Giorgio Vasari, *Le vite de' più eccellenti architetti, pittori, et scultori italiani, da Cimabue insino a' tempi nostri*, Luciano Bellosi and Aldo Rossi (eds), Turin, 1986.

Venice, Vienna and Bilbao 2004–05
The Era of Michelangelo: Masterpieces from the Albertina, Achim Gnann, exh. cat., Collezione Peggy Guggenheim, Venice; Albertina, Vienna; and Museo Guggenheim, Bilbao, 2004–05.

Vienna 1963
Konrad Oberhuber, *Parmigianino und sein Kreis: Zeichnungen und Druckgraphik aus eigenem Besitz*, exh. cat., Albertina, Vienna, 1963.

Vienna 1966
Die Kunst der Graphik III: Renaissance in Italien – 16. Jahrhundert, Konrad Oberhuber, exh. cat., Albertina, Vienna, 1966.

Vienna 1967–68
Die Kunst der Graphik IV: Zwischen Renaissance und Barock – Das Zeitalter von Bruegel und Bellange; Werke aus dem Besitz der Albertina, Konrad Oberhuber, exh. cat., Albertina, Vienna, 1967–68.

Vienna 1992
Die Beredsamkeit des Leibes: Zur Körpersprache in der Kunst, Ilsebill Barta Fliedl and Christoph Geissmar (eds), exh. cat., Albertina, Vienna; Salzburg and Vienna, 1992.

Vienna 2012–13a
Kaiser Maximilian I. und die Kunst der Dürerzeit, Eva Michel and Marie Luise Sternath (eds), exh. cat., Albertina, Vienna, 2012–13.

Vienna 2012–13b
Die Nacht im Zwielicht: Kunst von der Romantik bis heute, Agnes Husslein-Arco, Brigitte Borchhardt-Birbaumer and Harald Krejci (eds), exh. cat., Belvedere, Vienna, 2012–13.

Vienna and Munich 2011–12
Dürer, Cranach, Holbein: Die Entdeckung des Menschen – Das deutsche Porträt um 1500, Sabine Haag, Christiane Lange, Christof Metzger and Karl Schütz (eds), exh. cat., Kunsthistorische Museum, Vienna, and Kunsthalle der Hypo-Kulturstiftung, Munich, 2011–12.

von der Osten 1983
Gert von der Osten, *Hans Baldung Grien: Gemälde und Dokumente*, Berlin, 1983.

Washington 1987–88
Rosso Fiorentino: Drawings, Prints and Decorative Arts, Eugene A. Carroll, exh. cat., National Gallery of Art, Washington, 1987–88.

Washington and Boston 1983
The Prints of Lucas van Leyden & his Contemporaries, Ellen S. Jacobowitz and Stephanie Loeb Stepanek, exh. cat., Washington, National Gallery of Art, and Boston, Museum of Fine Arts, 1983.

Washington and New Haven 1981
Hans Baldung Grien: Prints and Drawings, James H. Marrow, Alan Shestack and Charles W. Talbot, exh. cat., National Gallery of Art, Washington, and Yale University Art Gallery, New Haven, CT, 1981.

Washington, Dallas and Detroit 1976–77
Titian and the Venetian Woodcut, David Rosand and Michelangelo Muraro, exh. cat., National Gallery of Art, Washington; Museum of Fine Arts, Dallas; and The Detroit Institute of Arts, 1976–77.

Washington, Mexico City and San Francisco 1997–98
Stanley Spencer: An English Vision, Fiona MacCarthy, exh. cat., Hirshhorn Museum and Sculpture Garden, Smithsonian Institution, Washington; Centro Cultural/Arte Contemporáneo, Mexico City; and California Palace of the Legion of Honor, Fine Arts Museums of San Francisco, 1997–98.

Weigel 1865
Rudolph Weigel, *Die Werke der Maler in ihren Handzeichnungen: Beschreibendes Verzeichnis der in Kupfer gestochen, lithographierten und photographierten Facsimiles von Originalzeichnungen grosser Meister*, Leipzig, 1865.

Weimar 1957
Italienische Farbenholzschnitte des 16. bis 18. Jahrhunderts: Chiaroscuri, Werner Schade, exh. cat., Schlossmuseum, Weimar, 1957.

Wescher 1974
Paul Wescher, 'Crispin van den Broeck as Painter', *Jaarboek van het Koninklijk Museum voor Schoone Kunsten Antwerpen*, 1974, pp. 171–85.

Wethey 1987
Harold E. Wethey, *Titian and his Drawings*, Princeton, 1987.

Winkelbauer 1954
Walter Winkelbauer, 'Kaiser Maximilian und St. Georg', *Mitteilungen des Österreichischen Staatsarchivs*, vol. 7, 1954, pp. 523–50.

Winkler 1916
F[riedrich]. Winkler, 'Floris, Frans', in Ulrich Thieme and Felix Becker, *Allgemeines Lexikon der bildenden Künstler von der Antike bis zur Gegenwart*, vol. 12, Leipzig, 1916, pp. 123–6.

Winkler 1927
F[riedrich]. Winkler, 'Key, Adriaen Thomasz.', in Ulrich Thieme and Felix Becker, *Allgemeines Lexikon der bildenden Künstler von der Antike bis zur Gegenwart*, vol. 20, Leipzig, 1927, pp. 227–8.

Winkler 1951
Friedrich Winkler, 'Hans Wechtlins "Schöne Maria"', *Berliner Museen*, n.s., vol. 1, nos 1–2, 1951, pp. 9–11.

Wittenberg 1998
Druckgraphiken Lucas Cranachs der Ältere: Im Dienst von Macht und Glauben, Jutta Strehle and Armin Kunz, exh. cat., Lutherhalle, Wittenberg, 1998.

Wood 2003
Christopher S. Wood, 'The Perspective Treatise in Ruins: Lorenz Stoer, Geometria et perspective, 1567', in Lyle Massey (ed.), *The Treatise on Perspective, Published and Unpublished*, Studies in the History of Art, vol. 59, Washington, New Haven, CT, and London, 2003, pp. 235–57.

Wood 2010–11
Jeremy Wood, *Corpus Rubenianum Ludwig Burchard, Part XXVI: Copies and Adaptations from Renaissance and Later Artists – Italian Artists*, 6 vols, London and Turnhout, 2010–11.

Wouk 2009
Edward H. Wouk, 'Frans Floris and disegno', *Ars*, vol. 42, 2009, pp. 47–63.

Wouk 2011
Edward H. Wouk, *Frans Floris*, The New Hollstein: Dutch and Flemish Etchings, Engravings and Woodcuts 1450–1700, Ger Luijten (ed.), 2 vols, Ouderkerk aan den Ijssel, 2011.

Wurzbach 1904
Alfred von Wurzbach, *Niederländisches Künstler-Lexikon*, vol. 1, Leipzig and Vienna, 1904.

Zanetti 1837
Alexandre Zanetti, *Le Premier Siècle de la calcographie ou catalogue raisonné des estampes du cabinet de feu M. le Comte Léopold Cicognara: Ecole d'Italie*, Venice, 1837.

Zava Boccazzi 1962
Franca Zava Boccazzi, *Antonio da Trento incisore (prima metà XVI sec.)*, Trent, 1962.

Zerner 1969
Henri Zerner, *The School of Fontainebleau: Etchings and Engravings*, New York, 1969.

Zerner 1979
Henri Zerner, *Italian Artists of the Sixteenth Century: School of Fontainebleau*, The Illustrated Bartsch, vol. 32, New York, 1979.

Zezza 2003
Andrea Zezza, *Marco Pino: L'opera completa*, Naples, 2003.

Photographic Acknowledgements

All works of art are reproduced by kind permission of the owners. Every attempt has been made to trace the photographers of works reproduced. Specific acknowledgements are as follows:

Berlin, © Martin Müller: fig. 6

Boston, © 2014 Museum of Fine Arts, Boston: fig. 20

Florence, © 2013. Photo Scala: figs 3, 5; figs 13, 4 (Galleria degli Uffizi/courtesy of the Ministero Beni e Att. Culturali)

London, © The Trustees of the British Museum. All rights reserved: figs 7, 8
London, © The National Gallery, 2013: fig. 30
London, Royal Collection Trust / © Her Majesty Queen Elizabeth II 2013: fig. 15
London, courtesy of Sotheby's: fig. 31

Paris, © RMN-Grand Palais/Musée du Louvre: fig. 11 (Thierry Le Mage); fig. 19 (Christophe Chavan)

Vienna, © Albertina, Peter Ertl and Caroline Heider: fig. 39

Warsaw, © University of Warsaw Library, Krystyna Dabrowska: fig. 35

Index of Names, Works and Places

All references are to page numbers; those in **bold** type indicate catalogue illustrations, those in *italic* type indicate other illustrations

Supporters of the Royal Academy

MAJOR BENEFACTORS

The President and the Trustees of the Royal Academy Trust are grateful to all its donors for their continued loyalty and generosity. They would like to extend their thanks to all those who have made a significant commitment, past and present, to the galleries, the exhibitions, the conservation of the Permanent Collection, the Library collections, the Royal Academy Schools, the Learning programme and other specific appeals.

HM The Queen
Her Majesty's Government
The 29th May 1961 Charitable Trust
The Aldama Foundation
The American Associates of the Royal Academy Trust
The Annenberg Foundation
Barclays Bank
BAT Industries plc
Sir David and Lady Bell
The late Tom Bendhem
The late Brenda M Benwell-Lejeune
John Frye Bourne
British Telecom
The Brown Foundation
John and Susan Burns
Mr Raymond M Burton CBE
Sir Trevor Chinn CVO and Lady Chinn
The Trustees of the Clore Foundation
The John S Cohen Foundation
Sir Harry and Lady Djangoly
The Dulverton Trust
Alfred Dunhill Limited
The John Ellerman Foundation
The Eranda Foundation
Ernst & Young
Esso UK plc
Esmée Fairbairn Charitable Trust
The Fidelity UK Foundation
The Foundation for Sports and the Arts
Friends of the Royal Academy
Jacqueline and Michael Gee
The Getty Grant Programme
Mr Thomas Gibson
Glaxo Holdings plc
Diane and Guilford Glazer
Mr and Mrs Jack Goldhill
Maurice and Laurence Goldman
The Horace W Goldsmith Foundation
HRH Princess Marie-Chantal of Greece
Mr and Mrs Jocelin Harris
The Philip and Pauline Harris Charitable Trust
The Charles Hayward Foundation
Heritage Lottery Fund
IBM United Kingdom Limited
The Idlewild Trust
Lord and Lady Jacobs
The JP Jacobs Charitable Trust
The Japan Foundation
Gabrielle Jungels-Winkler Foundation
Mr and Mrs Donald Kahn
The Lillian Jean Kaplan Foundation
The Kresge Foundation
The Samuel H Kress Foundation
The Kirby Laing Foundation
The Lankelly Foundation
The late Mr John S Latsis
The David Lean Foundation
The Leverhulme Trust
Lex Service plc
The Linbury Trust
Sir Sydney Lipworth QC and Lady Lipworth CBE
John Lyons Charity
Ronald and Rita McAulay
McKinsey and Company Inc
John Madejski OBE DL
The Manifold Trust
Marks and Spencer
The Paul Mellon Estate
The Mercers' Company
The Monument Trust
The Henry Moore Foundation
The Moorgate Trust Fund
The late Mr Minoru Mori HON KBE and Mrs Mori
Museums and Galleries Improvement Fund
National Westminster Bank
Stavros S Niarchos
Simon and Midge Palley
The Peacock Charitable Trust
The Pennycress Trust
PF Charitable Trust
The Pidem Fund
The Pilgrim Trust
The Edith and Ferdinand Porjes Trust
The Porter Foundation
John Porter Charitable Trust
Rio Tinto
John A Roberts FRIBA
Sir Simon and Lady Robertson
The Ronson Foundation
Rothmans International plc
RTZ Corporation plc
Dame Jillian Sackler DBE
Jillian and Arthur M Sackler
Mr Wafic Rida Saïd
Mrs Jean Sainsbury
The Saison Foundation
The Sammermar Trust
The Basil Samuel Charitable Trust
Mrs Coral Samuel CBE
Sea Containers Ltd
Shell UK Limited
Miss Dasha Shenkman
William and Maureen Shenkman
The Archie Sherman Charitable Trust
The late Pauline Sitwell
The Starr Foundation
Sir Hugh Sykes DL
Alfred Taubman
Sir Anthony and Lady Tennant
Ware and Edythe Travelstead
The Trusthouse Charitable Foundation
The Douglas Turner Trust
Unilever plc
The Weldon UK Charitable Trust
The Welton Foundation
The Weston Family
The Malcolm Hewitt Wiener Foundation
The Maurice Wohl Charitable Foundation
The Wolfson Foundation

and others who wish to remain anonymous

PATRONS

The Royal Academy is extremely grateful to all its Patrons, who generously support every aspect of its work.

Chair
Robert Suss

Platinum
Celia and Edward Atkin CBE
Mr and Mrs Christopher Bake
Mr and Mrs Patrick Doherty
Ms Ghizlan El Glaoui
Mr Hideyuki Osawa
Mr Mauirce Pinto
Mr and Mrs Jake Shafran
David and Sophie Shalit

Gold
Christopher and Alex Courage
Mr and Mrs Andrew Higginson
Mrs Elizabeth Hosking
Mr Michael Jacobson
Miss Joanna Kaye
Lady Rayne Lacey
Jacqueline and Marc Leland
The Licensing Company, London
Sir Sydney Lipworth QC and Lady Lipworth CBE
Mr and Mrs Ronald Lubner
Sir Keith and Lady Mills
Jean and Geoffrey Redman-Brown
Mrs Stella Shawzin
Mr Kevin Sneader and Ms Amy Muntner
Jane Spack
David Stileman
Mr and Mrs Pierre Winkler
Mr Robert John Yerbury

Silver
Lady Agnew
Miss H J C Anstruther
Lord Ashburton
Mrs Emma Avignon
Mr and Mrs Simon Bamber
Jane Barker
Ms Catherine Baxendale
The Duke of Beaufort
Mrs J K M Bentley, Summers Art Gallery
Mr Nigel Boardman
Eleanor E Brass
Mr and Mrs Richard Briggs OBE
Mrs Elie Brihi
Mrs Marcia Brocklebank
Sir Francis Brooke Bt
Mrs Joyce Brotherton
Jeremy Brown
Lady Brown
Lord Browne of Madingley
Mr Martin Burton
Mr F A A Carnwath CBE
Sir Roger Carr
Jean and Eric Cass
Suzy Castleman
Sir Charles and Lady Chadwyck-Healey
Sir Trevor Chinn CVO and Lady Chinn
Mr and Mrs George Coelho
Denise Cohen Charitable Trust
Sir Ronald Cohen
Ms Linda Cooper
Mark and Cathy Corbett
Mr and Mrs Ken Costa
Keith Craig
Andrew Crawley
Julian Darley and Helga Sands
The Countess of Dartmouth
Mr Daniel Davies
Peter and Andrea De Haan
The de Laszlo Foundation
Dr Anne Dornhorst
Lord and Lady Douro
Mr and Mrs Jim Downing
Ms Noreen Doyle
Mrs Janet Dwek
Lord and Lady Egremont
Bryan Ferry
Benita and Gerald Fogel
Mr Sam Fogg
Mrs Rosamund Fokschaner
Mrs Jocelyn Fox
Mr and Mrs Eric Franck
Arnold Fulton
The Lord Gavron CBE
Mrs Mina Gerowin Herrmann
Jacqueline and Jonathan Gestetner
Lady Getty
Mr Mark Glatman
Lady Gosling
Mr Stephen Gosztony
Piers Gough CBE RA
Mr Gavin Graham
Mrs Mary Graves
HRH Princess Marie-Chantal of Greece
Mr Jim Grover
Mrs Margaret Guitar
Mrs Jennifer Hall
Mrs Melanie Harris
Richard and Janeen Haythornthwaite
Sir John Hegarty and Miss Philippa Crane
Sir Michael and Lady Heller
Lady Heseltine
Mr and Mrs Alan Hobart
Mr Philip Hudson
Mr and Mrs Jon Hunt
Judy and Robert Huret
Mrs Deanna Ibrahim
S Isern-Feliu
Mrs Caroline Jackson
Sir Martin and Lady Jacomb
Mrs Raymonde Jay
Ignacio Jayanti
Fiona Johnstone
Mr Nicholas Jones
Mrs Ghislaine Kane
Skip Keesal
Dr Elisabeth Kehoe
Mr Duncan Kenworthy OBE
Princess Jeet Khemka
Mr D H Killick
Mr and Mrs James Kirkman
Mrs Aboudi Kosta
Mr and Mrs Herbert Kretzmer
Norman A Kurland and Deborah A David
Joan H Lavender
Mr George Lengvari and Mrs Inez Lengvari
Lady Lever of Manchester
Miss R Lomax-Simpson
The Hon Mrs Virginia Lovell
Mr and Mrs Henry Lumley
Mrs Josephine Lumley
Gillian McIntosh
Andrew and Judith McKinna
Mr Nicholas Maclean
Sir John Mactaggart
Madeline and Donald Main
Scott and Laura Malkin
Mrs Inge Margulies
Mr Charles Martin
Mr and Mrs Richard Martin
Zvi and Ofra Meitar Family Fund
Professor Anthony Mellows OBE TD and Mrs Anthony Mellows
Mrs Joy Moss
Dr Ann Naylor
Ann Norman-Butler
Mr Michael Palin
John H Pattisson
Nicholas B Paumgarten
Mr and Mrs D J Peacock
Mr and Mrs A Perloff
Mr Philip Perry
David Pike
Mr and Mrs Anthony Pitt-Rivers
Mr Basil Postan
John and Anne Raisman
Mr David Reid Scott
Lady Renwick
Rothschild Foundation
Miss Elaine Rowley
Mr and Mrs K M Rubie
The Lady Henrietta St George
Mr Adrian Sassoon
Mr and Mrs Christopher Satterthwaite
Mr and Mrs Kevin Senior
Christina Countess of Shaftesbury
Mr Robert N Shapiro
Victoria Sharp
Major General and Mrs Jonathan Shaw
Alan and Marianna Simpson
The Tavolozza Foundation
Lady Tennant
Dr Gillian Tett
Anthony Thornton
Mr Anthony J Todd
Miss M L Ulfane
John and Carol Wates
Mrs Angela Webb
Edna and Willard Weiss
Anthony and Rachel Williams
Mrs Isobel Williams
Christopher G Williams Esq
Mr William Winters

Patron Donors
Stephen Barry Charitable Settlement
Mr Peter Lloyd
Mrs Bianca Roden
The Michael H Sacher Charitable Trust
H M Sassoon Charitable Trust

and others who wish to remain anonymous

BENJAMIN WEST GROUP PATRONS

Chair
Lady Judge CBE

Platinum
Mr Tony Davis
David Giampaolo
Charles and Kaaren Hale
Mr and Mrs John R Olsen

Gold
Mr Steve Cardell
Lady Judge CBE
Mr Christian Levett
Ms Alessandra Morra
Mr John Peter Williams

Silver
Lady J Lloyd Adamson
Mr Dimitry Afanasiev
Poppy Allonby
Mrs Spindrift Al Swaidi
Ms Ruth Anderson
Ms Sol Anitua
Mr Andy Ash
Marco and Francesca Assetto
Mrs Leslie Bacon
Naomi and Ted Berk
Mrs Michal Berkner Jenrick
Jean and John Botts
Mr Simon Brocklebank-Fowler
Mrs Olga But-Gusaim
Mrs Sophie Cahu
Brian and Melinda Carroll
Mr and Mrs Paul Collins
Vanessa Colomar de Enserro
Ms Karla Dorsch
Mr and Mrs Jeff Eldredge
Mrs Stroma Finston
Cyril and Christine Freedman
Ms Moya Greene
Mr David Greenwald
Mr and Mrs Timothy Hart
Mr Andrew Hawkins
Ms Alexandra Hess
Katie Jackson
Suzanne and Michael Johnson
Lord and Lady Leitch
Mrs Stephanie Léouzon
Mrs Valerie Nataliya Levine
Mr Guido Lombardo
Charles G Lubar
Ted and Patricia Madara
Cornelius Medvei
Dean Menegas
Mrs Victoria Mills
Neil Osborn and Holly Smith
Lady Purves
Mr Aaron Rosenstein
Mrs Candice Schneider
Mr James B Sherwood
Mr Stuart Southall
Sir Hugh and Lady Sykes
Mr Ian Taylor
Miss Lori Tedesco
Mr and Mrs Julian Treger
Frederick and Kathryn Uhde
Mr Craig D Weaver
Prof Peter Whiteman QC
Mr and Mrs John Winter
Ms Regina Wyles

and others who wish to remain anonymous

SCHOOLS PATRONS

Chair
Mr Keir McGuinness

Platinum
Matthew and Sian Westerman

Gold
Sam and Rosie Berwick
Mrs Sarah Chenevix-Trench
Rosalyn and Hugo Henderson
Christopher Kneale
Mr William Loschert
Mr Keir McGuinness
Carol Sellars

Silver
Lord and Lady Aldington
Mrs Elizabeth Alston
Mr Nicholas Andrew

Lazard
Lindsell Train
Marie Curie
Moelis & Company
Oracle Capital Group
The Royal Society of Chemistry
Tanya Baxter Contemporary
Tiffany & Co.
Trowers & Hamlins
UBS
Weil, Gotshal & Manges

Associate
Bank of America Merrill Lynch
Bloomberg LP
BNP Paribas
Bonhams 1793 Ltd
Clifford Chance LLP
Credit Agricole CIB
DONG Energy
EY
Generation Investment Management LLP
Heidrick & Struggles
John Lewis Partnership
Lubbock Fine
Morgan Stanley
Pentland Group plc
Rio Tinto
Sykes & Son Limited
Timothy Sammons Fine Art Agents

SUPPORTERS OF PAST EXHIBITIONS

The President and Council of the Royal Academy would like to thank the following supporters and benefactors for their generous contributions towards major exhibitions in the last ten years:

2014
Sensing Spaces
Scott and Laura Malkin
AKT II
Arauco

2013
Bill Woodrow RA
Lead Series Supporter JTI
The Henry Moore Foundation
Daumier
2009–2013 Season supported by JTI
Australia
National Gallery of Australia
Qantas Airways
The Woolmark Company
Richard Rogers RA: Inside Out
Ferrovial Agroman
Heathrow Airport
Laing O'Rourke
Mexico: A Revolution in Art, 1910–1940
2009–2013 Season supported by JTI
Art Mentor Foundation Lucerne
Conaculta
James and Clare Kirkman
Mexican Agency for International Development Cooperation
Catherine and Franck Petitgas
Sectur
Visit Mexico
Mercedes Zobel
245th Summer Exhibition
Insight Investment
George Bellows
2009–2013 Season supported by JTI
Edwards Wildman
Premiums 2013, RA Schools Annual Dinner and Auction and RA Schools Show 2013
Newton Investment Management
Manet: Portraying Life
BNY Mellon, Partner of the Royal Academy of Arts

2012
Mariko Mori
JTI
RA Now
JTI
Bronze
Christian Levett and Mougins Museum of Classical Art
Daniel Katz Gallery
Baron Lorne Thyssen-Bornemisza
John and Fausta Eskenazi
The Ruddock Foundation for the Arts
Tomasso Brothers Fine Art
Jon and Barbara Landau
Janine and J. Tomilson Hill
Embassy of the Kingdom of the Netherlands
Eskenazi Limited
Lisson Gallery
Alexis Gregory
Alan and Mary Hobart
Richard de Unger and Adeela Qureshi
Rossi & Rossi Ltd
Embassy of Israel
244th Summer Exhibition
Insight Investment
From Paris: A Taste for Impressionism – Paintings from the Clark
2009–2013 Season supported by JTI
Edwards Wildman
The Annenberg Foundation
Premiums, RA Schools Annual Dinner and Auction and RA Schools Show 2012
Newton Investment Management
Johan Zoffany RA: Society Observed
2009–2013 Season supported by JTI
Cox & Kings
Building the Revolution: Soviet Art and Architecture 1915–1935
2009–2013 Season supported by JTI
The Ove Arup Foundation
The Norman Foster Foundation
Richard and Ruth Rogers
David Hockney RA: A Bigger Picture
BNP Paribas
Welcome to Yorkshire: Tourism Partner
Visit Hull & East Yorkshire: Supporting Tourism Partner
NEC

2011
Degas and the Ballet: Picturing Movement
BNY Mellon
Region Holdings
Blavatnik Family Foundation
Eyewitness: Hungarian Photography in the Twentieth Century. Brassaï, Capa, Kertész, Moholy-Nagy, Munkácsi
2009–2013 Season supported by JTI
Hungarofest
OTP Bank
243rd Summer Exhibition
Insight Investment
Premiums, RA Schools Annual Dinner and Auction and RA Schools Show 2011
Newton Investment Management
Watteau: The Drawings
2009–2013 Season supported by JTI
Region Holdings
Modern British Sculpture
American Express Foundation
The Henry Moore Foundation
Hauser & Wirth
Art Mentor Foundation Lucerne
Sotheby's
Blain Southern
Welcome to Yorkshire: Tourism Partner

2010
GSK Contemporary – Aware: Art Fashion Identity
GlaxoSmithKline
Pioneering Painters: The Glasgow Boys 1880–1900
2009–2013 Season supported by JTI
Glasgow Museums
Treasures from Budapest: European Masterpieces from Leonardo to Schiele
OTP Bank
Villa Budapest
Daniel Katz Gallery, London
Cox & Kings: Travel Partner
Sargent and the Sea
2009–2013 Season supported by JTI
242nd Summer Exhibition
Insight Investment
Paul Sandby RA: Picturing Britain, A Bicentenary Exhibition
2009–2013 Season supported by JTI
The Real Van Gogh: The Artist and His Letters
BNY Mellon
Hiscox
Heath Lambert
Cox & Kings: Travel Partner
RA Outreach Programme
Deutsche Bank AG

2009
GSK Contemporary
GlaxoSmithKline
Wild Thing: Epstein, Gaudier-Brzeska, Gill
2009–2013 Season supported by JTI
BNP Paribas
The Henry Moore Foundation
Anish Kapoor
JTI
Richard Chang
Richard and Victoria Sharp
Louis Vuitton
The Henry Moore Foundation
J W Waterhouse: The Modern Pre-Raphaelite
2009–2013 Season supported by JTI
Champagne Perrier-Jouët
GasTerra
Gasunie
241st Summer Exhibition
Insight Investment
Kuniyoshi. From the Arthur R. Miller Collection
2009–2013 Season supported by JTI
Canon
Cox & Kings: Travel Partner
Premiums and RA Schools Show
Mizuho International plc
RA Outreach Programme
Deutsche Bank AG

2008
GSK Contemporary
GlaxoSmithKline
Byzantium 330–1453
J F Costopoulos Foundation
A G Leventis Foundation
Stavros Niarchos Foundation
Cox & Kings: Travel Partner
Miró, Calder, Giacometti, Braque: Aimé Maeght and His Artists
BNP Paribas
Vilhelm Hammershøi: The Poetry of Silence
OAK Foundation Denmark
Novo Nordisk
240th Summer Exhibition
Insight Investment
Premiums and RA Schools Show
Mizuho International plc
RA Outreach Programme
Deutsche Bank AG
From Russia: French and Russian Master Paintings 1870–1925 from Moscow and St Petersburg
E.ON
2008 Season supported by Sotheby's

2007
Paul Mellon's Legacy: A Passion for British Art
The Bank of New York Mellon
Georg Baselitz
Eurohypo AG
239th Summer Exhibition
Insight Investment
Impressionists by the Sea
Farrow & Ball
Premiums and RA Schools Show
Mizuho International plc
RA Outreach Programme
Deutsche Bank AG
The Unknown Monet
Bank of America

2006
238th Summer Exhibition
Insight Investment
Chola: Sacred Bronzes of Southern India
Cox & Kings: Travel Partner
Premiums and RA Schools Show
Mizuho International plc
RA Outreach Programme
Deutsche Bank AG
Rodin
Ernst & Young

2005
China: The Three Emperors, 1662–1795
Goldman Sachs International
Impressionism Abroad: Boston and French Painting
Fidelity Foundation
Matisse, His Art and His Textiles: The Fabric of Dreams
Farrow & Ball
Premiums and RA Schools Show
The Guardian
Mizuho International plc
Turks: A Journey of a Thousand Years, 600–1600
Akkök Group of Companies
Aygaz
Corus
Garanti Bank
Lassa Tyres